SEEKING THE IMPERISHABLE TREASURE

SEEKING the IMPERISHABLE TREASURE

Wealth, Wisdom, and a Jesus Saying

Steven R. Johnson

Μὴ θησαυρίζετε
ὑμῖν θησαυροὺς
ἐπὶ τῆς γῆς

CASCADE Books • Eugene, Oregon

SEEKING THE IMPERISHABLE TREASURE
Wealth, Wisdom, and a Jesus Saying

Copyright © 2008 Steven R. Johnson. All rights reserved. Except for brief quotations in critical publications or reviews, no part of this book may be reproduced in any manner without prior written permission from the publisher. Write: Permissions, Wipf and Stock Publishers, 199 W. 8th Ave., Suite 3, Eugene, OR 97401.

Cascade Books
A Division of Wipf and Stock Publishers
199 W. 8th Ave., Suite 3
Eugene, OR 97401

www.wipfandstock.com

ISBN 13: 978-1-55635-244-7

Cataloging-in-Publication data:

Johnson, Steven R.

Seeking the imperishable treasure : wealth, wisdom, and a Jesus saying / Steven R. Johnson.

xvi + 184 p. ; 23 cm.

Includes bibliographical references.

ISBN 13: 978-1-55635-244-7 (alk. paper)

1. Q hypothesis (Synoptics criticism). 2. Bible. N.T. Gospels—Criticism, interpretation, etc. 3. Gospel of Thomas (Coptic Gospel)—Criticism, interpretation, etc. 4. Bible. N.T. James—Criticism, interpretation, etc. 5. Bible. N.T. Colossians—Criticism, interpretation, etc. 6. Wealth—Religious Aspects—Christianity. 7. Wisdom—Religious Aspects—Christianity. I. Title.

BS2555.2 J64 2008

Manufactured in the U.S.A.

To Ellen

You may not be what Jesus
and the sages of old were speaking of,
but to me

you are radiant and unfading,
more precious then jewels,
an unfailing treasure,
an enduring wealth,
better than silver or choice gold;
with you I am happy.

Contents

Acknowledgments ix

Abbreviations xi

List of Figures xv

1. Introduction 1
2. The Synoptics and Q 27
3. John, Thomas, and Luke 58
4. James and Colossians 80
5. Inferences and Reconstruction of an Archetype 124
6. Conclusion 148

Appendix: Reconstructed Text of Q 12:33 155

Bibliography 157

Index of Ancient Documents 171

Acknowledgments

I would like to recognize and extend my appreciation and gratitude to the following institutions and individuals for their support in this project.

The Institute for Antiquity and Christianity supported my work as a research associate with the International Q Project. Much of the thanks for this goes to the emeritus Director of the Institute, James M. Robinson. Jon Ma. Asgeirsson, a former Associate Director, provided support in many other ways—I'm glad to be able to thank him here.

Benjamin L. Hubbard, Religion Department Chair emeritus at California State University, Fullerton, provided me with a teaching assistant in my last year of adjunct teaching. James Robinson enabled my writing in innumerable ways, both financially and intellectually. It has truly been an education working with him. Gregory J. Riley provided me with fresh, new ways of looking at the Gospel of Thomas, ways that are reflected in this work. Douglas M. Parrott has been especially supportive as a reader and friend, providing both a sounding board and sound advice on numerous occasions in recent years.

A big thanks to K. C. Hanson, Editor in Chief at Wipf and Stock Publishers, for approaching me about publishing this study. Both his enthusiasm and his editing skills have been a tremendous help.

Blessings to my friend and colleague, C. Michael Robbins, who has been an ever-present reminder to me that scholarship is not the end-all—that a full life is a happier life. To my parents, Robert and Lois Johnson, whose love, enthusiasm, interest, concern, and support—both as parents and as friends—helped me to survive the program at Claremont. And finally, to my wife and sweetie, Ellen Davis, who has been a dear friend since the day I arrived in Claremont; for her love and support. She slowed me down in the courtin' years—*and I thank God.*

Abbreviations

AAR/SBL	American Academy of Religion/Society of Biblical Literature
AB	Anchor Bible
AcOr	*Acta Orientalia*
ANRW	*Aufstieg und Niedergang der römischen Welt*
APOT	*The Apocrypha and Pseudepigrapha of the Old Testament*. Edited by R. H. Charles
ASNU	Acta seminarii neotestamentici upsaliensis
BDAG	Walter Bauer, Frederick W. Danker, William F. Arndt, and F. Wilbur Gingrich, *A Greek-English Lexicon of the New Testament and Other Early Christian Literature* (the earlier, 2nd edition [1979] is referred to as BAGD)
BDF	Friedrich Blass, Albert Debrunner, and Robert W. Funk, *A Greek Grammar of the New Testament and Other Early Christian Literature*
BETL	Bibliotheca Ephemeridum Theologicarum Lovaniensium
BHT	Beiträge zur historischen Theologie
Bib	*Biblica*
BibS(F)	Biblische Studien (Freiburg)
BJRL	*Bulletin of the John Rylands University Library of Manchester*
BU	Biblische Untersuchungen
BWANT	Beiträge zur Wissenschaft vom Alten und Neuen Testament
BZ	*Biblische Zeitschrift*
BZENT	Beiträge zur Einleitung in das Neue Testament

BZNW	Beihefte zur Zeitschrift für die neutestamentliche Wissenschaft und die Kunde der älteren Kirche
CBQ	*Catholic Biblical Quarterly*
CBR	*Currents in Biblical Research*
CEQ	*The Critical Edition of Q*: Edited by James M. Robinson, Paul Hoffmann, and John S. Kloppenborg. Hermeneia Supplements
CNT	Commentaire du Nouveau Testament
Crum	W. E. Crum, *A Coptic Dictionary*
Ebib	Études bibliques
EGGNT	Exegetical Guide to the Greek New Testament
EKKNT	Evangelisch-katholischer Kommentar zum Neuen Testament
EvT	*Evangelische Theologie*
Exp	*The Expositor*
FB	Forschung zur Bibel
FFNT	Foundations & Facets: New Testament
Forum	*Foundations & Facets: Forum*
FRLANT	Forschungen zur Religion und Literatur des Alten und Neuen Testaments
GBS	Guides to Biblical Scholarship
GNT[4]	*The Greek New Testament*, 4th ed.
HTKNT	Herders theologischer Kommentar zum Neuen Testament
HTR	*Harvard Theological Review*
HTS	Harvard Theological Studies
IAC	Institute for Antiquity and Christianity
ICC	International Critical Commentary
Int	*Interpretation*
IQP	International Q Project
JBL	*Journal of Biblical Literature*
JSNTSup	Journal for the Study of the New Testament Supplement Series
KBANT	Kommentare und Beiträge zum Alten und Neuen Testament
KEKNT	Kritisch-exegetischer Kommentar über das Neue Testament

KlT	Kleine Texte für Vorlesungen und Übungen
KZNT	Kirchliche Zeitschrift zum Neuen Testament
LSJ	Henry G. Liddell, Robert Scott, and Henry S. Jones, *A Greek-English Lexicon*
LSJ Supp	E. A. Barber, editor, *Greek-English Lexicon: A Supplement*
LXX	Alfred Rahlfs, editor, *Septuaginta: Id est: Vetus Testamentum graece iuxta LXX interpretes*
MeyerK	H. A. W. Meyer, *Kritisch-exegetischer Kommentar über das Neue Testament*
MT	Masoretic Text—*Biblia Hebraica Stuttgartensia*
Mus	*Muséon*
NA^{27}	*Novum Testamentum Graece*, 27th ed.
NHMS	Nag Hammadi and Manichaean Studies
NHS	Nag Hammadi Studies
NIGTC	The New International Greek Testament Commentary
NovT	*Novum Testamentum*
NovTSup	Novum Testamentum Supplements
NRSV	New Revised Standard Version
NTAbh	Neutestamentliche Abhandlungen
NTD	Das Neue Testament Deutsch
NTR	New Testament Readings
NTS	*New Testament Studies*
NTTS	New Testament Tools and Studies
RSR	*Recherches de science religieuse*
RTP	*Revue de Théologie et de Philosophie*
SAC	Studies in Antiquity & Christianity
SBLSP	Society of Biblical Literature Seminar Papers
SBT	Studies in Biblical Theology
SecCent	*The Second Century*
SNT	Studien zum Neuen Testament
SNTIW	Studies in the New Testament and Its World
SNTSMS	Society for New Testament Studies Monograph Series
TDNT	*Theological Dictionary of the New Testament*
THKNT	Theologischer Handkommentar zum Neuen Testament
TRu	*Theologische Rundschau*
TS	*Theological Studies*

TU	Texte und Untersuchungen
UBSHS	United Bible Societies Handbook Series
UNT	Untersuchungen zum Neuen Testament
WMANT	Wissenschaftliche Monographien zum Alten und Neuen Testament
WUNT	Wissenschaftliche Untersuchungen zum Neuen Testament
ZNW	*Zeitschrift für die neutestamentliche Wissenschaft und die Kunde der älteren Kirche*
ZTK	*Zeitschrift für Theologie und Kirche*

Figures

1. Matt 6:19–20 and Luke 12:33 · 28
2. Treasure in Heaven—Gospel Versions · 63
3. Luke, Thomas (Coptic), and John Similarities · 72
4. Luke, Thomas (Greek), and John Similarities · 72
5. Q, Luke, and Thomas Adversity Clauses · 73
6. John's Use of Thomas · 75
7. James / Q Parallels · 89
8. Jas 2:5 and Q 6:20 · 90
9. Jas 1:22–25 and Q 6:46–49 · 92
10. Q 14:11 (Matt 23:12) and Jas 4:10 · 94
11. Figs and Grapes in James and the Synoptics · 95
12. Q 12:33 and Jas 5:2–3 · 97
13. Colossians / Thomas Parallels · 110
14. Col 3:1–2; GTh 76:3; and Q 12:33 · 117
15. Tradition and Redaction in Col 3:1–4 · 118
16. Col 3:1–2 and GTh 76:3 · 119
17. Q 12:33 and GTh 76:3 (Greek) · 133
18. Transmission History of the Treasure Saying · 151

CHAPTER 1 | Introduction

WHY THIS BOOK?

One of the more significant lessons we have learned from biblical scholarship is that traditions about Jesus were not passed down in any kind of linear or uniform fashion. We know with certainty that the teachings of Jesus were transmitted through a variety of media including, but not exclusive to, sayings collections, rules for church order, instructional and hortatory letters, liturgies, and apostolic word-of-mouth. We know that individual writings of the New Testament and other early Jesus movement literature usually reflect not singular, but multiple sources.

The most obvious example of this latter reality comes from gospel studies. Regardless of one's theory of the source relationships between canonical gospels, it is clear that a variety of sources are involved. Even if one begins with the most fundamental and widely-held hypothesis—the two-source hypothesis (Matthew and Luke used Mark and another source, "Q")—one is still faced with the likelihood of additional "M" and "L" sources used by Matthew and Luke respectively, as well as sources used in the composition of Mark and Q themselves.

Part and parcel of the problem of identifying sources and the forms they took is discerning in what ways and to what purposes oral tradents, collectors of traditions, and gospel writers modified their sources in order to address new and different social contexts. Simply put, sayings of Jesus found in more than one gospel are rarely identical. And while some differences can be readily identified as changes befitting the individual gospel writers' stylistic or grammatical preferences, other differences reflect their theological or cultural viewpoints—perspectives that become apparent through a close reading of the entire respective work and by comparison with other gospels.

Still other differences can be attributed to various pre-gospel stages of transmission. Form critics, beginning with Rudolf Bultmann and Martin Dibelius, have demonstrated the tendency of nascent Jesus movements to shape the sayings traditions according to their particular needs.[1] More recently, John Dominic Crossan showed how regularly the gospel writers shaped the core of aphoristic sayings by various means, such as contraction, expansion, substitution, transposition, and conversion, and then further shaped the interpretation of those sayings by combining or clustering them and then embedding them in larger speech units and narratives.[2] And so, with even the subtlest of modifications, an aphoristic saying can take different forms, such as maxim, rhetorical question, admonition, or prohibition and take on different meanings in different hermeneutical contexts.

With occasional exceptions (e.g., *The Lord's Prayer*, *Against Divorce*), Crossan deals only with gospel material. However, his arguments are appropriate to a wider range of material. Compare the following:

> "Are grapes gathered from thorn-bushes, or figs from thistles?" (Matt 7:16b)

> "Figs are not gathered from thorns-bushes, nor are grapes picked from a bramble bush." (Luke 6:44b)

> "Can a fig tree ... yield olives, or a grapevine figs?" (Ja 3:12a)

With regard to form, Matthew and James have rhetorical questions; Luke states a gnomic truth. With regard to content: Luke and James begin with figs, Matthew with grapes. Matthew and Luke contrast fruits with prickly plants that do not bear edible fruit; James contrasts fruits with plants bearing different edible fruit.

Advances in rhetorical criticism have since confirmed many of Crossan's observations, but gone beyond them as well. By focusing on the way ancient rhetoricians worked with the chreia, rhetorical critics have demonstrated how sayings of Jesus could be and were transformed for rhetorical effect (at *any* stage of transmission) according to the methods

---

1. Bultmann, *History of the Synoptic Tradition*; Dibelius, *From Tradition to Gospel*.
2. Crossan, *In Fragments*.

of chreia elaboration as outlined in the ancient *progymnasmata* (exercises preliminary to training in rhetoric).³

The relevant point for this study is that individual sayings of Jesus underwent significant transformations in form and meaning depending on how they were used—in much the same way ten Christian preachers can apply the same given lectionary passage, on the same Sunday, in ten different ways, depending upon their particular congregations' social and historical contexts and perceived needs. Compare again the previous New Testament examples, but with a little context added:

> "You will know them by their fruits. Are grapes gathered from thorn-bushes . . . ?"
>
> "For each tree is known by its own fruit. For figs are not gathered from thorn-bushes . . ."
>
> "Can a fig tree, my brothers, yield olives . . . ? Neither can salt water yield fresh."

The broader Matthean context has Jesus warning the crowd to beware of false prophets, who are to be identified in the metaphor as "thorn-bushes" and "thistles" that do not bear (good) fruit. Luke's context has Jesus admonishing listeners in the crowd to examine the "fruits" of their own lives and thereby consider their quality of character. The implied readers of James, who are viewed as religious family members, are exhorted to watch their tongues, because good and evil should not proceed from the same source. The contrast of the metaphor is less sharp here and more an issue of like producing like fruit. In each of the examples, however, what is essentially the same saying of Jesus—in this case an aphoristic teaching that applies a specific metaphor to express the necessary congruence between moral nature and resulting activity—is used in a different literary context, exists in a different form, and consequently has a different hermeneutic.

In subsequent chapters, I will track the development of the Treasure in Heaven saying of Jesus, a saying that is remarkable for its utility and breadth of interpretive applications in New Testament and other early Jesus movement writings. Elements of the Treasure in Heaven saying are found not only in the canonical Gospels of Matthew, Mark, Luke, and

---

3. An excellent introduction to the subject is found in Mack and Robbins, *Patterns of Persuasion*.

John, but also in extra-canonical Q and the Gospel of Thomas. It was used in the Pauline epistolary tradition (Colossians) as well as in the Letter of James. Not only are no two of these eight versions of the saying exactly alike, but the saying is broadly applied under two vastly different *topoi*, or motifs, of the Jewish Wisdom tradition: the proper disposition of wealth and the search for divine wisdom or knowledge. These different *topoi* are not particular either to gospels or to epistles; each *topos* is found in both genres. The saying functions as exhortation or prohibition—sometimes both—as a rationale for moral behavior, and as a prophetic warning against unethical behavior. In short, it is one of the most widely used and broadly interpreted sayings of Jesus and is therefore a prime candidate for studying the development of sayings traditions in the first century of the common or Christian era.

Thesis and Approach

My primary thesis in this study is that the Q and Thomas versions of the Treasure in Heaven saying (Q 12:33; GTh 76:3) are particularly relevant to discussion concerning the development of sayings traditions. It is my contention that, on the one hand, the Thomasine Treasure in Heaven saying was well known in the first century and played a pivotal role in the early transmission of the saying, influencing or being modified in three canonical versions (Luke 12:33; John 6:27; Col 3:1-2). And on the other hand, the use of the saying in James (5:2-3) reflects knowledge of Q, which was also an early and foundational version of the saying for the gospel tradition (cf. Matt 6:19; Luke 12:33). Ironically, both extra-canonical gospel versions of the Treasure saying may have found their earliest canonical expressions *in the epistles*.

One ramification of this thesis, if it holds up under close scrutiny, is important for our reconstruction of the development of early Christian texts and communities because there is the implication that some sayings traditions (as represented in the Gospel of Thomas, for example), eventually excluded for their perceived heretical theology or for their use by groups excluded from the mainstream, were recognized as authoritative in the first century. However, the point should not be overstated. This study focuses on one saying of Jesus, not an entire collection, such as we find in the Sayings Gospel Q, the Gospel of Thomas, or in the many non-Q collections of parables and aphoristic sayings found in, for example,

Matthew 13, Mark 4, and Luke. I stress this caveat later in the chapter by comparing pairs of studies by James M. Robinson and Risto Uro that lead to apparently contradictory results—results that are only contradictory, however, if one begins with the fallacious assumption that the Gospel of Thomas as we know it represents a relatively stable, unchanging tradition throughout the history of its oral and written transmission.

The International Q Project was formed in 1983 with two goals in mind. The first goal was to provide, for the first time, a relatively objective, non-idiosyncratic reconstruction of the text of Q—as far as this is possible—by an *international team* of scholars. The other was to provide a complete history of 200 years of research on Q reconstruction. The first goal was achieved in two stages: the publication of IQP reconstructions in the *Journal of Biblical Literature*[4] and the subsequent publication of *The Critical Edition of Q*.[5] The second goal is coming to fruition in the gradual publication of Documenta Q databases. Chapter 2 is largely a product of my work on the database for Q 12:33-34.[6] The advantage of chapter 2 is that it provides a running commentary on my reconstruction of Q 12:33-34—supported by judicious use of notes—as well as a brief review of Matthew's and Luke's theological purposes in redacting Q a brief discussion of Mark's adaptation of the Treasure saying (Mark 10:21). The reader can always refer to the Documenta Q volume for a complete survey of research on any given variation unit. Reference to the Gospel of Thomas and other non-synoptic versions of the saying is minimal and mostly relegated to the footnotes—the evaluations are largely based on issues specific to Matthew and Luke and their redactional tendencies.

Chapter 3 originated as an internal International Q Project paper looking at the relationship between Matthew, Luke, Thomas, and Q. When I discovered the importance of John 6:27 for understanding the transmission history of the saying, I revised and expanded the paper, presenting it to the Annual Meeting of the Society of Biblical Literature. It was subsequently published in a volume of collected essays commemo-

---

4. See the October issues of volumes 109 (1990); 110 (1991); 111 (1992); 112 (1993); 113 (1994); 114 (1995); and 116 (1997).

5. Robinson, Hoffmann, and Kloppenborg, eds., *The Critical Edition of Q*. The text of the *CEQ* occasionally differs from the IQP text because the *CEQ* text is the result of deliberations by the managing editors in consultation with the earlier IQP decisions. Every variation between the *CEQ* and the IQP is identified in the apparatus of the *CEQ*.

6. See Johnson, *Q 12:33-34*.

rating the discovery of the Nag Hammadi Library.[7] Chapter 3 represents a significant revision of the published essay.

I discovered an epistolary version of the Treasure saying that had been adapted and used in a paraenetic section of the Letter to the Colossians (Col 3:1–2). It seemed wise to investigate this version, along with the previously recognized version in James 5:2–3, particularly for their relevance to the issue of the transmission of sayings traditions in epistolary literature. Chapter 4 is a result of this investigation, with interesting implications for gospel studies. Chapters 5 and 6 summarize the results of preceding chapters and suggest several significant implications for New Testament studies.

Before I launch into the more detailed comparative studies of chapters 2–4, however, it seems prudent to introduce those studies by a brief and limited survey of the current state of research with regard to the Gospel of Thomas and the study of the New Testament and Christian origins. The remainder of this chapter will look at research into several specific areas: (1) contemporary studies of individual Thomasine sayings of Jesus and their connection, if any, to the synoptic sayings traditions; (2) studies of the relationship, if there is one, between the gospels of Thomas and John; and (3) an overview of what comparisons have been made between Thomas and epistolary literature.

Recent History of Studies in Thomas

With Wolfgang Schrage's seminal 1964 study, Gospel of Thomas studies all but died off in Europe and North America.[8] However, Thomas studies have experienced something of a renaissance in recent years for a couple of reasons. First, Schrage's study has been reassessed and found to be methodologically lacking.[9] These reassessments have led to a reopening of the issue of Thomas' date, provenance, and relation to synoptic sayings of Jesus traditions. Second, combined with these reassessments has been a convergence of Thomas and Q studies, especially in the fields of redactional analysis and social reconstruction of communities behind texts. Because of the growing recognition of the fluidity of sayings tradi-

---

7. Johnson, *"Gospel of Thomas 76:3."*
8. Schrage, *Das Verhältnis*.
9. See Sieber, "Redactional Analysis"; Patterson, *Gospel of Thomas*; idem., "Gospel of Thomas."

tions both in oral and written form, the history of the composition of Thomas has become an important area of study. In tracing the methods of composition of the text, scholarship is moving in at least two different directions: the search for redactional evidence of a stratigraphical development of the text on the one hand, and on the other, an analysis of the text, either rhetorical or hermeneutical, as it stands in the extant Coptic manuscript.[10] The literature is growing fast, and several attempts have been made through the years to mark the status of Thomas scholarship.[11] It is my intention to pick up from the most recent *Forschungsberichten* and see where scholarship stands in the tracing of the relative antiquity of the Thomas tradition, the development of the text over time, and the place of the non-canonical gospel in relation to the canon.

One idea that is beginning to find wider acceptance among scholars is the notion that the Gospel of Thomas was not composed in its entirety at any one place or time. Many studies seem to assume that it was, though there have been periodic calls to analyze the gospel one saying at a time.[12] Indeed, many studies have been made of individual sayings or small groups of sayings through the years, but often with overt or covert presuppositions that predetermined the results. The primary assumption seemingly held by a broad spectrum of commentators is that the Gospel of Thomas is either a first-century, non-gnostic document embodying traditions that are independent of canonical traditions, or it is a mid- to late-second century, thoroughly gnostic document, directly or indirectly dependent upon the synoptic gospels for parallel material. But need this strict dichotomy be maintained? Is not some sapiential and philosophical literature somewhat "gnostic" in character, literature that predates the first century? Could not the traditions behind the Gospel of Thomas have

---

10. Recent examples of stratigraphical analysis include Arnal, "Rhetoric"; McLean, "On the Gospel of Thomas and Q"; and DeConick, *Recovering*. Some of these studies use recent work on the stratigraphy of Q as models for understanding the composition history of Thomas. Examples of recent analyses of the text as a whole include Asgeirsson, "Doublets and Strata"; Robbins, "Rhetorical Composition"; and Valantasis, *Gospel of Thomas*.

11. E.g., Haenchen, "Literatur zum Thomasevangelium"; Fallon and Cameron, "Gospel of Thomas"; Riley, "*Gospel of Thomas* in Recent Scholarship"; and Perrin, "Recent Trends."

12. E.g., Cullmann, "Gospel of Thomas," 434–35; Chilton, "Gospel according to Thomas," 164; Fallon and Cameron, "Gospel of Thomas," 4237; Hedrick, "Thomas and the Synoptics," 56; Neller, "Diversity," 18.

been interpreted, and hence shaded, in a gnostic direction in the early first century, especially if they bore resemblance to Jewish wisdom literature? And need the text in its entirety have been written in one place and time? What sets apart some recent attempts to address the issue of Thomas' relationship to canonical tradition on the basis of individual sayings is the openness to seeing broader possibilities concerning the history of the composition of the text. These studies should be examined carefully.

Thomas and the Synoptic Gospels

Though research into the Gospel of Thomas has expanded into many different directions in recent years, the issue of its place in the history of sayings of Jesus traditions continues to be debated. Several recent works suggest that some scholars are finally taking seriously the many previous calls to approach the Gospel of Thomas by analysis of one or two sayings at a time. The result of this approach is different studies, sometimes by the same scholars, that yield potentially divergent conclusions with regard to the tradition history of Thomas sayings.

Risto Uro, in his 1990 essay "Neither Here Nor There: Luke 17:20–21 and Related Sayings in Thomas, Mark, and Q," finds that both GTh 113 and Luke 17:20–21 show signs of redaction, but that GTh 113 does not include any of the redactional elements of Luke 17:20–21.[13] On the contrary, Uro finds two specific differences between the texts that shows GTh 113 to be the more primitive version of the sayings complex.[14] Uro takes this evidence to suggest that GTh 113 and Luke 17:20–21 represent use of a common tradition.[15] Uro does not go beyond this to suggest a date for the Thomas versions of the saying, and this is perhaps wise. The evidence, as Uro has laid it out, does not warrant such a conclusion.

In his 1993 *Forum* article, "'Secondary Orality' in the Gospel of Thomas? Logion 14 as a Test Case," Uro discerns evidence of synoptic redaction in at least one of the sayings included in Thomas 14 (GTh 14:5;

---

13. Uro, "Neither Here Nor There," esp. 13–20, 30–31.

14. Ibid., 20. On the one hand, Thomas' conclusion appears to be a redactional expansion. Uro suggests that GTh 113 comes from the same textual source as GTh 3:3a. On the other hand, Luke's lack of a second "lo" (before "there") suggests to Uro Lukan redaction. Also, the identity of the questioners differs in GTh 113 (disciples) and Luke 17:20–21 (Pharisees). Uro argues that if there were a change in the tradition, it would likely be from disciples to Pharisees, not vice versa.

15. Ibid., 30.

cf. Matt 5:11's redaction of Mark 7:15).[16] At the same time, however, the evidence is not substantial enough to suggest to Uro direct use of a synoptic gospel in the construction of the logion. In fact, he argues that the structure of GTh 14 and the order of the sayings therein rule out direct dependence on the synoptic gospels. In trying to adjudicate between these two conflicting results, Uro develops a theory of "secondary orality."[17] In other words, Uro argues that sayings of Jesus found in the canonical gospel texts often circulated independently after the gospels were written as isolated sayings of Jesus in oral transmission among Jesus communities. Uro's thesis is an attempt to respect both the pervasive influence of oral tradition in the first century and the influence of the written gospels. While Uro does not come to any conclusions about the first two sayings of GTh 14 (he thinks Luke 10:8–9, circulating independently of the written gospel, may have been the source for GTh 14:4),[18] the implication of his study would be that the brief chreia elaboration-like sayings cluster of GTh 14 is a construction that postdates the writing of the Gospel of Matthew (and maybe Luke).

While the results of Uro's earlier study need not imply a written text of GTh 3 and 113 pre-dating the writing of the synoptics, they do imply that the composition of the Gospel of Thomas involved sources for the sayings of Jesus other than the synoptic gospels. The evidence of Luke's redactional elements in Luke 17:20–21 and the lack of these elements in GTh 113 does not rule out Uro's later theory of "secondary orality" for this particular saying of Jesus, but there is no evidence to support it. To summarize, Uro has provided evidence for Thomas' use of oral tradition that ultimately goes back both to the synoptic gospels and to oral tradition that lies behind or is independent of the synoptic gospels.

James M. Robinson has likewise presented evidence that precludes any easy resolution regarding the history of traditions behind the Gospel of Thomas. In his evaluation of Q (Luke) 12:52 for the International Q Project, he argues that the Gospel of Thomas does not provide inde-

---

16. Uro, "'Secondary Orality,'" esp. 317–20, 22–24. This article was revised as "*Thomas and Oral Gospel Tradition.*" Uro expands on the interaction of orality and textuality in *Thomas: Seeking the Historical Context*, 106–33.

17. For the concept and term, Uro cites Haenchen, "Literatur," 178; Snodgrass, "The Gospel of Thomas," 27–28; and Kelber, *Oral and the Written Gospel*, 197.

18. "Uro, "'Secondary Orality,'" 20–22, 24.

pendent testimony of this saying being in Q.[19] Rather, GTh 16:3 lacks elements that would make its version of the Children against Parents pericope fully understandable, elements that are found only in Luke's redactional expansion of Q 12:51–53 (Luke 12:52's number of antagonists in the house). While Robinson concedes that the history of the transmission of GTh 16:1–2 is probably much more complicated, he finds, quite simply, that GTh 16:3 is dependent upon Luke (whether directly or indirectly he does not indicate). From this, one can conclude that the chreia elaboration-like clustering of sayings in GTh 16 postdates the writing of the Gospel of Luke, even if the traditions behind GTh 16:1–2 are potentially earlier and remain obscure.

On the other hand, Robinson, with Christoph Heil, believes he has identified a rare instance where one can actually observe the *literary* redaction of a saying of Jesus by the author of Q.[20] Central to Robinson and Heil's argument is the version of the Free from Anxiety like Ravens and Lilies pericope found in P. Oxy. 655 (GTh 36; cf. Q/Luke 12:22–31 and Matt 6:25–34; cf. esp. Q 12:27), a version that is more primitive than the abridged Coptic version and which contains two words (οὐ ξαίνει) that stand behind the version of the saying in Q 12:27 (specifically, Q 12:27's αὐξάνει). They argue that the P. Oxy. 655 version of the Free from Anxiety like Ravens and Lilies pericope shows no signs of Gnostic theological development—if anything, the P. Oxy. version of GTh 36 is *anti*-Gnostic and closer to Jesus' intention than Q—and that the Q version of the pericope shows more theological development in its parallel text (Q 12:22–24; e.g., its body-soul pairing vis-à-vis P. Oxy. 655's food-clothing pairing).[21] In constructing a chart of textual and chronological relations

19. Robinson, "Evaluation of Q 12:49–53," 119–21.

20. Robinson and Heil, "Zeugnisse."

21. Ibid., 36–39, 42–44. Robinson argues elsewhere that P. Oxy. 655 (GTh 36) preserves many details of this pericope that are more primitive than Q and can be used to reconstruct a pre-Q aphoristic core of sayings. See Robinson, "Pre-Q Text"; idem, "A Written Greek Sayings Cluster." Robinson's and Heil's findings have not gone unchallenged. Jens Schröter addressed them in "Vorsynoptische Überlieferung." Robinson and Heil responded with "Noch einmal." Stanley E. Porter challenged the thesis in "P.Oxy. 655." Robinson and Heil responded with "P.Oxy. 655 und Q"; and "The Lilies of the Field," esp. 9–21. Robinson provides a thoroughgoing English response to Schröter in "A Pre-Canonical Greek Reading." There, he also addresses the concerns of Robert H. Gundry, "Spinning the Lilies." The most recent critique comes from Dirk Jongkind, "'The Lilies of the Field' Reconsidered." All of the Robinson (and Heil) articles on this subject are contained in Robinson, *The Sayings Gospel Q*.

among the versions of the saying of Jesus about the unconcern of the crows, Robinson and Heil date a written pre-Q text to 30–70 CE and the written Gospel of Thomas at ±100 CE, though they give no reason for this comparatively late dating of Thomas. Their own evidence, however, leaves open other possibilities, and Robinson's further expansion on the "scribal error" in Q makes a turn of the century date for GTh 36 (Oxyrhynchus version) seem even more unlikely.[22]

Uro and Robinson both demonstrate that the source and composition history of the Gospel of Thomas is complex. They provide one example of the dependence of Thomas on a synoptic gospel[23] and one of indirect dependence through secondary orality.[24] Conclusions from their other two studies are less clear.[25] Do Luke and Thomas reflect use of a common tradition?[26] Do Q and Thomas reflect independent developments of oral and literary traditions?[27] What *is* clear from these studies is that the source history of sayings in Thomas defies simplistic answers, and that perhaps we should consider the composition history of the written text of Thomas as having undergone a developmental process, not as a product of a one-time scribal effort.

Gregory J. Riley has added another dimension hitherto lacking in the discussion and certainly complicating it. Using historical-critical methods usually reserved for the study of inter-synoptic relationships, methods that are also observed, however, in the works of Uro and Robinson discussed above, Riley, in his 1996 article "Influence of Thomas Christianity on Luke 12:14 and 5:39," looked for instances where elements in the Gospel of Thomas that are indicative of Thomasine emphasis, and hence of redaction or modification of tradition, might be reflected in the Gospel of Luke.[28] He found two such instances in Luke 12:13–14 (cf. GTh 72) and Luke 5:39 (cf. GTh 47:3–4). In the first case, Riley points out that the word for "divider" in Luke 12:14 rarely occurs in known Greek literature. Its presence does not add much to the saying in Luke.[29] However, it is

22. Robinson, "Pre-Q Text."
23. Robinson, "Evaluation."
24. Uro, "'Secondary Orality.'"
25. Uro, "Neither Here nor There"; Robinson and Heil, "Zeugnisse."
26. Uro, ibid., 30.
27. Robinson and Heil, "Zeugnisse," chart.
28. Riley, "Influence."
29. Ibid., 230–31. On μεριστής, see LSJSupp, 98b.

perfectly understandable in the Gospel of Thomas, where the unification of two into one is a central theme and Jesus is most definitely not to be understood as a divider.[30] The most logical conclusion from this, considering Luke's propensity for collecting from disparate sources, is that Luke has conflated two versions of a traditional saying, one of them represented by GTh 72.[31] In the other case, Luke's redaction of Mark 2:21–22 by adding a positive statement about old wine, while creating a generally true statement about good wine, contradicts the Markan emphasis on the value of the new over the old.[32] Where did Luke get this idea? Thomas 47 provides a complex of Jesus' sayings where a decision must be made between two choices, and in GTh 47:3–5 the choice is decidedly for the value of the old over the new. Riley sees this emphasis in Thomas to be redactional, epitomized by the recasting of the New Patch saying so that one is (incredibly) more concerned for an old patch than a new garment.[33] According to Riley, Luke's contradictory complex of sayings makes most sense if one understands Luke 5:36–39 to be a conflation of GTh 47:3–5 and Mark 2:21–22.

Riley chose perhaps the clearest and strongest cases for Lukan dependence on the Thomas tradition. And, while his argument that Luke was in contact with an actual community developing a Thomasine tradition of exegesis of Jesus' sayings needs further development to be persuasive—Luke may have simply been working from a written collection of sayings that had found its way into the Lukan community from traveling apostles who had passed through a Thomasine community[34]—Riley has provided strong evidence concerning two sayings in Thomas (72, 47) which stands in sharp contrast to the findings of Uro (GTh 14:5) and Robinson (GTh 16:3). In light of Riley's findings, Luke's aggregation of two similar sayings in Luke 17:20–21, 23 might also be re-examined in light of the pos-

---

30. Riley, "Influence," 231–32.
31. Ibid., 232.
32. Ibid., 233.
33. Ibid., 233–34.
34. On the one hand, knowledge of a particular community privileging this sayings tradition may have given the collection more authority in the eyes of the Lukan editor. On the other hand, unlike what Riley finds in his book *Resurrection Reconsidered*, a study which provides evidence of hermeneutical polemics between communities, Luke wouldn't appear to have a particular theological bone to pick with the Thomas tradition, judging by the examples Riley gives in the *HTR* article ("Influence").

sibility that Luke has preceded the Q "Coming of the Son of Humanity" pericope (Q 17:23–37) with a saying from the Thomas tradition (GTh 113), or even with a conflation of two sayings from the tradition (GTh 3 and 113).[35] Indeed, perhaps parallel Lukan *Sondergut* material as a whole should be reconsidered on a saying-by-saying basis.[36]

An equally important implication of Riley's study is that one must reconsider the composition history of Thomas in a new light. Whereas the results of Uro's (1990) and Robinson and Heil's studies (1998) do not necessarily speak to the dating of the composition of Thomas, Riley's study suggests that at least part of a distinctly Thomasine sayings tradition predates the composition of the Gospel of Luke. Hence, even if one suggests that the sayings of the Gospel of Thomas were written down for the first time at the end of the first century or early in the second century, if Riley's study holds up under closer scrutiny, then the Gospel of Thomas as a developing tradition of sayings of Jesus transmitted *with a particular theological perspective* at the very least predates the Gospel of Luke. At the same time, the conclusions of the preceding studies also require that one consider the Thomas tradition, even the written Gospel of Thomas itself, as developing over time. A mid-to-late first century oral collection or written text of the Gospel of Thomas *did* exist, but did *not* include *all*

---

35. See Robinson, "The Study of the Historical Jesus after Nag Hammadi," esp. 50–53. Robinson sees GTh 3 as evidence for an early tradition perhaps taken up by Q. Patterson rules out dependence in either direction on the basis of lack of verbal correspondence (Patterson, *Gospel of Thomas and Jesus*, 71–72). However, what he shows is that neither thesis is ultimately demonstrable on the basis of verbal comparison, especially when moving between Greek and Coptic. In noting the differences in the way Luke 17:20 and GTh 113:1–2 introduce the dominical saying, however, he fails to recognize that the difference in one could be due to alteration of the text of the other to create a different literary context for a similar saying, even using a typically more complex sentence structure for the introduction For example, inasmuch as 17:21 and 17:23 could be perceived as somewhat repetitious statements to the disciples, the author of Luke, in including the Thomasine material at this point, may have placed 17:20a on the lips of another group, the Pharisees, before redactionally prefacing the Q speech on the Coming of the Son of Humanity with a reference to the disciples (17:22), creating two separate conversations. Furthermore, there is almost verbatim similarity between Luke 17:21b and P. Oxy. 654.15–16 (GTh 3:3a), with Luke using a redactional ἰδοὺ γάρ to introduce the saying in its new context as an explanation for 17:20–21a (ἰδού possibly even coming from GTh 113:3's second "behold"). Hence, Lukan conflation of two sayings in Thomas is not only *not* ruled out, but is quite plausible, despite the perceived lack of verbal correspondence between Luke 17:20–21a and GTh 113:1–2. This hypothesis would answer the question of Luke's otherwise unknown source for 17:20–21 and ought to be explored further.

36. Cf. Schürmann, "Thomasevangelium."

of the sayings of Jesus found in the fourth century Coptic manuscript bearing the gospel title.

Finally, an important implication of the previous studies, when taken as a whole, is that the Thomas text and tradition and synoptic texts and traditions did not develop in isolation from each other.

Thomas and John

While New Testament scholars have mostly focused on the relationship between Thomas and the synoptic traditions, the similarities between the Gospel of Thomas and the Gospel of John have long been recognized.[37] In contrast to the synoptic similarities, however, similarities between Thomas and John lie less in clear and distinct sayings parallels, and more in theological conceptuality and symbolism. Nevertheless, the parallels that exist invite comparison, and scholars have suggested a multitude of possibilities. Hugh Evelyn-White looked at the Oxyrhynchus papyri and determined that similarities to John could not come from direct use of the Gospel: "The two fragments [P. Oxy. 1, 654] do not contain a single passage which can be regarded as derived either from the Fourth Gospel or from any other Johannine work."[38] Instead, he suggested that similarities were due to the Oxyrhynchus fragments having been compiled in a pre-Johannine gospel milieu:

> I do not see why the Oxyrhynchus Collection may not have been indebted to the same source (whether traditional or documentary) as St John, or to some nearly related source. At the same time Johannine influence is distinctly traceable in the Sayings. . . .
>
> . . . Johannine influence is distinctly present, though definite dependence on any of the Johannine works or literary use of any of them is not likely . . . the Sayings were formed at a pe-

---

37. E.g., Evelyn-White, *Sayings of Jesus*, xxxiv–xxxvi; Doresse, *Secret Books*, 339, 342, 350, 375–83; Wilson, *Studies*, 87; Kasser, *Thomas*; Brown, "Gospel of Thomas"; Koester, "Gnostic Writings"; idem, "Dialog"; Sell, "Johannine Traditions"; Davies, "Thomas," esp. 106–16; Koester, "Gnostic Sayings"; idem, "Les discours d'adieu," esp. 269–71, 275; idem, *Ancient Christian Gospels*, 113–24, 256–67; Patterson, "Gospel of Thomas"; Koester, "Story"; Riley, "Gospel of Thomas," 239–40; idem, *Resurrection*; De Conick, "Blessed"; Pagels, "Exegesis of Genesis 1"; Attridge, "'Seeking' and 'Asking,'"; DeConick, *Voices of the Mystics*; idem, "John Rivals Thomas"; Pagels, *Beyond Belief*; Popkes, "'Ich bin das Licht.'" Translations and commentaries have noted similarities, be they a word, a phrase, or an idea, from Doresse to the present (Doresse, *Thomas*).

38. Evelyn-White, *Sayings of Jesus*, xxxv.

riod when Johannism was already in the air but still nascent and undeveloped.[39]

Robert McL. Wilson, having the Coptic Gospel of Thomas at his disposal, still found Evelyn-White's proposal to be plausible, arguing that similarities between Thomas and John exist "in the realm of ideas, not citation."[40] Surprisingly, these suggestions of White and Wilson were not picked up and developed in several subsequent decades of Thomas research.

Raymond E. Brown was the first to do a systematic comparison of parallels between John and Thomas. He began with the assumption that the Gospel of John predated the Gospel of Thomas.[41] However, he also recognized that "the affinity to John in *GTh* is not nearly so clear or so strong as the affinity to the Synoptic Gospels." In fact, he argues that "many of the parallels . . . are so tenuous that they would be of significance only after a clear relationship between John and *GTh* had already been established."[42] He offered four ways of understanding the relationship between Thomas and John:

> (1) The author(s) of *GTh* may have read John in the past and have been influenced, consciously or unconsciously, by recollections. (2) The author(s) of *GTh* may have had some familiarity with memories of the oral preaching that underlay the Fourth Gospel. There have been attempts to localize both *GTh* and John in Syria. (3) The author(s) of *GTh* may have drawn on a source which in turn drew on John. . . . (4) *GTh* and John may both be drawing on a third source like Bultmann's hypothetical *Offenbarungsreden* source.[43]

In the end, Brown argues that the Gospel of Thomas originally contained a collection of synoptic-like sayings that were overlaid with Johannine themes indirectly derived from the Gospel of John itself.[44]

Jesse Sell rejected Brown's thesis (and his caution), arguing that Thomas was directly dependent upon John.[45] Unfortunately, as Riley

---

39. Ibid., xxxv–xxxvi.
40. Wilson, *Studies*, 87.
41. Brown, "Gospel of Thomas," 157.
42. Ibid., 174.
43. Ibid., 175.
44. Ibid., 175–77.
45. Sell, "Johannine Traditions," 25.

has pointed out, "he makes no comment on why the author of Thomas should never quote a saying or sentence from John, although the GTh is half full of such 'quotations' from the Synoptics."[46]

Helmut Koester has approached the Thomas-John relationship from the direction of genre development. Koester has argued in a series of studies that the Gospel of John represents a development of the dialogue or discourse genre two steps removed from the Gospel of Thomas—that is, two steps *beyond* the genre of Thomas, not prior to it.[47] In these studies, Koester deals especially with the gospels of Thomas and John, the *Dialogue of the Savior*, and the *Apocryphon of James*. According to Koester, the Gospel of Thomas "exhibits the first stage of transition from sayings collection to dialogue. The *Dialogue of the Savior* shows the initial stages of larger compositions."[48] Koester further argues that John "contains fully developed dialogues and discourses. Earlier stages could be reconstructed by using the analogies of the Gospel of Thomas and the *Dialogue of the Savior*, both with respect to form and structure and with respect to themes and topics."[49] Koester calls this earlier stage the Dialog as Exposition of Sayings ("Dialog als Spruchauslegung") and includes the Gospel of Thomas, the *Dialogue of the Savior*, the *Apocryphon of James*, and the *Book of Thomas* as Nag Hammadi texts belonging to this form.[50] Yet, the *Apocryphon of James* is seen by Koester as possibly dependent upon the Gospel of Thomas, and the form of the Gospel of Thomas shows us how the *Dialogue of the Savior* has combined sayings in the construction of discourses.[51] Furthermore, the *Dialogue of the Savior* is even less developed than the Gospel of John in terms of discourse development. Koester concludes:

---

46. Riley, "*Gospel of Thomas*," 239.

47. See esp. Koester, "Gnostic Writings"; idem, "Dialog"; idem, "Traditions"; idem, "Les discours d'adieu"; and idem, "Johannine Tradition."

48. Koester, "Gnostic Writings," 253.

49. Ibid.

50. Koester, "Dialog," 534, 544.

51. Ibid., 545–51. Koester and Elaine Pagels have argued that the *Dialogue of the Savior* is constructed using the saying found in GTh 2 as a framework, though they also state that the *Dialogue of the Savior* witnesses to a sayings tradition that "appears to be an independent parallel to the one used in *The Gospel of Thomas* and the Gospel of John" (Koester and Pagels, "Dialogue of the Savior," 244–45).

1. The speeches and dialogs of John's gospel are composed on a greater scale than hitherto received and transmitted sayings of Jesus. 2. The sayings dialogs from the Nag Hammadi writings as well as previously known apocryphal gospel material have preserved such sayings independently of the Gospel of John and thus provide a means to better discern the sayings that are foundational to the Johannine dialogs and speeches.[52]

At this point, Koester makes what many have considered to be a radical claim for the Gospel of Thomas: "A date in the second half of the first century C.E. can certainly be assumed for an older version of this writing."[53] What is often missed in this claim, however, is the fact that Koester is not claiming that the Gospel of Thomas *as represented by the Coptic manuscript* is to be dated this early.[54] Rather, he argues for an earlier version of the sayings collection. Such a qualified claim fits with the data collected in the recent comparisons of Thomas to synoptic sayings parallels noted above. Koester is usually careful not to make an outright claim that the Gospel of John has used the Gospel of Thomas.[55] Most recently he has suggested that Thomas and John have shared a common tradition, developing it in different directions.[56] However, he is clear that he thinks the author of John is combating gnostic responses to the teaching of Jesus and the search for life—gnostic responses reflected in the Gospel of Thomas, the *Apocryphon of James*, and the *Dialogue of the Savior*.[57] More to the point of our survey, Koester argues that "these dia-

---

52. Koester, "Dialog," 553–54: "1. Die Reden und Dialoge des Johannesevangeliums sind in größerem Umfang als bisher angenommen auf überlieferten Sprüchen Jesu aufgebaut. 2. Die Spruchdialoge aus den in Nag Hammadi gefundenen Schriften sowie bereits bekanntes apokryphes Evangelien-Material haben solche Sprüche unabhängig vom Johannesevangelium aufbewahrt und geben so eine Handhabe dafür, die den johanneischen Dialogen und Reden zugrunde liegenden Sprüche besser zu erkennen."

53. Ibid., 554. "Ein Datum in der zweiten Hälfte des 1. Jh. nChr. läßt sich für eine ältere Fassung dieser Schrift durchaus annehmen."

54. Koester, Gnostic Writings," 243–44: "Although the Johannine attestations [of Thomas sayings] assure a first-century date for their incorporation into the sayings tradition of Jesus, it would be hazardous to consider these Johannine occurrences as proof for a first-century date of the Gospel of Thomas *in the form in which it is preserved in its Coptic translation*. The Greek fragments from Oxyrhynchus demonstrate the instability of text and context of such sayings collections" (italics mine).

55. E.g., Koester, "Gnostic Writings," 243, 259.

56. See Koester, *Ancient Christian Gospels*, 119, 122–23.

57. See, e.g., Koester, "Les discours d'adieu," 269–75; idem, *Ancient Christian Gospels*,

logues were shaped by a theological interpretation of Jesus' sayings that is comparable to that of the *Gospel of Thomas*, a theology that emphasized the recognition of one's divine self and the return to one's heavenly origin."[58]

Stevan L. Davies returned to the thesis of Evelyn-White that the Gospel of Thomas as a saying collection derived from an early stage of the Johannine community.[59] This sayings collection was developed by the author of John (à la Koester) in the discourse material of the gospel. Where Davies appears to depart from Koester is in his insistence that the Gospel of Thomas is not gnostic but, like John, relies on and develops the Jewish wisdom tradition.[60] Rather than being about a return to one's heavenly origin, the Gospel of Thomas is about a return to the pre-Fall state of Genesis creation.[61]

Riley has argued that the Gospels of John and Thomas represented separate and distinct communities that were in dialogue, but that were also in fundamental disagreement over aspects of christology and soteriology.[62] That they were in dialogue is evident by the many similarities in cosmology, literary symbolism, and, especially, anthropology. The Gospel of John gives specific indications of the conflict, however, in its portrayal of Thomas as first doubter, then believer in the physical resurrection of Jesus. More specifically,

> The Doubting Thomas pericope is evidence within the Gospel of John for the prior existence of the community of Thomas. The elements present and positions countered in the pericope cohere well with those in the *Gospel of Thomas*, and lead to the conclusion that the *Gospel of Thomas* itself was already at some stage of completion, either written or oral, and that its contents were known to the author of John, probably through verbal contact

---

264–67; idem, "Johannine Tradition," 19–23.

58. Koester, "Johannine Tradition," 23.

59. Davies, *Gospel of Thomas*, 115–16.

60. Ibid., 106–16. Actually, Koester agrees that both texts develop wisdom traditions. In fact, gnostic thought clearly develops out of the wisdom tradition inasmuch as both emphasize the search for wisdom and enlightenment as the path to one's salvation. The question is how far along in the development from wisdom speculation to gnostic speculation, and from wisdom forms to gnostic interpretation of those forms, the Gospel of Thomas has moved.

61. Davies, "Christology and Protology." Cf. Koester, "Johannine Tradition," 23.

62. Riley, *Resurrection*, 69–179.

with members of this rival community. In addition, the *Gospel of Thomas* contains evidence of reciprocal debate with the community of John, although in a form which predates the Gospel.[63]

April D. De Conick agrees wholeheartedly with Riley that analysis of John reveals "a discourse between the Thomasine and Johannine Christians"—one that reflects a dispute over soteriology.[64] However, she argues this for very different reasons. She has argued that the Gospel of John contains a polemic against Thomasine ascent mysticism.[65] In John's insistence that the disciples cannot follow Jesus where he goes, she sees an argument against Thomas' call to mystical ascension to the place where Jesus is. She also refutes Riley's understanding of John 20:24–29 as an argument for the fleshly resurrection of Jesus. She sees the exchange between Thomas and Jesus as an example of a common topos of identifying the hero through touch, and argues that John 20:29 "criticizes visionary experience in favor of faith."[66]

Ismo Dunderberg questions whether the argument has been demonstrated that the Gospel of John was written in part as polemic against a Thomas community. He is not persuaded largely because the conflict exists on an implicit level in the two gospels.[67] Dunderberg argues that there are problems with Riley's thesis related to the inconsistent use of Judas/Thomas terminology in the Thomas tradition, the lack of a distinctive characterization of Thomas in John, and problems Dunderberg sees with Riley's analysis of the Doubting Thomas pericope in John (John 20:24–29).[68] While he is right that the case has not been *proven*, none of the problems noted are decisive.

Dunderberg extends his critique of the thesis of a literary relationship between Thomas and John in two more recent articles.[69] In

---

63. Ibid., 178. Cf. Ron Cameron's critique of Riley's thesis in "Ancient Myths and Modern Theories," esp. 239–44.

64. De Conick, "Blessed," 397.

65. De Conick, *Seek*, 92–93. DeConick's more recent *Voices of the Mystics* contains a more extensive and thorough treatment of her thesis.

66. "Blessed," 396.

67. Dunderberg, "John and Thomas in Conflict?"

68. Ibid., 370–78.

69. Dunderberg, "*Thomas'* I-Sayings"; and idem, "Thomas and the Beloved Disciple." Dunderberg extensively critiques the theories of DeConick, Pagels, and Riley in *The Beloved Disciple in Conflict?*

"*Thomas*' I-Sayings and the Gospel of John," he surveys the different theories of Thomas' relationship to John and finds definitive evidence of a literary relationship lacking. Occasionally, he finds closer verbal or thematic parallels to John or Thomas in other literature.

In "*Thomas* and the Beloved Disciple," Dunderberg argues that the disciple Thomas in the so-named gospel is not literarily related to the Beloved Disciple of John. Rather, both reflect the use of authorial fiction to gain authority for the text. Whereas late second century writers attached the names of disciples or early apostles to the gospels to give them authority, John and Thomas reflect a more primitive tradition of placing a key figure, even the author, into the narrative itself.[70] Nevertheless, Dunderberg sees Thomas and John working in different ways and reflecting "a more broadly attested phenomenon in early Christianity."

Apart from Dunderberg's studies, what distinguishes research into the relationship between Thomas and John from Thomas-synoptic research is the broad and general recognition that the two texts/traditions are somehow related. For the most part, there is also recognition that this relationship is not simply one of direct literary influence. This latter point should again make us hesitate before making general claims concerning specific sayings of Jesus. Nevertheless, the aforementioned studies provide a number of possibilities for understanding the relationship or lack of relationship between the texts, and should be kept in mind when undertaking a saying-by-saying analysis of sayings of Jesus found in both Thomas and John.

Thomas and the Pauline Tradition

There has been relatively little discussion of connections between the Gospel of Thomas or a Thomasine tradition and the epistolary corpus of the New Testament. This is due in part to the fact that Thomas is a collection of sayings of Jesus and the bulk of its similarities to the New Testament canon are to the gospels, in part to the lack of consensus on the history and development of the Gospel of Thomas, and in part to the larger historical problem of assessing connections between gospel traditions and the Pauline tradition. The first problem should not deter

---

70. An earlier study argues that the author of Mark also places the author in the narrative in a similar but even more subtle way than the redactor of John (Johnson, "Identity"). Mark may have even provided the model for the redactor's work in John.

scholarship. The second problem is, of course, an on-going discussion, but perhaps can be dealt with by a study of similarities between Thomas and the New Testament letters. It is the third issue that ought to be addressed here since it is relevant to a discussion of Thomasine and epistolary traditions. Therefore, the following survey of literature on possible connections between the Gospel of Thomas and the Pauline tradition is prefaced by the review of a more basic and ongoing discussion concerning Paul's knowledge and use of sayings of Jesus.

Biblical scholarship is divided on how much acquaintance Paul had with traditions of sayings of Jesus.[71] Several problems contribute to this disagreement. For one, Paul shows little interest in the earthly Jesus outside of his death, burial, and resurrection. For another, Paul never cites sayings of Jesus by name; only occasionally does he cite sayings as words of "the Lord." These problems have not stopped many from searching for allusions to sayings of Jesus throughout the Pauline corpus. D. M. Stanley and John Pairman Brown are two good examples of this.[72] Works like theirs have largely been rejected because of the extent and lack of defensibility of their claims.

Perhaps more important, *where and how* Paul uses different sayings of Jesus in the letters is not often discussed, as though the rhetorical context makes little difference. By "where and how" I am not referring to the common observation that apparent allusions are found grouped in isolated passages such as Romans 12–14, 1 Thessalonians 4–5, or 1 Corinthians 1–4. More specifically, I am referring to the type of epistolary material in which the supposed sayings are embedded. The exceptions—some have observed that possible sayings are never found in sections where Paul is expounding upon central theological issues, but are found rather in sections of "ethical paraenesis"—are usually stated in general terms, and still leave us with the question of why Paul almost never attributes sayings tradition material to Jesus.[73] However, observing

71. For a comprehensive bibliography and overview of the discussion up to 1986, see Neirynck, "Paul."

72. Stanley, "Pauline Allusions"; John Pairman Brown, "Synoptic Parallels."

73. E.g., Walter, "Paul." Walter cites Schürmann, "'Das Gesetz des Christus' (Gal 6,2)," esp. 285–86; and Gräßer, "Der Mensch Jesus," esp. 133–36. Martin Dibelius argues that paraenetic sections of epistolary literature—even full documents like the Epistle of James—use community paraenesis, an oral form of teaching that does not usually cite Jesus directly (Dibelius, *James,* 28–29; idem, *From Tradition to Gospel,* 238–44. He also argues that texts like James are themselves examples of the genre "community paraene-

the context in which the material is used may help to explain how Paul is using it and why he does not cite Jesus, or even "the Lord," when adapting material from sayings collections.

In three cases, there is little debate about Paul's use of Jesus' teaching. Paul cites traditions of Jesus' teaching in 1 Cor 7:10–11 (divorce and remarriage), 9:14 (evangelists earning a living), and 11:23–25 (the Last/Lord's Supper).[74] In a fourth case, 1 Thess 4:15 (order of eschatological ascension), it appears that Paul is citing a saying of Jesus. In each of these cases, Paul uses teachings of Jesus as authoritative teaching within the rhetorical structure of his arguments and exhortations. To be more explicit, Paul is addressing particular problems in the Corinthian community in 1 Corinthians 5–7; 8–10; and 11:17–34. Sayings parallels (1 Cor 7:10–11; 9:14; 11:23–25) are embedded within the extended arguments of these larger passages. The citations in 1 Corinthians function as appeals to authority usually do within rhetorical arguments (though Paul, to make a point about humility and other-centeredness, rejects for the commonweal the implications of the chreia in 1 Cor 9:14). First Thess 4:15 is also embedded in a discussion about the eschaton, though the context is less argumentative in structure and tone. In fact, Paul has already established his own authority at length in 1 Thessalonians 1–3.

Disagreement becomes prominent when one looks beyond these four citations for further uses of a sayings tradition. Possible scattered allusions can be found throughout Romans, 1 and 2 Corinthians, 1 Thessalonians, and disputed Pauline letters like Colossians. More cre-

---

sis." However, Dibelius too facilely slips between oral forms and written genres without adequately explaining *why* paraenesis—be it oral form or written genre—does not tend to cite Jesus' authority (especially when texts like James *do* cite scriptural authority). His argument that "all the sayings of Christian exhortation were regarded as inspired by the Spirit or by the Lord" cannot be taken seriously as an explanation.

74. According to Furnish, "Chapters 7 and 11 of 1 Corinthians supply firm evidence that, at the very least, Paul was acquainted with Jesus' words as mediated in the catechetical and liturgical traditions" (Furnish, "Jesus-Paul Debate," 375). That liturgy is a source is true at least for 1 Cor 11:23–25. For the other two, Neirynck observes that "there is no 'quotation' of the saying" by Paul. "Paul produces in his own formulation 'a halakah based on such a saying'" ("Paul and the Sayings of Jesus," 320; in the latter sentence quoting Gerhardsson, *Memory and Manuscript*, 318 n. 93). Considering his largely negative assessment of other potential allusions in the letter based on a close analysis of verbal parallels, Neirynck's observation here is important. To wit, based on 1 Cor 7:10–11 and 9:14, where Paul actually cites teachings of Jesus but doesn't "quote" him, one should not expect extensive verbal parallels between Paul and synoptic sayings of Jesus elsewhere when Paul does not even cite "the Lord."

dence is gained, however, when attention is focused on clusters of potential sayings within specific sections of Paul.[75]

In Romans 12-14, alongside of the abbreviated recapitulations of teachings also found in 1 Corinthians 12 (Rom 12:3-8) and 1 Cor 6:12-11:1 (Rom 14:1—15:6), Paul compiles a number of wisdom admonitions and prohibitions to exhort his readers—some of these admonitions are very close to teachings of Jesus in the Q Sermon and Mark 12.[76] A close comparison of verbal similarities between Pauline and synoptic texts would undercut any claims to proof that Paul has used sayings of Jesus here. The similarities between individual exhortations and known sayings of Jesus usually extend as far as common theme and common form, but with only a few lexical parallels. More important than looking for lexical parallels, however, is observing the generic context in which these "allusions" are found. In Romans 12-14, Paul is clearly using a collection (or collections) of sayings, not for the purpose of defending his ministry, disputing with snobbish Gentile converts in Rome, or addressing particular ethical problems that he has heard about, but for the purpose of general exhortation; and so he appears to have the freedom to expand and adapt his source(s). Since the nature of the material in Rom 12:9-21 especially is *not* rhetorical argumentation, but rather a string of general wisdom admonitions and prohibitions, there is no need to cite the source of the admonitions in order to establish authority.[77] If the readers/hear-

---

75. Ferdinand Hahn lists the following as paraenetic sections in the canonical epistles: 1 Thess 4:1-9; 5:(1-11, 12-14,)15-22; Gal 5:14—6:10; Phil 4:4-9; Rom 12:9—13:14; Col 3:5—4:6; Eph 4:17—6:17; Heb 13:1-9, 17; 1 Pet 2:11—4:11; (5:1-11); Jas 1:3—5:11 (Hahn, "Die christologische Begründung," 89, n. 13).

76. E.g., cf. the following: Rom 12:14/Luke 6:27-28/Matt 5:44; Rom 12:17, 21/Luke 6:29/Matt 5:39-40; Rom 13:7/Mark 12:17 par.; Rom 13:9/Mark 12:28-30 par. (cf. Mark 10:17-22); Rom 14:10, 13/Luke 6:37/Matt 7:1. See Neirynck ("Paul and the Sayings of Jesus," 270) for a table of allusions and a number of scholars who argue for each of them. Included in this table is Rom 12:21/Luke 6:27ff/Matt 5:39ff; Rom 14:14(20)/Mark 7:15 par.; and Rom 16:19/Matt 10:16b. Romans 14:13 is usually compared to Mark 9:42 par. with their common use of σκανδαλ-. Walter and Patterson include Rom 12:18/Mark 9:50/Matt 5:9 (Walter, "Paul," 56; Patterson, "Paul," esp. 29 n. 26).

77. Even in Romans 13-14, where Paul returns to argumentative style, the "allusions" are usually the point of the rhetoric, not supportive material in the body of the argument. Rom 13:7 is a rhetorical recapitulation, giving the elaboration pattern of 13:1-7 a specific, practical focus. Rom 13:8-10 stands on its own, though it is smoothly connected to the preceding thought. Rom 14:10a is the issue subsequently defended in 14:10b-12, and this issue of judging others is the essential departure in theme from Paul's more elaborate discussion in 1 Cor 6:12-11:1.

ers have accepted Paul's claims to authority in the letter thus far, they will certainly accept these general exhortations without need of higher authority. This would also be the case for 1 Thess 5:12–22, where we find two possible sayings of Jesus, 1 Thess 5:12 (cf. Rom 12:18) and 1 Thess 5:15 (cf. Rom 12:17), embedded in a string of general exhortations that close out the letter.

In 1 Corinthians 1–4, a different situation prevails. Here Paul is at odds with opponents who seem to be preaching a message laden with eloquence, power, and a focus on words of divine wisdom. Observing that sayings collections like Q have a strong sapiential overtone, some scholars have tried to uncover parallels to Q in Paul's rhetoric against his opponents.[78]

Christopher Tuckett has questioned some of the cases cited for a Q tradition in 1 Corinthians.[79] At the same time, Robinson is right to note the importance of the wisdom orientation of the opponents and to ask whether a sayings tradition is represented in Paul's rhetoric against his opponents.

Robinson, Koester, and Heinz-Wolfgang Kuhn also note certain affinities in 1 Corinthians 1–4 to the Gospel of Thomas.[80] Koester, while focusing his discussion on Q 10:23–24 (Matt 13:16–17), notes a much closer parallel to 1 Cor 2:9 in GTh 17, though a literary relationship between the texts is difficult to maintain.[81] Stevan L. Davies and Stephen J. Patterson have both picked up on these hints and argued that the collection of say-

---

78. E.g., Robinson, "Kerygma and History," esp. 40–46; Kuhn, "Der irdische Jesus," esp. 308–18; Koester, "Gnostic Writings," esp. 244–50.

79. Tuckett, "1 Corinthians and Q." Tuckett is right to question a Q relationship to the three citations in 1 Corinthians, as well as Koester's 1 Cor 2:9/Matt 13:16–17 (Q 10:23–24) parallel, though he appears to miss the point when he observes the different uses of νηπίοις in 1 Cor 3:1 and Q 10:21–22. If Paul's opponents understood themselves as enlightened "newborns" due to their recent baptism and spiritual instruction, then Paul's condescending use of "newborn" makes an effectively snide attack on their self-understanding. In effect, Paul is saying "Yes, they are newborns, but for that very reason they are spiritually *immature* (or, as he puts it, σαρκίνοις) and ought to be treated as such."

80. Kuhn goes as far as to suggest a tradition-historical connection between the opponents of 1 Corinthians, the tradents of Q, the opponents in the letter of Polycarp, and the Gospel of Thomas ("Der irdische Jesus," 518).

81. Koester, "Gnostic Writings," 248. But see also idem, "One Jesus," 230. On GTh 17 specifically, see Onuki, "Traditionsgeschichte." For a critique of Onuki, see Dunderberg, "John and Thomas in Conflict?" 365–70.

ings in the Gospel of Thomas, not Q, is perhaps best represented by Paul's rhetoric against his opponents in 1 Corinthians 1–4.[82] Davies cites two of the Corinthian passages most crucial to Robinson's analysis, 1 Cor 3:1 and 4:8, and finds even stronger parallels in the Gospel of Thomas.[83] In each case cited in 1 Corinthians (except perhaps 1 Cor 2:9—but even there, it is possible that Paul changes the last line of a traditional saying to bring it more in line with Isa 64:3 [LXX]), Paul appears to be using his opponents' teaching *against* them. It is certainly significant that the Gospel of Thomas provides an even better picture of Paul's rhetorical opponents than do the sapientially-oriented Q tradents. The evidence so far presented suggests the possibility that the opponents of Paul taught from a sayings collection very similar to what is found in parts of the Gospel of Thomas. For this very reason, Paul would not likely cite sayings of Jesus himself, but rather would focus—as he does—on the apparent folly of the cross and the *kerygma* with its message of divine power expressed in weakness.

In summary, detailed studies like Neirynck's help to clarify just how much can be claimed when using lexical parallels as the primary datum for determining what constitutes use of a saying of Jesus. At the same time, Romans 12–14, 1 Thessalonians 5, and 1 Corinthians 1–4 appear to provide evidence for Paul's use of sayings traditions *when one observes how and where he uses them*. Paul uses great freedom in adapting and modifying sayings traditions for his didactic needs. More to the point, Paul does not need to cite "the Lord" in the general exhortations of Romans 12–14 (or 1 Thessalonians 5) anymore than he would *want* to cite "the Lord" when condemning his opponents with their own sayings tradition in 1 Corinthians 1–4.

Regardless of how one decides for the authorship of letters such as Colossians and James, the foregoing survey has implications for the

---

82. Patterson, "Paul and the Jesus Tradition"; Davies, *Gospel of Thomas*, 138–45. See also Kelber, who argues that substantial similarities in the Gospel of Thomas support the existence of a sayings tradition at Corinth (*Oral and Written Gospel*, 176).

83. Davies, *Gospel of Thomas*, 141–43. "Paul writes of them, 'you are completely satisfied . . . , you have grown rich . . . , and you have begun your reign . . . .' These are three distinct metaphors for present fulfillment, and Paul's opponents apparently applied them to themselves" (141). Cf. esp. Thomas 109 and 110 on becoming rich, and 2 and 81 on becoming rulers. As discussed above, Paul's opponents may have called themselves babes in a positive sense, a self-designation that Paul derides. For an example of this kind of self-designation, Davies notes Thomas 4, 21, 22, 37, and 46 (p. 143).

present study. Chapter 4 includes a comparison of similarities between specific sections of Colossians and Thomas and suggests the use by the author of Colossians of sayings material also found in Thomas. The similar material in Colossians is found at what is almost universally recognized among commentators as the beginning of an extended section of community paraenesis.[84] As seen above with Romans 12–14, 1 Thessalonians 5, and 1 Corinthians 1–4, a collection of sayings parallels is found to be isolated in a particular section of the letter (Col 3:1–11). If Paul authored this letter, then the parallels potentially argue for a Thomasine sayings tradition that can be dated to the 50's CE. If a follower of Paul is writing in his name, then the parallels are at least indicative of a tradition dating to the second half of the century in a location where a collection of Paul's letters are known.

Summary

The foregoing survey of literature points to several issues to be addressed in the following analysis of the Treasure in Heaven saying. (1) Some of the sayings of Jesus in the Gospel of Thomas may reflect a primitive, first-century sayings tradition, one that may have influenced canonical texts in some places, while other Thomas sayings may derive—directly or indirectly—from the canonical gospels. When dealing with a sayings collection that represented the traditions of living communities behind it, these two observations are not contradictory, but point to a complex history of development. (2) While a strictly literary relationship between Thomas and John probably cannot be proven, there may be either a relationship between tradent communities, or evidence of the use of one sayings tradition in the writing of two different types of literary text. (3) The use of sayings traditions in the canonical letters is an ongoing debate, one that will not be determined by reference to lexical parallels alone. Isolating possible sayings sources in specific letter sections, especially paraenetic sections, appears to be a fruitful approach. Of course, James is almost entirely paraenetic, which is why James's relationship to gospel traditions is an important topic for research today.

---

84. Col 3:1–4:6. See, e.g., Pokorny, *Colossians*, 157.

CHAPTER 2 | The Synoptics and Q

INTRODUCTION

For most biblical commentators, the primary point of departure in the study of the Treasure in Heaven saying is the content and interpretation of this saying in Matthew and Luke, where we find the clearest and most elaborate expressions among canonical parallels. Intimately connected to the issue of how Matthew and Luke employ this saying is the issue of how they adapt their primary source for this saying, the sayings gospel Q. In order to understand how they have altered the content and, hence, intended meaning of the Q version of the saying, one must first reconstruct this earlier Q version. In the process of reconstruction, by noting some of the redactional tendencies of Matthew and Luke, some of the answers to the question of how Matthew and Luke use and adapt the Treasure saying will begin to become clear. Subsequent to the reconstruction of Q will be a discussion of the following: (1) how the composers of these three texts used the Treasure in Heaven saying; (2) how these texts might be related to the larger context of Jewish wisdom and eschatology; (3) the place of Mark 10:21 in the history of the transmission of this saying.

Q 12:33

Q 12:33⁰: Is Luke 12:33 par. Matt 6:(19–)20 in Q?

This variant is occasioned by the different positions of the sayings in Matthew and Luke, the difference in the internal order of the adversity clauses in the two versions, and the lack of verbal agreement between the versions (relative to most Q texts in Matthew and Luke). The only signifi-

Figure 1

Matt 6:19-20[1]	Luke 12:33
⁰⌐	⁰⌐
¹⌠	¹⌠
6:19 (μὴ θησαυρίζετε ὑμῖν θησαυροὺς ἐπὶ τῆς γῆς, ὅπου σὴς καὶ βρῶσις ἀφανίζει καὶ ὅπου κλέπται διορύσσουσιν καὶ κλέπτουσιν·)[2]	[πωλήσατε τὰ ὑπάρχοντα ὑμῶν καὶ δότε ἐλεημοσύνην·][2]
6:20	
(θησαυρίζετε)[3]	[ποιήσατε][3]
(δὲ)[4]	( )[4]
(ὑμῖν)[5]	[ἑαυτοῖς][5]
[ ][6]	[βαλλάντια μὴ παλαιούμενα][6],
θησαυρο(ὺς)[7]	θησαυρὸ[ν][7]
[ ][8]	[ἀνέκλειπτον][8]
ἐν [ ][9]	ἐν [τοῖς][9]
οὐραν(ῷ)[10],	οὐραν[οῖς][10],
ὅπου	ὅπου
¹¹⌠ (οὔτε)[12] σὴς (οὔτε βρῶσις)[12] (ἀφανίζει)[13] ⌡¹¹	¹¹⌠κλέπτ[ης][15] οὐ[κ ἐγγίζει][16] ( )[17] ⌡¹¹
(καὶ ὅπου)[14]	[οὐδὲ][14]
¹¹⌠ κλέπτ(αι)[15]	¹¹⌠( )[12] σὴς ( )[12]
οὐ (διορύσσουσιν)[16]	[διαφθείρει][13]
(οὐδὲ κλέπτουσιν)[17] ⌡¹¹.	⌡¹¹.
⌡¹	⌡¹
⌡⁰	⌡⁰

cant "minimal Q" words and phrases are θησαυρο- ("treasure"), ἐν οὐραν- ("in heaven), ὅπου ("where"), σής ("moth"), and κλέπτ- ("rob").[2]

1. The format for identifying the variants of this saying is that of the International Q Project. See Johnson, *Q 12:33-34*, 2-3. See also Robinson, Hoffmann, and Kloppenborg, eds., *The Critical Edition of Q*, 328-31 (henceforth *CEQ*).

2. "Minimal Q" refers to words common to both Matthew and Luke. Include here the second person plural ending -τε for the main verbs followed by a second person plural dative pronoun. GTh 76:3 parallels Matthew and Luke in the use of the plural imperative, but places the pronoun before the imperative as part of the transition from the parable of

A number of arguments, however, support Luke 12:33/Matt 6:(19–)20 as coming from Q. (1) This saying is found in Matthew and Luke, but not in Mark—the fundamental premise for identifying Q material.[3] (2) Both versions of the saying have Q 12:34 ("For where you treasure is, there will your heart be also") attached as a rationale for the behaviors recommended in the Treasure saying (against GTh 76:3 and all other versions of the saying to be identified in this study). It is not likely that the two sayings would be attached independently in pre-gospel oral traditions. (3) Both gospels group Q 12:33–34 with the Free from Anxiety like Ravens and Lilies pericope of Q 12:22–31 (Matt 6:19–21, 25–34). (4) A catchword connection exists between Luke 12:33/Matt 6:19–20 and the Son of Humanity Coming as a Robber saying of Luke 12:39/Matt 24:43 ("thief" and Matt 6:19–20's "dig through"). This connection is most especially significant since Matt 24:43 is located quite some distance from the sayings clusters of Matthew 6.[4] Taking into account the cumulative force of these observations, and starting with the presupposition of the Q hypothesis, there should be little doubt that this saying existed in Q.

Q 12:33[1]: *Position of the Pericope in Q*

Determining the position of Q 12:33(–34) in Q must take into consideration several issues. Are there good redactional rationales for Matthew or Luke to have moved the saying to its present position in one or the other gospel? Matthew's present position preceding the Generous Eye and Two Masters sayings (Matt 6:22–24) is almost universally recognized as being secondary. But what if Matt 6:19–21 (Q 12:33–34) immediately preceded

---

GTh 76:1–2 to the admonition of 76:3.

3. Herbert Braun argues that Mark 10:21 is a version—indeed, the most primitive version—of the Treasure in Heaven saying (Braun, *Radikalismus*, 56–58 n. 1; 74 n. 2; 75 n. 1; 76 n. 1). He may be right that it represents a version of the saying, but the saying exists in barely recognizable form and there is no possibility that both Matt 6:19–20 and Luke 12:33 could have been created from the Markan saying. For Luke's use of Mark 10:21, see below, p. 33.

4. Since there is no apparent connection between Luke 12:22–34 and 12:35–38, it must otherwise be argued that Luke, upon attaching 12:35–38 to 12:33–34, also brought forward 12:39–40 from later in Q, creating the catchword connection ("thief") between Luke 12:33 and 12:39–40. The connection between Q 12:39 and Matt 6:19–20 would then have to be considered coincidental. It seems far more likely that Luke 12:39–40 immediately followed 12:33–34 (with "dig through" in Q 12:33) in Q, and that Luke inserted 12:35–38 on the basis of a common theme and catchword connection to Q 12:39 (Matt 24:43, φυλακή, "watch" [Matt 24:43] being transferred to Luke 12:38).

Matt 6:25–34 (Q 12:22–31) in Q?[5] How well do the respective positions fit in the larger context of Q 12:2–40?

Ordinarily, one would expect the issue of redactional rationales to provide the strongest argument for one choice or the other. Such is not the case here. It could be argued that Matthew has very good reasons for placing Q 12:33–34 (Matt 6:19–21) ahead of Q 12:22–31 (Matt 6:25–33).[6] This repositioning is suggested by the last saying in the "Cult Didache" (Matt 6:1–18) on the Father's reward for proper and pious behavior and/or by the antithetical parallelism of Matt 6:1–18. After repositioning Q 12:33–34, Matthew then would have added Matt 6:22–24 to create a three-saying aphoristic collection on the subject of greed and divided loyalties.[7] Matthew 6:19–24 would thus provide an apt transition from the "Cult Didache" to the Free from Anxiety like Ravens and Lilies pericope (Matt 6:25–33/Q 12:22–31), which addresses concerns about obtaining food and clothing.[8] All of these redactional arguments, however, are mitigated by the simple fact that if Q 12:33–34 already preceded Q 12:22–31 in Q, then all of the above advantages would have been gained merely by inserting Q 12:33–34, 22–31 as a block into the Sermon on the Mount after Matt 6:18 and inserting Q 11:34–36 and Q 16:13 (Matt 6:22–24) between them.[9]

On the other hand, one could argue that Luke has moved Q 12:33–34 to its present position in Luke, modified Q 12:33, and inserted a complex of sayings and parables (Parable of the Rich Fool, etc.—Luke 12:13–21) in 12:33's former position in order to frame the Q Free from Anxiety like Ravens and Lilies pericope with Lukan ethical interests regarding the hoarding of possessions and almsgiving.[10] The addition of Luke 12:32 ("Do not be afraid, little flock, for it is your Father's good pleasure to give you the kingdom") creates a summary that frames the speech ("do not be anxious" [12:22]/"fear not" [12:32]), and exposes the lack of a good original connection between Q 12:31 and Q 12:33. If Luke 12:33–34's

---

5. Hoffmann, "Jesu 'Verbot des Sorgens,'" esp. 128; reprinted in *Tradition und Situation*, esp. 119; idem, "Mutmassungen," 267, 278.

6. See, e.g., Castor, *Matthew's Sayings of Jesus*, 85. Günther Bornkamm argues that it is based on the structure of the Lord's Prayer (Bornkamm, "Aufbau," 426–27).

7. Marriot, *Sermon on the Mount*, 66–67.

8. Schmid, *Matthäus und Lukas*, 237.

9. Hoffmann, *Tradition und Situation*, 119.

10. Cf. Hoffmann, "Verbot," esp. 124–25; idem., *Tradition und Situation*, 116.

position is original, however, then framing the Free from Anxiety like Ravens and Lilies pericope with Lukan concerns would have been accomplished merely by redacting Q 12:33 and inserting 12:13-20 into its present position, with a Lukan moral, 12:21, created from Q 12:33's original vocabulary. In short, redactional rationales in either direction are mitigated by simpler arguments based on the sayings being located in their present positions. Having thus disposed of the issue of redactional rationales, the following arguments seem most cogent to me:

1. Obvious catchword connections exist with Q 12:2-12/12:22-24[11] and Q 12:33/12:39,[12] but not with either Q 12:2-12/12:33-34 or Q 12:22-31/12:39-40.

2. Conceptual and metaphorical connections exist between Q 12:4-7, 11-12 (Not Fearing the Body's Death, Hearings before the Synagogues) and 12:22-24: God's providence in a crisis or concerning daily needs and God's care for birds as an *a minore ad maius* ("from the lesser to the greater") argument for God's concern for people.[13]

3. The assertion of God's providence in Q 12:11-12 provides a strong rationale for the transitional διὰ τοῦτο ("for this reason") in Q 12:22, which allows for the rhetorical development of the argumentation in Q 12:22-31 without explicit mention of God's providence until Q 12:24. The location of Q 12:33-34 preceding 12:22-31 would interrupt this (and the μεριμνάω ["be anxious"] catchword) connection.[14] Luke's insertion of 12:13-21 also interrupts this development of thought in favor of Luke's thematic

---

11. Q 12:2-12 and 12:22-31, dealing with the issues of public proclamation and the basic necessities of life respectively, are connected by the catchwords μή and μεριμνάω ("do not be anxious"—12:11; 12:22). Further catchword and thematic connections are found between 12:4-7 and 12:22. Both contain ψυχῆς ("soul, life") and σῶμα ("body") in similar (but nonetheless distinct) contexts of fear or anxiety about them.

12. Κλέπτης ("thief"); possibly διορύσσω ("dig through"; cf. Matt 6:19-20). The two passages share a common metaphor but otherwise deal with completely different interpretive issues. See Kloppenborg, *Excavating Q*, 126; Fleddermann, *Q: A Reconstruction and Commentary*, 621, n. 160.

13. Q 12:7—πολλῶν στρουθίων διαφέρετε; Q 12:24—μᾶλλον ὑμεῖς διαφέρετε (τῶν πετεινῶν). This catchword connection is even closer if Q 12:8-9, 10 represent a secondary stratum in Q. See Lührmann, *Redaktion*, 51-52; Kloppenborg, *Formation*, 207-8, 211-14.

14. Compare the following:

concern for dealing with wealth. The issue of earthly/heavenly concerns is shared by Q 12:22–31, but Q 12:22 and its διὰ τοῦτο ("for this reason") does not logically follow Luke 12:21.

4. There *is* a thematic connection between Q 12:31 and 12:33 in that the two imperatives call for seeking divine or heavenly things over earthly things. However, the redactional Luke 12:32 creates a *better* summary to 12:22–31 as a whole, and in the process obscures this thematic connection between Q 12:33 and 12:31 that may have been part of the original reason for placing the two pericopae together in Q. Any such connections noted here or in (1) and (2) above would have been lost with Matthew's relocation of Q 12:22–31, 33–34 in the Sermon on the Mount.

5. Consideration should also be given to the reminiscence theory, that Luke 12:21 recalls the original position of Q 12:33 (as found

---

When they bring you «before» synagogues, *do not be anxious* about how or what you are to say; for ⟦the holy Spirit will teach⟧ you in that .. hour what you are to say. For *this reason* I tell you, *do not be anxious* about your life, what you shall eat, nor about your body, with what you are to clothe yourself. Is not life more than food, and the body more than clothing? Consider the ravens: They neither sow nor reap nor gather into barns, and yet God feeds them. Are you not better than the birds? (Q 12:11–12, 22–24)

When they bring you before synagogues, *do not be anxious* about how or what you are to say; for ⟦the holy Spirit will teach⟧ you in that .. hour what you are to say. Do not treasure for yourselves treasures on earth, where moth and gnawing deface and where robbers dig through, but treasure for yourselves treasure«s» in heaven, where neither moth nor gnawing defaces and where robbers do not dig .. through nor rob. For where your treasure is, there will also be your heart. For *this reason* I tell you, do not be *anxious* about your life, what you are to eat, nor about your body, with what you are to clothe yourself with. Is not life more than food, and the body more than clothing? Consider the ravens: They neither sow nor reap nor «gather into barns», and yet God feeds them. Are you not better than the birds? (Q 12:11–12, 33–34, 22–24)

Texts are adapted from *CEQ*, 314–17, 330–38.

The διὰ τοῦτο ("for this reason") of 12:22 implies that prior to the Free from Anxiety like Ravens and Lilies pericope, the reader is given a reason *why* one need not worry about food and clothing. Though the issue there is ostensibly different, Q 12:12 still gives this assurance: God will provide. This assurance is then affirmed in 12:24ff. Q 12:34, on the other hand, does not provide a very adequate motive for the Free from Anxiety like Ravens and Lilies pericope. Cf. Hoffmann, "Verbot," 124–25. For a good summary of arguments for the position of Q 12:33–34 before Q 12:22–31, see Hoffmann's evaluation of Q 12:33[1] in "Evaluation," 16, 53–57, 104–5, 114, 117, 120, 127, 133, 138, 142–45, 150–52, 156–57, 162, 168, 171–72, 176, 182, 187, 194–95, 197; esp. 53–57.

in Matthew), since Luke *does* appear to frame Q 12:22-31 with Luke 12:13-21 and Q 12:33-34.[15] However, Luke 12:21 may now stand as an indication of Luke's ethics-based intentionality in framing Q 12:22-31, not as a reminiscence of 12:33's prior position in Q.

Q 12:33²: Luke's πωλήσατε... ἐλεημοσύνην or Matthew 6:19

The Lukan introduction to Q 12:33 reflects Lukan thematic interests concerning the stewardship of one's possessions and the giving of alms to the poor.[16] While the specific terminology is not especially Lukan (except ὑπάρχω),[17] the framing of Luke 12:22-31 with 12:13-21 and 12:32, 33-34 suggests that Luke has a different audience in mind—one that actually has appreciable disposable wealth—than that which is reflected in Q. The addition of Luke 12:33a reflects this different audience. The fact that Luke uses different words elsewhere in reference to almsgiving does not provide an effective counter-argument to the obvious Lukan interest in both the gospel and Acts. As to the source for Luke 12:33a, the initial imperative is probably taken from Mark 10:21, with minor alterations (cf. Luke 18:22).

---

15. In the IQP discussion of this saying, Robinson suggested that Luke 12:21, the moralizing conclusion to Luke's Parable of the Rich Fool, is possibly a reminiscence of Q 12:33's prior position before the Free from Anxiety like Ravens and Lilies pericope, the key words being θησαυρίζων ἑαυτῷ ("treasure up for yourself"; cf. Matt 6:19-20—θησαυρίζετε ὑμῖν), and the key theme being an implied contrast between heavenly and earthly wealth. Since the key word θησαυρίζω is found in Matthew's version of the saying but not in Luke 12:33, it could be that Luke left the word and attendant theme of earthly/heavenly possessions at Luke 12:21 to summarize the parable, while moving and modifying 12:33 to address the corresponding Lukan theme of giving alms to the poor. Cf. Schürmann, *Traditionsgeschichtliche Untersuchungen*, 119-20. Cf. also Grundmann, *Lukas*, 262, who argues that Luke 12:15-21 and 12:33-34 originally belonged together in the Lukan *Sondergut* (source material special to Luke); and Haupt, *Worte Jesu*, 64.

16. Harnack, *Sprüche*, 49; Hawkins, *Horae Synopticae*, 195; Haupt, *Worte Jesu*, 237; Klostermann, *Lukasevangelium*, 137; Dupont, *Béatitudes*, 80 n. 1; Pesch, "Zur Exegese," 358-59; Zeller, *Die weishheitlichen Mahnsprüche*, 77-78; Horn, *Glaube und Handeln*, 45, 64, 67-68, 89-90, 193; Luz, *Matthäus*, 356; Moxnes, *Economy*, 113; and Fleddermann, *Q*, 617.

17. The use of ὑπάρχω as a participle with article ("possessions") is distinctly Lukan style (8 times). Cf. Schulz, who argues that *every* word in Luke 12:33a is Lukan (Schulz, *Q*, 142).

The Matthean prohibition of 6:19 is another issue. It is an almost exact mirror of the positive admonition in Matt 6:20. Such close verbal similarity in an antithetical parallelism is rare in the gospels, and may have partially led to Luke's replacement with 12:33a.[18] However, there is antithetical parallelism in Matthew's immediate context, both in Matt 6:2-4, 6:5-6, and 6:16-18, and in 6:31-33 (Q 12:29-31). The question is whether Matthew retained this parallelism from Q and placed it with 6:22-24 in its present location as a transition from 6:1-18 (Matthew's "Cult Didaché") to 6:25-34 (Q's Free from Anxiety like Ravens and Lilies pericope) or created the parallelism for this very purpose when relocating the saying to the Sermon on the Mount.

Matthew, Luke, and Thomas all contain introductions to this saying, though the introductions differ from each other both in form and content (Matthew a prohibition, Luke an exhortation, and Thomas the Parable of the Pearl of Great Price). The fact that they all have introductions can be taken as an argument for there having been one in Q as well. The Epistle of James, which reflects knowledge of a Q-like version of this saying (Jas 5:2-3), is interested in the eventual destruction of *earthly* treasures and those who hoard them, just as Matt 6:19 warns against storing up earthly treasures. Luke 12:21 contrasts the storing of earthly riches with being rich toward God. Both texts may therefore reflect an original contrast in Q. The antithetical parallelism in Q 12:33 (Matt 6:19-20) may have originally followed the passage of Q 12:29-31. The interpretation of the two passages is very different, but the general theme of dealing with possessions and the contrast of earthly concerns as opposed to the seeking of the Reign of God may have been reasons for the original grouping of 12:22-31 and 12:33-34 in Q. John Dominic Crossan even suggests that the negative admonition of Matt 6:19 is more original than the positive one in 6:20, which he considers to be a secondary elaboration.[19]

On the other hand, a positive admonition that contains an implied contrast to present, earthly concerns invites expansion by means of a saying dealing with earthly goods. As will be shown later, John modifies the Thomasine version of this saying by using elements of the saying to create a prohibition and an exhortation (John 6:27; cf. GTh 76:3).[20] Thomas at-

---

18. Burney, *Poetry*, 76. Cf. Robinson, "Evaluation of Q 12:33-34," esp. 102-4; Hoffmann, "Evaluation," 104-5; and Verheyden, "Evaluation," esp. 105-7.

19. Crossan, *Historical Jesus*, 275-76. See also Kloppenborg, *Formation*, 222.

20. See below, Chapter 3: "John, Thomas, and Luke."

taches this saying to a parable about the selling of all one's merchandise to buy a single pearl. Matthew and Luke may have "taken the bait" as well and prefaced the saying with their own introductions, each introduction dealing with earthly possessions. So the fact that Matthew and Luke both have introductions that deal with possessing earthly goods is not surprising, and the usual argument that since both Matthew and Luke have something there, so Q probably had something as well, is not relevant here. The question remains whether Q received or created a negative admonition that Luke replaced, or whether Matthew and Luke created introductions independently.

The use of μή ("Do not") in Matt 6:19 is the primary link between Matt 6:1–18 and 6:20–34, and μή (with imperatives) appears to be the primary catchword for the entire sixth chapter of Matthew, a compilation of antitheses and contrasts in attitude and piety.[21] While continuing in the antithesis style of the "Cult Didache," Matt 6:19–21 begins a new section that focuses on greed, earthly possessions, and ultimate loyalties. So Matt 6:19 may have been created in the process of constructing the Matthean sermon in order to bridge two large sections of material. The addition of Matt 6:19 would also fit Matthew's interest in pairing or contrasting heaven and earth. On the other hand, Matt 6:19–21 may have been placed at this point in the Matthean text on the very basis of its pre-existing antithetical parallelism.

Most of the arguments that are given for or against Matt 6:19 can be countered with equally plausible counter-theories. The arguments have been:

- Matt 6:19–20 is an example of Semitic parallelism;[22]
- there is no parallel material between Matthew and Luke; hence, Matt 6:19–20 comes from M;[23]

---

21. So Brooks: "Verse 17 contains elements of Matthean style. Matthew frequently begins a sentence using μή and the second person plural (imperative or subjunctive; 6.19; 7.1; 7.6; 10.26).... The style of [Matt 7:6] fits well the command style of the entire section. Matt 6.19, 25, 34; 7.1 all use the negative command form of μή plus the second plural subjunctive"; *Matthew's Community*, 26, 91).

22. Cadbury, *Style*, 85, 88; Burney, *Poetry*, 87–88; Creed, *Luke*, 175; Pesch, "Zur Exegese," 358; Bonnard, *Matthieu*, 89. But, as Philip Sellew points out, "Matthew might well have constructed 6:19 out of Q 12:33–34 to provide a more structured parallelism" (Sellew, "Reconstruction," 624). See also Kilpatrick, *Origins*, 21–22, 75.

23. Manson, *Sayings of Jesus*, 114; Deppe, *Sayings of Jesus*, 123–24.

- parallelism reflects oral tradition;[24]
- Matthew likes antitheses and parallelism;[25]
- only a few heaven/earth contrasts are attributable to the author;[26]
- the implied contrast to earthly goods in the positive exhortation invites explication by Matthew and Luke;[27]
- Luke 12:21 contains a reminiscence of Matt 6:19;[28]
- Matthew creates 6:19 to bridge the "Cult Didache" antitheses of Matt 6:1–18 and the other inserted material of Matt 6:22–34;[29]
- both texts have something there, so Q probably had something there, too.[30]

As a result, I find only a few arguments that are persuasive on either side of the issue.

On the one hand, as I will argue below, Matthew has made very few changes to Q 12:33/Matt 6:20. This is probably true for Matt 6:22–24 as well. I find this to be a strong argument that Matthew found 6:19 in Q. This is supported by James's sole emphasis on the eschatological self-condemnation of those who hoard earthly wealth. On the other hand, Q pericopae that contain both "heaven" and "earth" do not contrast them as Matthew does. The Matthean preference for juxtaposing these locations redactionally is a good argument for Matthew adding the prohibition here. The almost perfectly symmetrical parallelism of Matt 6:19–20 makes me particularly suspicious.[31]

---

24. Wrege, *Überlieferungsgeschichte*, 110. But there is parallelism within the Q saying already.

25. Kilpatrick, *Origins*, 21–22, 75. But cf. Knox, *Sources*, 2:27–28, n. 2.

26. Knox, *Sources*, 27–28, n. 2. But Knox is focusing too strictly on explicit contrasts. Cf. Gundry, *Matthew*, 113.

27. However, if the explication is so inviting, why would the composer of Q have not made this move already?

28. Yet, the verbal parallel is also to Matt 6:20 and the contrast is implicit in 6:20.

29. However, if Q 12:33 already had the negative admonition as well, it would be all the better reason for Matthew to locate the saying after the "Cult Didache" with its antithetical parallelism.

30. Verheyden, "Evaluation," 106. But cf. Sellew: "Perhaps the differences between Matthew and Luke here suggest that Q had no equivalent to either Matt 6:19 or Luke 12:33a (cf. lack of parallel in *Gos. Thom.* 76b)" ("Reconstruction," 625).

31. Gundry, *Matthew*, 113.

The result is that I find arguments for and against Matthew somewhat equally balanced. I am undecided as to whether Q created a second admonition that Luke replaced, or whether Matthew and Luke created introductions independently.

Q 12:33³: Luke's ποιήσατε or Matthew's θησαυρίζετε

It is not uncommon for Q to use verbs in conjunction with cognate nouns and adjectives, as is found in Matt 6:20's θησαυρίζω ("treasure up") and θήσαυρος.[32]

Luke's ποιήσατε ("provide") appears to be dependent upon the subsequent βαλλάντια μὴ παλαιούμενα ("purses that do not wear out"), which itself appears to be of Lukan construction. The only thing that seems to speak for Luke's verb is the rarity of the expression ποιήσατε ἑαυτοῖς ("provide for yourselves"), which is found elsewhere in Luke only in 16:9.[33] Yet, even there, it appears to form part of a redactional summary interpretation of the Parable of the Dishonest Manager (16:1-8). In Luke 16:9, one "makes for oneself" friends for the purpose of securing lodging in "the eternal tents." Hence, the idea of giving away goods now to gain benefits in the hereafter is common to both passages.

The Parable of the Rich Fool, Luke 12:15-20, is probably taken from Lukan *Sondergut*, since it is not found in Matthew and its theme is consistent with themes found in *Sondergut* material. Luke 12:21 appears to be a redactional formulation of Luke.[34] The point is relevant because Luke 12:21 is similar in theme and wording to Matthew's version of Q 12:33.[35] Specifically, the term θησαυρίζω is used by Luke for contrasting the storing of treasures for oneself with being rich toward God. Since Luke appears to be intentionally framing the Free from Anxiety like Ravens and

---

32. Q 6:38 (μετρέω, μέτρον); 7:31-32 (ὁμοιόω, ὅμοιος); 11:39, 41 (καθαρίζω, καθαρός); 12:22-23 (ἐνδύω, ἔνδυμα); 12:33 (κλέπτω [IQP; CEQ], κλέπτης); 17:1-2 (σκανδαλίζω, σκάνδαλον).

33. Jeremias argues for its originality on this basis (*Sprache*, 218).

34. The IQP rejects all of Luke 12:13-21 as not coming from Q. See *CEQ*, 318-27. Cf. Schürmann, *Traditionsgeschichtliche Untersuchungen*, 119-20.

35. Schürmann has suggested two possibilities for the similarities between Luke 12:21 and Matt 6:19-20: (1) Luke 12:21 is a secondarily-added concluding image based on an original form of Q 12:33 that may have been similar to Matt 6:19-20; (2) Matt 6:19-20's θησαυρίζω was taken from the pre-Lukan version of Luke 12:21 (*Traditionsgeschichtliche Untersuchungen*, 119-20). Schürmann sides for Matt 6:19-20 being the reminiscence of Luke 12:21.

Lilies pericope with Luke 12:16–21 and 12:33–34, it is quite likely that the verb in Luke 12:21 is a reminiscence of its prior use in Q 12:33, a use evidenced by Matt 6:19–20.[36]

Overall, strong arguments exist for Matthew's verb and against Luke's being that of Q, but not vice versa.

Q 12:33[4]: Matthew's δέ

The existence of the particle δέ ("but") in Q is partly dependent upon a decision regarding variant Q 12:33[2].[37] If Matt 6:19 was originally in Q, then there certainly existed an adversative conjunction in 6:20. Yet, the weak particle could have existed without a prior negative admonition.[38] Q 12:31 reads "but seek his kingdom, and these things will be added to you" (ζητεῖτε δὲ τὴν βασιλείαν αὐτοῦ, καὶ ταῦτα προστεθήσεται ὑμῖν). Q 12:33 follows with a similar admonition to seek heavenly things and might have been connected to 12:31 with a conjunction (without negative connotation) like δέ or καί. Luke's omission would be due to the redactional addition of 12:33a ("Sell your possessions and give alms"), which does not allow for its use at this position in the saying.

On the other hand, if Matt 6:19 was not in Q, one is left with only the connective argument, which is itself quite weak. Matthean creation of 6:19 would provide a clear and obvious reason for δέ being in Matt 6:20. I am left undecided on this variant.

Q 12:33[5]: Luke's ἑαυτοῖς or Matthew's ὑμῖν

Three texts seem particularly relevant: Luke 12:21; 16:9; Q 12:31. Luke 12:21 has θησαυρίζων ἑαυτῷ ("the one who lays up treasure for himself") in what appears to be a saying based on Q 12:33. Q 12:31 immediately precedes Q 12:33 and uses the dative pronoun ὑμῖν. Luke 16:9 appears to be a redactional addition of Luke, and is the only other place in the NT where the expression ποιήσατε ἑαυτοῖς is found.

---

36. James 5:2–3 reflects use of a Q tradition that developed in the community that likely spawned the Gospel of Matthew; no one has yet supplied a plausible argument for Matthew's verb being secondary. Cf. Gundry, *Matthew*, 112.

37. So Robinson and Hoffmann in Johnson, *Q 12:33–34*, 116, 117. Kloppenborg ties the decision against Luke to Q 12:33[3] (ibid., 117).

38. Cf. also Q 3:9; 4:1; 6:41; 7:24; 9:59; 10:5, 7; 12:11, 25, 39, 45. Verheyden agrees that δέ is not uncommon in Q as an introductory particle—and therefore sees no good reason to exclude it from Q ("Evaluation," 117).

Several arguments support Luke's reflexive as the Q reading. Though 12:21 is a redactional creation of Luke, if it was suggested by Q 12:33 and includes Q's θησαυρίζω ("treasure"), then the reflexive may have been taken from Q as well. Ὑμῖν ("for yourselves") is found more often in Q, but ἑαυτο- is found in Q in at least nine places, and ὑμῖν is never used reflexively elsewhere in Q.[39] Ὑμῖν is used in Q 12:31, but not reflexively. Assuming previous arguments for the position of the pericope (see above, Q 12:33[1] above), it seems peculiar for Q to have used ὑμῖν twice in the space of four words, but with different grammatical functions.[40]

On the other hand, Luke might have preferred a proper reflexive for both 12:21 and 12:33, changing ὑμῖν in Q 12:33 and adding ἑαυτοῦ redactionally in 12:21.[41] The slight discomfiture between Q 12:31 and Matt 6:(19-)20 may have been a result of Q's placing two previously unrelated sayings side-by-side, if 12:31 existed prior to its incorporation in Q. Luke would have eliminated this difficulty both by changing Q 12:33's ὑμῖν and by inserting Luke 12:32. In Luke 16:9, Luke uses the full expression ἑαυτοῖς ποιήσατε ("provide for yourselves") redactionally in a saying that is very similar to Luke 12:33a in its eschatologically-based ethic.

One other observation seems pertinent to the discussion. The personal pronoun is almost never used reflexively in the NT without a preceding preposition.[42] Matthew 6:19-20 is unique in this, lending weight to Matthew's ὑμῖν being the more difficult and hence more original reading. One of Matthew's tendencies *is* to use the personal pronoun as a reflexive, but *always* with a preceding preposition (Matthew uses the reflexive with prepositions as well).[43] It has been suggested that referring back to a Semitic original might be of help, since "Hebrew and Aramaic pronominal suffixes do not allow the distinction between personal and

---

39. Verheyden observes that Matthew is by no means averse to using the reflexive, taking it over six times from Q and twice from Mark, and introducing it another 19 times ("Evaluation," 120-21).

40. Cf. Q 12:31, 33: . . . προστεθήσεται ὑμῖν. θησαυρίζετε δὲ ὑμῖν . . . (or, if Matt 6:19 = Q, . . . προστεθήσεται ὑμῖν. μὴ θησαυρίζετε ὑμῖν . . .).

41. Kloppenborg observes that Luke adds ἑαυτοῦ redactionally elsewhere: 9:25, 47; 11:21; 12:1; 20:20; 21:30, 34; 22:17; 23:2, 28 (and probably at 13:19, 34; 14:26, 27). See Johnson, *Q 12:33-34*, 120. Robinson sees it as a refinement here (120). See also Fleddermann, *Q*, 619.

42. BDF, §283.

43. Ibid.

reflexive."[44] In other words, a translator may have accidentally translated a pronoun suffix as a personal pronoun, rather than a reflexive. This observation assumes, however, that Q was being translated *in written form* from an Aramaic original (be it oral or written). This is highly unlikely.[45]

Matthew's reading is therefore the *lectio difficilior* (more difficult reading) in at least two different ways (suggesting that it is the more original reading). Matthew's tendency to use the personal pronoun as a reflexive would balance Luke's probable redactional preference for a proper reflexive if not for the fact that Matthew always uses a preceding preposition elsewhere. Hence, the evidence leans in favor of ὑμῖν in Q.

Q 12:33[6]: Luke's βαλλάντια μὴ παλαιούμενα

The phrase βαλλάντια μὴ παλαιούμενα ("purses that do not wear out") is decidedly Lukan vocabulary. Βαλλάντιον ("purse") is found in the NT only in Luke (4 times!).[46] Its presence in Q 10:4 is due to Lukan redaction.[47] Παλαίοω ("wear out") is also found only in Luke among the gospels.[48] Since Luke's initial verb ποιήσατε ("provide") appears tied to this subsequent phrase, it, too, should be rejected as Lukan redaction.[49]

A general problem with Luke's version of the saying is that minimal Q words like "treasure," "in (the) heaven(s)" (i.e., a place), "moth," and "thief" (κλέπτης, "thief"; not λῃστής, "bandit") imply a treasure to be found in a somewhat fixed location, whereas Luke's version with "purses" that do not "wear out" (from regular use?) and a thief that "approaches" (presumably the treasure in the purse) suggests the mobility

---

44. Davies and Allison, *Matthew*, 629.

45. For a thorough discussion of the language of Q, see Kloppenborg, *Formation*, 51–64. In short, the presence of a handful of translational variants or possible translational mistakes is far outweighed by the extent of verbatim agreement between Matthew and Luke in Q passages.

46. Creed, *Luke*, 175: "The heavenly purses which do not wear out are peculiar to Luke, and are perhaps his own addition. Lucan only in N.T., cf. x.4, xxii.35,36." So also Kilpatrick: "βαλλάντιον is peculiar to Luke, while Mark, Luke, Matthew, and possibly Q use πήρα" (*Origins*, 22). Cf. Gundry, *Matthew*, 112.

47. See Robinson, "Work Session 1990," 496; and Hoffmann, "Evaluation," 127 (but cf. *CEQ*, 164–65!). To obtain the most current database for Q 10:2–12, 13–16 (and any other as-yet-unpublished volumes), contact the Institute for Antiquity and Christianity, Claremont Graduate University, Claremont, CA, 91711).

48. Schulz, *Q*, 142.

49. Cf. Polag's reconstruction in *Fragmenta Q*, 62.

of the treasure. Matthew's version, on the other hand, is consistent with minimal Q terminology: moths and other things eat away at a sedentary treasure—like fine linen, perhaps—and thieves break into homes or storehouses to steal such treasures. In other words, while Lukan redaction scores style points for creating an appositive parallelism in Luke 12:33b ("make purses that do not wear out, a treasure unfailing in the heavens") and a tighter structure in Luke 12:33c (the adversity clauses), it does so by using Q terminology that better fits another context, one which is best represented by Matthew (as well as the Gospel of Thomas).

Q 12:33⁷: Luke's θησαυρόν or Matthew's θησαυρούς

An attempt to determine whether Q had the singular or plural of "treasure" is hampered by the ability to read evidence in different ways. For instance, Crossan suggests that the chiastic pattern in 12:33–34 of *treasure/where//where/treasure* demonstrates Q's linkage of 12:33 and 12:34.[50] Yet, Luke may have created the agreement in number (the sg. "treasure"). Robert Gundry argues that Matthew created the agreement in number with the plural "thieves" and the plurality of eating agents.[51] However, it is just as likely that Luke has done the same, since Luke appears to have switched the order of adversity clauses in 12:33c to contrast ἀνέκλειπτον ("unfailing") with κλέπτης ("thief") in a creative word-play.[52] Matthew has the only plurals in the gospels, but Luke appears to prefer the singular.[53] Luke may have been influenced by the text of Mark 10:21.[54] Luke may have taken the singular from the Gospel of Thomas version of the saying, but agreement between Luke and Thomas may instead reflect agreement in their sources.[55]

---

50. Crossan, *In Fragments*, 130. Crossan's argument raises the following question: When Luke agrees with Thomas against Matthew, is this reflective of common tradition, Thomas' use of Luke, or Thomas' influence on Luke? For discussion of this issue, see below, chapter 3, pp. 66–76.

51. Gundry, *Matthew*, 111.

52. So argues Anderson, quoted in Johnson, *Q 12:33–34*, 155.

53. Ibid. Luke prefers the singular in every instance (6:45 [Q]; 12:33 [?], 34 [Q]; 18:22 [Mark]). Matthew usually goes with the source (6:21 [Q]; 12:35 [Q]; 19:21 [Mark]), but otherwise varies (2:11 [pl.]; 13:44, 52 [sg.]).

54. Klostermann, *Lukasevangelium*, 138; Horn, *Glaube und Handeln*, 280.

55. Crossan, *In Fragments*, 130.

The most pertinent observations would seem to be the following: (1) The difference in person between Matt 6:20 and 6:21 may be a sign of the prior combining (by Q) of two independent sayings, an inconsistency smoothed out in Luke. Hence, probability is with Matthew's θησαυρός being the Q version. (2) In adding "purses which do not wear out," Luke may have shifted the plural to the first object of the main verb, leading to agreement in number with "treasure" in 12:34 (Q) and 18:22 (Mark).[56] (3) If Matt 6:19 was originally part of Q, then the replacement of Matt 6:19 and Q's θησαυρίζω with the selling of possessions and giving of alms for the sake of gaining a heavenly reward provides a theological rationale for Luke's shift from the plural "treasures" to the singular "treasure."[57]

Q 12:33[8]: Luke's ἀνέκλειπτον

Adolf Harnack argued that ἀνέκλειπτον ("unfailing") is literary Greek, and so was added by Luke.[58] It could be argued that Matthew eliminated the word to smooth out the saying, but that does not answer Harnack's argument. Ἀνέκλειπτον is also Lukan terminology. Robinson has noted the similarity in thought to Luke 16:9's "unjust mammon" which "fails" (ἐκλίπῃ).[59] Hans-Theo. Wrege has noted Luke's use of the related ἐκλείπω in Luke 16:9; 22:32; and 23:45, but he assumes that 16:9 and 22:32 are from Lukan *Sondergut* and not a result of Lukan redaction. Hence, he argues that ἀνέκλειπτον is traditional here.[60] In fact, both verses show evidence of being Lukan redaction. Hence, it appears that ἐκλείπω is Lukan vocabulary after all, and by extension, ἀνέκλειπτον as well. By redactionally adding ἀνέκλειπτον, Luke has created parallelism by means of apposition in the construction βαλλάντια μὴ παλαιούμενα, θησαυρὸν ἀνέκλειπτον ἐν τοῖς οὐρανοῖς.[61]

---

56. Sellew, "Reconstruction," 626.

57. Horn, *Glaube und Handeln*, 64–65, 280.

58. Harnack, *Sprüche*, 49. See also Schulz, *Q*, 142; Sellew, "Reconstruction," 626; Steinhauser, *Doppelbildworte*, 236–37. Cf. Pesch: "ἀνέκλειπτος ist Hapaxlegomenon der Bibel und geläufiges hellenistisches Wort" ("Exegese," 359). However, ἀνέκλιπὴς γὰρ θησαυρός is found in Wis 7:14. There is no apparent connection between this passage on personified Wisdom and Q 12:22–34.

59. Robinson, "Evaluation of Q 12:33–34," 138.

60. Wrege, *Überlieferungsgeschichte*, 112.

61. Sellew, "Reconstruction," 626. In chapter 3 I will propose where Luke found the idea for this and several other additions and modifications of the Q text.

Q 12:33⁹: Luke's τοῖς

Q normally uses the article with οὐρανός ("heaven"), but occasionally does not.⁶² Both Matthew and Luke prefer the article with οὐρανός,⁶³ though to different degrees they are both flexible in usage as well.⁶⁴

The overwhelming preference for the article in Acts (24 of 26x, 92%) suggests that Luke prefers the article when redactionally adding οὐρανός. In the gospel, the article is lacking in ten cases, but there it appears that the deciding factor is most often the preposition used before the noun.⁶⁵ Hence, except when ἐκ or ἀπό precede the noun, Luke has a strong preference for the article.⁶⁶ Matthew omits the article when following a source.⁶⁷ Otherwise, Matthew prefers the article with οὐρανός.

On the other hand, Matthew possibly has a tendency to omit the article after ἐν ("in").⁶⁸ The article is missing 18 times in Matthew, 5 times in agreement with Mark or Q (only 1x following ἐν), 1 time with the preposition ἐκ ("from, out of," 28:2), and 12 times elsewhere with the preposition ἐν.⁶⁹

62. Cf. 7 or 9 times with article; Q 10:15; 11:13 without article (on 11:13, see CEQ, 220–21).

63. **Matthew:** 64 of 82 times, 78% (minus 32x with kingdom of heaven, still 32 of 50x, 64%); **Luke:** 24 of 34 times, 70.6% (but with Acts [24 of 26x, 92%], 48 of 60x, 80%).

64. While Matthew is always consistent in number with the formulae "kingdom of the heave*ns*," "Father in the heave*ns*," and "birds of the *sky*" (and even with the formulaic pairing of heaven and earth—8x singular, 2x plural), Matthew is not always consistent in using the article with "Father in the heavens" (8x w/art., 5x w/o) and the pairing of heaven and earth (5x w/art., 5x w/o). In the eight places where Matthew adds οὐρανός redactionally or from an unknown source, 5 times are with article, 3 times are without.

65. When Luke uses ἐκ or ἀπό, the article is lacking in 8 of 9 cases. In the other two places where Luke lacks the article, Luke is following Q (10:15—ἕως) or intentionally reworking Luke 2:14 in 19:38 by replacing δόξα ἐν ὑψίστοις θεῷ καί ἐπὶ γῆς εἰρήνη with ἐν οὐρανῷ εἰρήνη καὶ δόξα ἐν ὑψίστοις.

66. See Anderson, quoted in Johnson, Q 12:33-34, 140. For a thorough cataloging of articular or anarthrous use of οὐρανός in Luke, see Hoffmann, "Evaluation," 142–45.

67. Cf. Matt 11:23 (ἕως); 19:21 (ἐν); 21:25 (2x, ἐκ); 24:31 (ἀπ' ἄκρων). Verheyden provides a complete discussion of Matthew's tendency to follow sources with respect to using or not using an article in a prepositional phrase with οὐρανός in "Evaluation," 145.

68. Of the 18 times Matthew omits the article, 13 times follow the preposition ἐν. However, Matthew has ἐν before the noun 26 times, meaning that Matthew is split 50%—50% in cases with or without the article.

69. 6 times with the singular; 6 times with the plural (5x with the formula "Father in the heavens" and 1x with "his angels in heaven"). Of particular note is the fact that two

In short, we have redactional reasons for both Luke and Matthew to alter the other's reading of Q 12:33. Luke strongly prefers the article, though not with the prepositions ἐκ and ἀπό ("from"). Luke alters sources according to this preference, omitting the article after ἐκ in 2:22 and 11:16, and possibly adding the article after ἐν in 18:22 (there is a text-critical problem there). Matthew often omits the article with the preposition ἐν, but also leaves out the article when following a source. Overall, however, Luke's alterations according to preference, Matthew's tendency to follow sources,[70] Matthew's slight preference for the article, and Q's lack of consistency with regard to preference, suggest that Matthew has the Q reading (no article) here.

Q 12:33[10]: Luke's οὐρανοῖς or Matthew's οὐρανῷ

Q prefers the singular "heaven." In the six places where Matthew and Luke agree, Q uses the singular. In the two places where they disagree outside of Q 12:33, the IQP has decided with Luke's singular.[71] Hence, all eight cases outside of Q 12:33 appear to reflect the singular in Q.

According to Heinz Schürmann, Luke dislikes the plural and only uses it, at most, four times.[72] Luke keeps only one of Mark's five plurals, changing the number in Luke 3:21, 22 (cf. Mark 1:10, 11), eliminating the word by restructuring the sentence in 20:36 in order to clarify the nature of resurrected people (cf. Mark 12:25), and eliminating all of Mark 11:20–26 (hence Mark 11:25). Of course, one could therefore interpret the same evidence as suggesting that Luke only intentional avoids Mark's plurals twice, in Luke 3:21, 22. Schürmann argues that the plural with article in Luke 18:22 is a reminiscence of Q 12:33 (hence, Luke 18:22 reflects the use of one source, Q 12:33, over against another, Mark 10:21).[73] But if Schürmann is correct, then Luke still used a Markan plural once, retained one plural from Q, *added* one plural based on prior Q use, and inexplica-

---

cases in Matt 18:18 are repetitions of 16:19, but both of 16:19's plurals with article are changed to singulars without article (all 4 cases following the preposition ἐν). In other words, it would appear that Matthew has used a source in 16:19, but in redacting the saying in 18:18, has omitted the articles.

70. Luke has the article 1 time without ἐκ following Q 10:15 (ἕως).

71. See Q 6:23; 11:13 (*CEQ*, 52–53, 220–21); however, the decision for 6:23 was based on the six agreements between Luke and Matthew.

72. Schürmann, *Traditionsgeschichtliche Untersuchungen*, 115.

73. Ibid.

bly used the plural once in Luke 10:20, (The Return of the Seventy; Luke uses Q's singular in the very next verse). Luke's redactional use of the plural in 10:20 and 18:22 should give one pause to reconsider 12:33.

Matthew shows a preference for the plural, but is comfortable with the singular. In all but two cases, Matthew uses the singular when pairing or contrasting heaven and earth, demonstrating a redactional preference.[74] The two exceptions are found in Matt 16:19. In Matt 18:18, almost a verbatim doublet of 16:19, the plurals are changed to singulars. This suggests that Matthew let the source stand in 16:19, but preferred the singular when repeating the saying later in the gospel. Matthew can also be understood to have changed the plural in 6:20 to agree with the singular 'on the earth' in 6:19, whether Matt 6:19 is original to Q or not;[75] in other words, the plural is the more difficult reading and is corrected by Matthew.

Despite Matthew's redactional preference, the clear preferential use of the singular in all other Q sayings argues for the singular in 12:33.[76]

Q 12:33[11]: The Sequence of Adversities

There are a number of reasons for assuming that Luke has changed the order of the agents in creating a new version of the saying. Though the words are not etymologically related, a word-play is created by bringing κλέπτης ("thief") closer to the redactionally added ἀνέκλειπτον ("unfailing").[77] Consequently, the "unfailing treasure" is implicitly contrasted with the treasure that can be readily stolen by an approaching thief. In Luke's form of the saying, a nice parallelism, almost poetic in its tight, metrical structure, has been created: ὅπου κλέπτης οὐκ ἐγγίζει οὐδὲ σὴς διαφθείρει. A good argument for Matthean redaction at this point is en-

---

74. Davies and Allison, *Matthew*, 631: "Matthew, who is more fond of the plural, has here chosen the singular to underline the parallel with 'on the earth' (cf. 6:10)."

75. Schürmann, *Traditionsgeschichtliche Untersuchungen*, 115 n. 18.

76. For more extensive discussions of Lukan and Matthean use, see Hoffmann and Verheyden, respectively, in Johnson, *Q 12:33-34*, 150-52, 152-53.

77. Anderson in Johnson, *Q 12:33-34*, 155.

tirely lacking.⁷⁸ On the contrary, in Matthew's position, κλέπται is closer to its fellow catchword (κλέπτης) in Q 12:39.⁷⁹

Q 12:33¹²: *Matthew's (οὔτε) . . . (οὔτε βρῶσις)*

Two arguments favor Matthew's second adversary originating in Q. First, Matt 6:19–20, Jas 5:2–3, John 6:27, and GTh 76:3 all use some form of the stem βρωσ–, though with different meaning in each version.⁸⁰ Matthew has the noun βρῶσις ("eating" or "eating thing"); James uses a compound adjective σητόβρωτα ("your riches have rotted [σέσηπεν] and your garments are *moth-eaten*" [σητόβρωτα]); John has βρῶσις ("work not for the *food* [βρῶσις] that perishes"); and Thomas has ⲈⲞⲨⲰⲘ ("to eat" or "for eating").⁸¹ Matthew, James, and Thomas all use this word with the idea of a stationary treasure, unlike Luke's mobile, purse-carried treasure.⁸²

Second, elimination of this word provides Luke with a much tighter construction of 12:33c and helps focus the interpretation of the saying on the previous (in Luke) thief clause, which is itself shorter and more in line with Luke's conception of a treasure carried about in a purse. There is little to speak for Matthean redaction here.⁸³ Βρῶσις most likely was in Q.

---

78. Gundry's argument for Lukan order, based on the imagery engendered by Luke's metaphor, assumes that moths are eating a purse (not a treasure, such as fine fabrics, that might be stored away). See Gundry, *Matthew*, 113.

79. Robinson, "Evaluation of Q 12:33–34," 156.

80. Greek retroversions of the Coptic text typically use some form of φαγεῖν to translate ⲈⲞⲨⲰⲘ. See, e.g., in Aland, *Synopsis*, 538: "ὅπου σὴς οὐκ ἐγγίζει φαγεῖν." This translation does not take into account the likely transmission history of the text. See below, Chapter 3, p. 73, Figure 5 and n. 45.

81. According to Hartin, "James also refers to riches rotting and the garments being moth-eaten (σητόβρωτα), a form in which the two words in Q are now combined" (Hartin, *James*, 180). So also Davies and Allison, *Matthew*, 628–29. The infinitive in Thomas appears to have been the Coptic translator's attempt to retain the implication of eating while not finding a Coptic equivalent for the Greek expression εἰς βρῶσιν. See below, chapter 3, p. 73, n. 45.

82. Kloppenborg ("Evaluation," 162) also sees a connection to Q 12:22–31, which addresses concerns for food and clothing—precisely the kind of "treasures" likely to be eaten.

83. Gundry, *Matthew*, 112, provides a rationale for Matthean redaction, but does not explain how a purse that is carried around gets eaten by moths.

Q 12:33¹³: Luke's διαφθείρει or Matthew's ἀφανίζει

Adolf Harnack considered διαφθείρω to be classical Greek, and therefore Lukan redaction.[84] The verb is only found here in the gospels, but the substantive (διαφθορά) is used six times in two locations in Acts, and is *only* found in Acts.[85] Four of the occurrences of the substantive are in the same passage as Acts' use of ἀφανίζω, suggesting the interchangeability of the words for Luke. Hence, the root can be considered Lukan vocabulary.[86]

Matthew's ἀφανίζω ("destroy") is found elsewhere in Matt 6:16, Acts 13:41, and Jas 4:14. There is possibly a word-play between Matt 6:16 and 6:19. Schweizer and Gundry argue that 6:19–20's ἀφανίζω is derived from 6:16, creating the word-play, but the alternative, that 6:16 is based on 6:19, is just as likely.[87] On the other hand, Acts 13:41 shows that Luke is not averse to the word, and its use in Jas 4:14, near to where we find remains of the Q saying (5:2–3), suggests the possibility that the verb was also in Q.[88]

With strong arguments both for Matthew's verb and against Luke's verb, and only the inconclusive argument of Matt 6:16's priority in opposition, it seems clear to me that Matthew retained the Q verb.

Q 12:33¹⁴: Luke's οὐδέ or Matthew's καὶ ὅπου

Luke's creation of a tight, metrical construction in Luke 12:33c (the adversity clauses) is aided by replacing καὶ ὅπου with οὐδέ. At the same time, he statistical tendencies slightly favor Matthew's καὶ ὅπου ("and where") as original.[89] It is possible that Matthew found the use of οὐδέ ("nor") to

---

84. Harnack, *Sprüche und Reden Jesu*, 49. See also Cadbury, *Style and Literary Method*, 183.

85. Wrege, *Die Überlieferungsgeschichte*, 112 n. 4; Jeremias, *Sprache*, 218.

86. Schulz, *Q*, 142; Jeremias, *Die Sprache*, 218.

87. Schweizer, *Matthäus*, 102; Gundry, *Matthew*, 112. Verheyden ("Evaluation," 168) observes that ἀφανίζω has different meanings in 6:16 and 6:20, arguing against 6:16 being the source for 6:20.

88. Its use in James may have been suggested by the possibility of a word-play with φαίνω—ἀτμὶς γάρ ἐστε ἡ πρὸς ὀλίγον φαινομένη, ἔπειτα καὶ ἀφανιζομένη or φαίνω may have been suggested by Q's ἀφανίζω.

89. Both Matthew and Luke eliminate almost all Markan uses of ὅπου (Mark 15x// Matt 3x, Luke 0x). Luke uses it only 4 times, all in Q passages that agree with Matthew. Matthew uses it 4 times more in Q contexts and once in the Passion narrative. Therefore:

be repetitive here, but the same could be said for using ὅπου a second time.⁹⁰ Overall, there is no apparent rationale for Matthean redaction, but a good case can be made for Lukan stylistic redaction.

Q 12:33¹⁵: Luke's κλέπτης or Matthew's κλέπται

Luke's use of the singular can also be seen as a stylistic improvement of 12:33c in accordance with the omissions of βρῶσις and κλέπτουσιν and the replacement of καὶ ὅπου with οὐδέ and διορύσσουσιν with ἐγγίζει, all of which results in the tightening-up of the parallelism in Q 12:33. Specifically, a switch to the singular would shorten the verb and cause it to agree in number with the verb "destroy" (οὐκ ἐγγίζει ... διαφθείρει). These omissions and abbreviations improve the readability of the adversity clauses of 12:33c while helping to focus attention on the initial redactional admonitions of Luke 12:33a ("sell ... and give alms") and the Lukan parallelism of Luke 12:33b ("make ... purses that do not wear out, a treasure unfailing in the heavens").

It is possible that Matthew has changed to the plural in order to parallel the multiple number of agents in the first adversity clause.⁹¹ In so doing, Matthew would have smoothed out a difficulty in Q's parallelism. This would also mean that Q 12:33 was originally in agreement with Q 12:39's singular. The opposite argument, however, is much more likely: when eliminating βρῶσις ("eating or eating thing" see above under Q 12:33¹²), Luke changed the plural "thieves" to the singular to agree with

---

1) Q uses ὅπου 4-8 times, and Matthew and Luke rarely use it elsewhere; and 2) either Luke has eliminated it from several Q positions or Matthew has added it in Q contexts. Since Matthew uses ὅπου only 4 times outside of a Q context, and three of those cases following Mark, it does not appear that Matthew particularly likes or dislikes using the word (avoiding Markan usage 12x). However, Luke *does* appear to dislike it, never using it apart from Q. The evidence here weighs slightly on the side of Lukan elimination of ὅπου from Q.

As for οὐδέ, Matthew and Luke again tend to avoid Markan usage (Mark 9 or 10x// Matt 2x, Luke 2x). Yet, they both use Q five times, and each uses the particle in other Q contexts (Matt 4x, Luke 6x: hence in Q 5-15x—notice that one of Matthew's uses is in 6:20). Each uses the term three to four times on their own, and follow their special sources two to three times. Matthew also uses it seven times in a Markan context where Mark does not use the term (Luke 1x). Therefore, while both see the need to improve Mark by eliminating or replacing οὐδέ on many occasions, neither writer is above using it in other locations.

90. Verheyden ("Evaluation," 172) qualifies Luke's avoidance of ὅπου, emphasizing Luke's probable avoidance of repetitive use of ὅπου in Q 12:33-34.

91. See Gundry, *Matthew*, 112.

the singular σής ("moth"). In so doing, Luke would have coincidentally harmonized 12:33 with Q 12:39.

Q 12:33[16]: Luke's ἐγγίζει or Matthew's διορύσσουσιν

Ἐγγίζω ("approach") is Lukan terminology.[92] It is found only once in a Q location (Q 10:9). Most Q scholars see Luke's verb as a colorless abbreviation of Matthew's colorful expression in order to refine Luke's concise parallelism.[93] The verb also fits Luke's conception of the treasure encased in the purse. The problem, as noted above, is that the action of approaching someone with a purse is more commonly associated with a ληστής than with a κλέπτης. The fact that Matthew uses ἐγγίζω on seven occasions (3 Markan, 1 Q) suggests that Matthew is not averse to the term and is not likely to eliminate it on stylistic grounds.[94]

Διορύσσω ("dig through") is found elsewhere in the NT only in Luke 12:39/Matt 24:43, suggesting a prior catchword connection in Q. Q 12:39 otherwise has very little in common with Q 12:33 thematically. Luke inserted Luke 12:35-38 between them, disrupting any previous catchword connection. Διορύσσω is more appropriate to the *locative context* of this saying as determined by other Q vocabulary (including words argued for above: "store up"; "in heaven"; "moth"; "eating thing"; "thieves" [κλέπται]).

Gundry sees a possible Semitic paranomasia behind the verbs "approach" (קרב, *qrb*) and "destroy" and (רקב, *rqb*), but this may be coincidental to Luke.[95] Yet to be determined is Luke's precise relationship to GTh 76:3, where the *moth* does not "approach to eat," and the verbs

---

92. Harnack, *Sprüche*, 49; Kilpatrick, *Origins*, 22; Jeremias, *Sprache*, 218.

93. E.g., Harnack, *Sprüche*, 49.

94. Verheyden ("Evaluation," 182–83), observes that, while Luke's typical use of ἐγγίζω is locative in function, the only minimal Q use of the verb is temporal.

95. Gundry, *Matthew*, 112. Cf. Davies and Allison: "For διορύσσουσιν Luke has ἐγγίζει, and this may well be original. Compare Gos. Thom. 76: 'where no moth comes near' (ⲧ2ⲛⲟ ⲉ2ⲟⲩⲛ). If Luke is in fact original, it is the more likely that assonance characterized the Semitic original, for 'draw near' could be *qereb*, 'moth' could be *ruqba*, 'destroy' could be *reqab*, and 'worm' could be *raqqaba*" (*Matthew*, 631). Though Davies and Allison seem to be arguing here for the originality of Luke, their speculation concerning a hypothetical Aramaic *Vorlage* would seem to argue for the originality of GTh 76:3's vocabulary and structure and for the secondarily-abbreviated nature of Luke 12:33.

"approach" and "destroy" are in the same order as Luke, suggesting that one version has had influence on the other.[96]

Overall, Matthew's verb has precedence in Q and Luke's verb appears to be a redactional smoothing out of the parallel adversity clauses in Q. Matthew's verb is also consistent with Q vocabulary that creates the image of a stationary, stored treasure.

Q 12:33[17]: Matthew's οὐδὲ κλέπτουσιν

Matthew's additional verb gives balance to Matt 6:20b, with its 2 subjects/1 verb//1 subject/2 verbs. It has already been shown that the other three elements of this parallelism were in Q, so this balance was probably original to Q. Likewise, with its cognate κλέπται, κλέπτουσιν ("steal") frames the whole saying with the initial imperative and its object θησαυρίζετε and θησαυρούς, which have also been shown to be in Q. The construction would appear to be original to Q, not Matthew. Once again, we can see Luke's hand at work in the abbreviation of the text.

The result of the foregoing analysis is the following reconstruction:

Q 12:33

«Μὴ θησαυρίζετε ὑμῖν θησαυροὺς ἐπὶ τῆς γῆς,
ὅπου σὴς καὶ βρῶσις ἀφανίζει
καὶ ὅπου κλέπται διορύσσουσιν καὶ κλέπτουσιν·»

θησαυρίζετε «δὲ» ὑμῖν θησαυροὺς ἐν οὐρανοῖς,
ὅπου οὔτε σὴς οὔτε βρῶσις ἀφανίζει
καὶ ὅπου κλέπται οὐ διορύσσουσιν οὐδὲ κλέπτουσιν.

〚Do not treasure up for yourselves treasures on the earth
where moth and eating thing destroys
and where thieves break in and steal.〛

〚But〛 treasure up for yourselves treasures in heaven
where neither moth nor eating thing destroys
and where thieves do not break in and steal.

---

96. Notice, however, that Thomas' use of ⲧ2ⲛⲟ ⲉ2ⲟⲩⲛ (cf. Luke's use of ἐγγίζω) implies a stationary treasure (moths, not thieves, approach).

Q, Matthew, and Luke

It is most likely that the composer of Q was the one to place the two pericopae Q 12:22–31 and Q 12:33–34 together for the first time. Q 12:33 is consistent with the reference to Solomon's finery (Q 12:27), in that luxurious clothing and the like seem to be implied in the treasures that are moth-eaten. The "storing up" of treasures may remind one that crows do not gather up into barns (Q 12:24). At the same time, the composer of Q appears to have unified what were possibly two different original audiences: while both pericopae admonish the readers/hearers to seek the divine good, Q 12:22–31 seems to be directed to those who do not have much to live on, while Q 12:33 is a warning to those who can afford to lay up extraneous finery (Matthew and Luke both speak to the latter class of audience).

It is apparent that the composer of Q understood Q 12:33 as being concretely applicable for dealing with life's concerns, especially regarding material needs. Q 12:33 follows a speech that warns against being anxious for the needs of day-to-day living and recommends, instead, the seeking of God's reign, since God will provide for day-to-day needs. In the same way, Q 12:33 is practical, and the image of earthly treasures is to be understood quite literally.[97] In this way, Q 12:33 functions as a typical wisdom admonition. What places the saying in its historical context is the heavenly goal, which reflects the conceptual development of Hellenistic Jewish soteriological thought that can be seen in the movement from Ben Sira to the Wisdom of Solomon to the various forms of Jewish eschatology (employing wisdom forms) current in the first centuries BCE and CE.[98]

The preceding reconstruction of Q 12:33 indicates that Matthew has made very few changes to the content of this saying. Especially with Matt 6:19, the saying retains Q's concern for focusing on heavenly concerns over against earthly cares. What is significant is Matthew's relocation of the saying. By placing Matt 6:19–21 (Q 12:33–34—Storing up Treasures in Heaven) immediately after the "Cult Didache" (Matt 6:1–18), Matthew focuses the interpretation of the sayings on the *intentionality* of one's ac-

---

97. Θησαυρίζω ("treasure") may even have been the creation of Q, replacing ζητέω ("seek") in Q's source. See the discussion of a possible pre-Q, pre-Thomas version below, chapter 5, pp. 131–47, esp. 135–39.

98. Treasures in heaven, especially as stored up for the "last times": 2 Esdr 7:77; 8:33; 2 Bar. 14:12–14; 24:1; *Ps. Sol.* 9:5; etc.

tions. Matthew is interested in pious and devout living, and in the eternal rewards that such a righteous life attain (and the punishment that results from impiety). The placement of Q 12:33–34 at this point also moves the direction of the Sermon specifically toward one's attitude concerning wealth. By framing Matt 6:22–23 (Q 11:34–35—The Light of the Body) with Matt 6:19–21 and Matt 6:24 (Q 16:13—God and Mammon), Matthew interprets the contrast between the ἁπλοῦς ("generous") eye and the πονηρός ("evil") eye as a contrast between generosity and greed, and the context makes clear that the saying is dealing with *financial* generosity.[99] Matthew 6:24 argues that one must choose between God or material goods as one's first priority in life. Matthew then follows with Q's Free from Anxiety like Ravens and Lilies pericope (Q 12:22–31; Matt 6:25–34), itself an extended admonition to seek God's kingdom and not worry about earthly, day-to-day needs.

Like Q 12:33, Matt 6:19–20 understands the image of storing up treasures quite literally and, even more than Q, understands the saying as calling for a lifestyle not founded on the accumulation of wealth, but on the living of the pious, virtuous life that will receive its reward in due time. Interestingly, Matt 6:19 does not differ in any significant way from the Greek and Hellenistic moral commonplace of "everything in moderation," especially as it is applied by Greco-Roman moralists to the proper use of money.[100] Matthew 6:20, on the other hand, presupposes an es-

---

99. There is disagreement over the translation of ἁπλοῦς (cf., e.g., BDAG, "ἁπλοῦς," 104; Bauernfeind, "Ἁπλοῦς, ἁπλότης," 386). Yet, Cadbury is surely right in arguing that the context of Matt 6:19–24 requires a translation with the implication of "generous" (Cadbury, "Single Eye," 71–72). The evil eye is usually associated with greed, both in the Hebrew Bible (ibid., 71) and in Greek literature, and this reflects the social phenomenon of the "evil eye" in Mediterranean and Middle Eastern cultures; see Elliott, "Fear of the Leer," and idem, "Evil Eye." Cadbury suggests that the "characteristic Hellenistic Greek words for generousness in giving are the adverb ἁπλῶς, or the noun ἁπλότης (Cadbury, "Single Eye," 70). Use of ἁπλοῦς in the LXX and early Christian writings suggests the implication of generosity as well. While ἁπλῆ in Prov 11:25 (LXX) does not directly translate its counterpart in the MT (דשנה), the word as used in the LXX has the implication of generosity, as does the context of the proverb in the MT. It is usually translated "simple" or "sincere" in *Barn.* 19:2; *1 Clem.* 23:1; and *Hermas Sim.* 9.24.2; but in each case the context suggests the implication of generosity. Luke's cluster of sayings in 11:33–36 is based on the catchwords of "lamp" and "light," reflecting the more primitive Q connection, but the redactional 11:36 shows Luke's awareness of the generous vs. greedy implications of ὀφθαλμὸς ἁπλοῦς and ὀφθαλμὸς πονηρός in 11:34–35 in the concluding phrase "it will be as full of light as when a lamp gives you light with its rays (NRSV)."

100. E.g., Aristotle, *Eth. Nic.* IV and Plutarch, *Moralia.*

chatological reward in heaven for one's pious obedience to God on earth in these matters, and in this way is distinguished from the moralists.[101] The antithetical form of prohibition/admonition is very much at home in Jewish wisdom literature, as is the practicality of the hermeneutic.

Even with Luke's many modifications of this saying, the concern for seeking and accumulating the divine good over against earthly goods is still apparent. But where Matt 6:19–20, in its context, seems to be more concerned with attitude and intentions regarding money and possessions, Luke 12:33 proposes specific and radical actions regarding one's lifestyle: selling all of one's possessions and giving to the poor. In a way, Luke 12:33 is even more closely tied to the Free from Anxiety like Ravens and Lilies pericope than either Matt 6:19–20 or Q 12:33 in that it proposes actions—selling all and giving the money away—that allow one to better follow the exhortations of Q 12:22–31 to rely on God for one's daily needs.

As argued earlier (re: Mark), and as will be demonstrated later (re: Thomas), Luke has been influenced in the redaction of this saying by sources other than the Q version of the saying. However, Luke's understanding of the saying is primarily governed by the Q version and Luke's own social concern regarding the use of wealth and the needs of the Lukan community. Like Q 12:33 and Matt 6:19–20, Luke 12:33 understands the image of the treasure literally, but like Mark 10:21 and its radical contextual ethic, Luke 12:33 is even more concrete and practical in its application. Whereas in Q and Matthew the contrast of heavenly and earthly concerns is somewhat balanced (due, in part, to the balanced parallelism in Matthew [and maybe Q]), the hermeneutic of Luke 12:33 is dominated by the imperatives of 12:33a. Though the metaphor of the treasure is expanded upon by Luke, the treasure is no longer the aim of the main imperative of the saying, but is presented as merely the motivation for following the very concrete admonitions to sell all and give the proceeds away. Ironically, in the process of expanding upon the treasure metaphor, Luke's reconstruction of the saying makes any interest in knowing the nature of the reward recede from view.

While we have seen that Q 12:33 is very much at home in Jewish wisdom, aspects of Luke 12:33a are equally at home in that world. Abundant parallels can be found for the importance of almsgiving and the

---

101. Pesch, "Zur Exegese," 361–62.

rewards that it offers.[102] What sets Luke 12:33a (and Mark 10:21) apart from earlier Jewish wisdom literature, as well as from Hellenistic morality, is the radicality of selling all that one has prior to almsgiving.[103] It is this command that has inspired some scholars to argue that Luke 12:33 (or Mark 10:21) represents the original words of Jesus.[104] It flies in the face of traditional Israelite religion, which emphasized—especially in the Deuteronomistic literature—that success, financial or otherwise, was a sign of obedience and God's favor. This perspective is largely shared by Proverbs and Ben Sira—almsgiving is important and its rewards are most valuable, but certainly not the giving away of everything one owns. In later literature, we continue to find the admonition to give alms and the rewards that giving bestows. Tobit 4:7-11 (esp. 8-10) possibly even provides the conceptual background for Luke 12:33a (and Mark 10:21):

> As you possess much, give alms according to your plenty; if you have little, do not be afraid to give according to the little you have. So you will be laying up a good treasure for yourself against the day of necessity. For almsgiving delivers from death and keeps you from going into the darkness. (NRSV)

But Tobit is clear here that almsgiving does not entail the sacrifice of all one owns.

Luke 12:33a also flies in the face of typical Hellenistic morality, which is tempered by the dictum "everything in moderation"—the so-called "golden mean" of the moral philosophers.

In summary, Q 12:33, Matt 6:19-20, and Luke 12:33 all share a literal understanding of earthly treasure as wealth, and suggest a concrete, practical orientation in their application much in the same way as typical Jewish wisdom admonitions. At the same time, we can detect in Luke (and Matthew, if 6:19 is not from Q) a movement away from consideration of the nature of the treasure with the increasing stress on the fulfillment of the imperative. Whereas Q neatly connects the treasure (of 12:33) to the seeking of the Reign of God (in 12:31), Matthew's relocation of the saying places stress on the importance of living out the imperatives in day-to-

---

102. E.g., Sir 29:10-13; Tob 4:6b-11; 12:8-9; 2 *Enoch* 50:5—51:3; *T. Levi* 13:5.

103. See Pesch, "Zur Exegese," 361-66.

104. Braun, *Radikalismus*, 56-58 n. 1; 74 n. 2; 75 n. 1; 76 n. 1. See below, pp. 55-57.

day life, and Luke's version further concretizes the saying by the use of imperatives that are quite specific and radical in their application.

The concrete understanding of the images and the practical application of the imperative suggested by the use of the Treasure saying in Q, Matthew, and Luke is certainly not the only way it can be understood, as Chapter Three should make abundantly clear.

Mark 10:21

Herbert Braun has argued that Mark 10:21 represents the most primitive version of the Treasure in Heaven saying and may even go back to Jesus himself. Braun asserts that the renunciation of possessions is a primary focus of Jesus' teachings, while the less stringent Matthean version (6:20) is atypical of Jesus.[105]

Braun finds in this saying an expression closest to Jesus' thinking, which in turn was very close to the teaching of the Qumran community. Matt 6:19–21 embodies nothing characteristic of Jesus, while Luke 12:33 sharpens the admonition (on the basis of Mark 10:21).[106] Whether or not Braun thinks the whole of Mark 10:17–22 describes an actual event in the life of Jesus is not clear, since Braun argues that "Mark 10:17–22 par. . . . is a typical scene, by means of which the tradent community elucidates the authentic words of Jesus (Mark 10:23, 25) concerning the dangers of wealth."[107] The answer is probably negative, if Braun's reliance on Bultmann is indicative.

The major problem with Braun's claim is that Mark 10:21 is embedded in a pronouncement story that shows numerous signs of Markan redaction (if not Markan construction).[108] Mark 10:21 itself is evidence of this redaction. The demand of Jesus to the rich young man to "follow me" is probably Markan. The theme of following Jesus is a constant

---

105. Braun, *Radikalismus*, 56 n. 1.

106. Ibid., 74 n. 2; 76 n. 1. With regard to Matt 6:19–21, Braun refers to Rudolf Bultmann (*History*, 104).

107. Braun, *Radikalismus*, 75 n. 1: "Mk 10,17–22 par . . . wird eine typische Szene sein, durch welche die tradierende Gemeinde die echten Jesusworte über die Gefahr des Reichtums, Mk 10, 23. 25 . . . erläutert."

108. Bultmann sees Mark 10:17–22 as a unitary composition (*History*, 21–22) and appears to argue that this "apophthegm" was created at an oral stage (*History*, 54). He lists only 10:17a as coming from the hand of Mark (*History*, 22).

thread throughout the Markan narrative.[109] The inclusion of this Markan demand in 10:21e should make one suspicious about the originality of the attachment of the previous comment "and you will have treasure in heaven," to the demand to sell possessions and give to the poor. Jesus' pronouncement, "you lack one thing; go, sell what you have and give to the poor," is itself a shocking answer to the rich man who thinks he has done it all. The rejoinder "and you will have treasure in heaven" appears to be an addition that softens the harshness of the command of Jesus, immediately presenting the rich man (and the readers/hearers of Mark) with an eternal reward in return for such an earthly, financial sacrifice.[110] Mark 10:28–31 continues the softening of the impact of Jesus' sayings after the similarly shocking statements of Jesus in Mark 10:23b, 25.

This is not to say that Mark 10:17–21c could not have existed as a pronouncement story prior to Mark—in fact, this is quite possible. And, it is not to say that Jesus himself did not command someone to give all they had to the poor—such a concept was relatively unknown in Jewish literature prior to Mark.[111] Nor is it to say that the "treasure in heaven" addition is itself a Markan creation—it could very well reflect the gospel author's knowledge of the Treasure saying as it is found in Q, Thomas, or some other source. The fragmentary application of the saying in the Markan context could even be taken as evidence for Matthew's two-strophe version of the saying coming from Q, which in an early form may predate Mark by some years. The specific issue raised by the man's wealth is how one should deal with earthly wealth, or, abstractly, anything that one holds most dear. In this way, the Markan version of the Treasure saying clearly understands earthly treasure as just that—treasure to be disposed of, in contrast to heavenly, abiding treasure. This literal understanding of treasure accords with the synoptic tradition represented by Q, Matthew, and Luke, which understands the saying as contrasting earthly and heavenly wealth (whatever heavenly wealth consists of) and focus-

---

109. Mark 1:17 (!), 18; 2:14, 15; 3:7; 5:24; 6:1; 8:34 (!); 9:38; 10:28 (!), 32, 52; 15:41.

110. In breaking down the rhetorical structure of Mark 10:17–31, Burton Mack recognizes the artificiality of the construction of 10:21, identifying the "treasure in heaven" phrase in 10:21d as providing the rationale that supports the thesis of 10:21bc. Mark 10:21 is not even the chreia upon which 10:17–21 is elaborated—that distinction belongs to 10:18, which may or may not have existed prior to construction of the pronouncement story as a whole (Mack, *Rhetoric*, 54–56, esp. 55).

111. Pesch, "Zur Exegese," 363–65.

ing the interpretation of the saying on ethical and pious living.[112] This concordance of perspective on wealth led to Luke's use of Mark 10:21 in the redaction of Q 12:33.

What is unlikely is Braun's thesis that Mark 10:21 provides the most primitive form of the Treasure saying. Jesus may have told someone to sell what they had and give to the poor, but probably not with the rationale that they would earn heavenly jewels in their crowns by doing so. The only way out of this difficulty would be to speculate that Jesus reprised the concept of earning treasures in heaven on different occasions and in different contexts.

---

112. Surprisingly, Mark appears to define the heavenly treasure as eternal life in 10:30, and so returns to the content of the rich person's question of 10:17. Not only that, but Mark has Jesus promising abundant wealth in this life as well. Mark 10:29–30 reads: "Jesus said, 'Truly I tell you, there is no one who has left house or brothers or sisters or mother or father or children or fields, for my sake and for the sake of the good news, who will not receive a hundredfold now in this time—houses and brothers and sisters and mothers and children and fields with persecutions—and in the age to come eternal life.'"

CHAPTER 3 | John, Thomas, and Luke

INTRODUCTION

The purpose of this chapter is to investigate the tradition- and redaction-history of the Treasure in Heaven saying as it has been utilized in GTh 76:3, Luke 12:33, and John 6:27. The outline is as follows: (1) establishing John 6:27 as a version of the "Treasure in Heaven" saying; (2) addressing problems engendered by assuming Thomas' relative isolation from or direct dependence upon the canonical gospels, and proposing an alternative solution; (3) clarifying relationships between the three gospels with respect to their treatment of this saying.

JOHN 6:27

To date, there is no agreement on the source of John 6:27. Most commentators simply ignore the source issue with regard to this verse. For those who do address the issue, however, opinion is divided. Some commentators consider John 6:27 to have been a redactional addition to the Bread of Life Discourse in connection with the eucharistic section of 6:51b–58.[1] Others see Johannine terminology in the verse and thus, by implication, appear to consider the whole verse as redactional.[2] On the other side of the coin, some commentators consider John 6:27 to have been part of a source used by the author of the gospel.[3] Still others appear to consider it source material by implication, arguing that 6:27b (ἦν ὁ

---

1. E.g., Becker, *Johannes*, 201, 204; Schnelle, *Antidoketische*, 227 (cited in Roulet and Ruegg, "Étude de Jean 6," 241–42).

2. E.g., Brown, *John*, 261, 264; possibly Barrett, *John*, 286.

3. E.g., Bultmann, *John*, 222 n. 5; Wilkens, *Entstehungsgeschichte*, 92–93 (cited in Kysar, *Fourth Evangelist*, 44); Temple, *Core*, 141–44, esp. 143.

υἱὸς τοῦ ἀνθρώπου ὑμῖν δώσει· τοῦτον γὰρ ὁ πατὴρ ἐσφράγισεν ὁ θεός) is a redactional addition to 6:27a in connection with 6:51b–58.[4]

Raymond Brown perhaps best summarizes the position that John 6:27 is redactional when he suggests that the expression "perishable food . . . may be an echo of vs. 12, where the fragments were collected so that nothing would perish."[5] Likewise, "food that lasts . . . is the favorite Johannine verb *menein.*" He makes his point especially by comparison with John 4:

> In vs. 27 Jesus presses the lesson home in terms of the familiar Johannine dualism: perishable food and the food that lasts for eternal life. In ch. iv the contrast was between water that could quench thirst temporarily and the water for eternal life that would satisfy thirst forever. Although the expression is Johannine, such symbols are frequent in the Bible.[6]

There are problems with considering this saying to be wholly a creation of the author. First, ἀπόλλυμι is not particularly Johannine in this instance. John 3:16; 6:39; 10:28; 17:12; and 18:9 all explicitly rehearse or develop the theme of Jesus giving life to and protecting the souls of every believer lest they "perish." John 6:12; 10:10; and 11:50 develop this theme through metaphor and allusion. John 6:27 appears to be used only because the saying can be modified to fit this theme *indirectly*. The "food" which abides—and by implication, "does not perish"—is subsequently interpreted in John 6:30–34 as Jesus himself, and it is only through the addition of 6:27b and subsequent interpretation that the saying can be made to refer to Jesus as the giver and guardian of life. In other words, the author must modify and elaborate upon the saying in order to give it a

---

4. E.g., Richter, *Studien*, 105 n. 56; Haenchen, *Johannesevangelium*, 320. Those who argue for a pre-Johannine source for the Bread of Life Discourse, but consider John 6:27 to be an addition in accordance with the addition of 6:51b–58, ignore the issue raised by the distinction between 6:27a and 27b. When John 6:27b is removed, discontinuity with 6:28 is also removed, and 6:27's connection with what follows becomes more obvious (Temple, *Core*, 143; Bultmann, *John*, 225 n. 1—Bultmann attributes the addition of 6:27b not to the author of John, but to the redactor, based on the improbability that the audience would identify him with the υἱὸς τοῦ ἀνθρώπου [12:34]).

5. Brown, *John*, 261. Dodd, on the other hand (who considers 6:26–34 to be part of a discourse source, but εἰς ζωὴν αἰώνιον in 6:27 to be Johannine), sees the use of ἀπόλλυμι in 6:12 as a redactional addition recalling 6:27 (Dodd, *Historical Tradition*, 207; idem, *Interpretation*, 146). Cf. Fortna, *Fourth Gospel*, 89.

6. Brown, *John*, 264.

Johannine interpretation. Grammatically, the use of "perish" (ἀπόλλυμι) in 6:27 is not typically Johannine. With the exception of John 6:27 and 12:25, all cases of ἀπόλλυμι in Johannine literature use the aorist tense, and John prefers the subjunctive in 7 of 11 cases (3:16; 6:12; 6:39; 10:10; 10:28; 11:50; 2 John 8). Only John 6:27 and 12:25 use the present tense— John 12:25 is source material and ἀπόλλυμι there comes from tradition (cf. Matt 10:39; Luke 17:33; Mark 8:35 par.). Finally, in all of Johannine literature, only John 6:27 uses ἀπόλλυμι as a participle. For these reasons, if ἀπόλλυμι was in fact Johannine redaction, then it most likely replaced a synonymous participle in a pre-Johannine source for the saying.

Likewise with μένω: at first glance the attributive clause "which abides" in John 6:27 would appear to be Johannine, μένω being a favorite Johannine verb.[7] However, it is not used here in the familiar way of furthering John's theology of immanence.[8] It only begins to take on this implication in a spiritualizing interpretation of the subsequent Bread of Life Discourse.[9] Grammatically, the form of the verb as it is used here differs from its use anywhere else in the Johannine corpus. Only here is μένω used as an accusative attributive participle. This is one of only four times μένω is used as an attributive participle in all of the Johannine literature (cf. John 15:5; 1 John 3:6; 2 John 9). Only here is μένω used with an article adjectivally, not replacing an assumed substantive. More importantly, this is also one of the few places where μένω is not connected with a preposition of immanence (ἐν, ἐπί, or παρά). Instead, John's implied second imperative, "(work) for the food which abides," is supplemented by the favorite Johannine expression "into eternal life" (εἰς ζωὴν αἰώνιον) in a manner reminiscent of John's elaboration on sayings traditions elsewhere.[10] In short, μένουσαν is probably not redactional, but comes rather from John's source. In 6:27a, only εἰς ζωὴν αἰώνιον is clearly Johannine.

---

7. Ibid., 261, 510–11.

8. Brown seems to recognize this by citing John 6:27 as an example of "the atmosphere of the permanence of the divine," but not including it in the subsequent discussion of John's theology of immanence (ibid., 510).

9. John 12:24–25 is the only other place in the gospel where one finds ἀπόλλυμι and μένω used in close proximity. Yet, both words appear to belong to their source(s). The use of μένω in 12:24 is appropriate to the parable and has no typically Johannine implication of a divine abiding presence.

10. Cf. the addition of the comparable εἰς ζωὴν αἰώνιον to the likewise-modified traditional saying of Jesus in John 12:25: "Those who love their life shall lose it, and those who hate their life in this world will keep it into eternal life." The insertion of εἰς ζωὴν

Further considerations ensure that John 6:27a is traditional. First, John 6:27 stands out as the first synoptic-like wisdom admonition used in the gospel. John uses very few general wisdom admonitions of Jesus as it is.[11] This particular admonition, however, is then used as part of the introduction to the Bread of Life Discourse (John 6:26–58); it is indeed the *keystone* for the construction of the entire sixth chapter of John. John 6:26 connects 6:27 to the previous Feeding of the 5,000 (6:1–5) and sets up the comparison of perishable vs. abiding food, the guiding theme for the rest of the chapter.[12] C. K. Barrett recognizes the importance of 6:27 in the narrative and even suggests that "the whole discourse is summarized here. Jesus is the Son of man, and it is in communion with him that men have eternal life." However, Barrett's choice of wording is unfortunate: John 6:27 cannot be a Johannine summary of the discourse since it is *only understandable in a Johannine way with subsequent interpretation*. Verses 28–33 begin the interpretation of 6:27 by defining the main verb and its object: "working" is defined in 6:28–29 as "believing"; "food" is then defined in 6:30–33 as the "true bread from heaven," the "manna" which "gives life to the world" (unlike manna that lasts for a day and gets worm-eaten overnight).

The subsequent Bread of Life Discourse is an extended commentary on especially these two issues. While there are a number of ways to break down the structure of the Bread of Life Discourse into constituent parts in order to analyze its thematic and theological development, here I would simply note how 6:35–47 focuses on the concept of believing, while 6:48–58 develops the bread motif.[13] Verses 51–55 in particular return to the previous definition of "food" as the "bread from heaven" and provide further definition—the bread from heaven is Jesus' flesh. Hence, the saying of Jesus in John 6:27 is the starting point of an extended theological exposition on the power and efficacy of mystical participation in Jesus as

---

αἰώνιον disrupts a form that otherwise parallels the Q form found in Matt 10:39. Cf. also John 4:14: "But those who drink of the water I will give them will never thirst (οὐ μὴ διψήσει εἰς τὸν αἰῶνα). The water that I will give will become in them a spring of water gushing up into eternal life (εἰς ζωὴν αἰώνιον)."

11. Other examples include John 7:24; (12:26;) 12:35; 14:27; 16:24. For other non-narrative-specific imperatives, cf. 7:37; 14:1; 15:4–9.

12. John 6:26–27: "You seek me . . . because you ate of the loaves and were filled. Do not work for the food which perishes."

13. For a discussion of the structure, see Brown, *John*, 293–94.

giver of life, and (perhaps secondarily) on the efficacy of partaking of the eucharistic elements. The point is that either the author of John or the composer of a pre-Johannine discourse source recognized the authenticity of the saying in 6:27 and proceeded to use it as the keynote saying of the Bread of Life Discourse.

If John 6:27 comes from a source of Jesus' sayings, then it remains to be seen what form the saying took originally.[14] Whether or not 6:27 belonged to a discourse source prior to its inclusion in the Bread of Life Discourse, Koester's observations are apropos:

> The discourses of the Gospel of John have been developed on the basis of traditions which consisted primarily of sayings. The purpose of the discourses is to explore and discuss critically the meaning and interpretation of such sayings. This is accomplished through changes of the wording of such sayings as well as by placing sayings into a particular context in the composition of a discourse so that the context becomes a critical commentary.[15]

Certain considerations suggest that John 6:27 was a version of the Treasure in Heaven saying. Figure #2 compares John 6:27 to the other gospel versions of the saying (see the following page).

All of these sayings of Jesus involve a contrast between striving for or storing up earthly, material goods and striving for or storing up what is heavenly and/or eternal.[16] All five sayings are wisdom admonitions in the second person imperative form. All use the clausal form *imperative—object—object qualifier* (the qualifiers being adjectives, prepositional phrases and/or attributive clauses).

Like Matthew, John consists of two antithetically parallel admonitions, though the use of earthly images in the saying and thus the implicit contrast between earthly and heavenly, or perishable and imperishable, lends itself to an expansion of the saying into parallel admonitions (as I

---

14. Bultmann suggests that "v. 27 is probably based on a saying taken from the source . . . ; it is doubtful whether it is quoted word for word, since the style of the source would lead us to expect a verb in the second half verse as well" (*John*, 222, n. 5).

15. Koester, *Ancient Christian Gospels*, 114.

16. In other words, it is not just that the sayings all involve a conceptual dualism ("this warning is . . . delivered against the background of Johannine 'dualism'" [Bultmann, *John*, 222); the *content* of the contrast is similar as well.

Figure 2: Treasure in Heaven—Gospel Versions

Q 12:33	Matt 6:19-20	Luke 12:33	GTh 76:3	John 6:27
(...	Μὴ θησαυρίζετε ὑμῖν θησαυροὺς ἐπὶ τῆς γῆς, ὅπου σὴς καὶ βρῶσις ἀφανίζει καὶ ὅπου κλέπται διορύσσουσιν καὶ	Πωλήσατε τὰ ὑπάρχοντα ὑμῶν καὶ δότε		ἐργάζεσθε μὴ τὴν βρῶσιν <u>τὴν</u> <u>ἀπολλυμένην</u>
...?)	κλέπτουσιν·	ἐλεημοσύνην·	N̄TΩTN̄ 2ΩT THYTN̄	
θησαυρίζετε δὲ ὑμῖν	θησαυρίζετε δὲ ὑμῖν	ποιήσατε ἑαυτοῖς βαλλάντια μὴ παλαιούμενα,	ϢINE N̄CA	ἀλλὰ
θησαυροὺς	θησαυροὺς	θησαυρον ἀνέκλειπτον	Π{Єϥ}Є2O ЄMAϤΩA͞N	τὴν βρῶσιν
<u>ἐν</u> <u>οὐρανοῖς,</u> ὅπου οὔτε σὴς <u>οὔτε βρῶσις</u> ἀφανίζει	<u>ἐν</u> <u>οὐρανῷ,</u> ὅπου οὔτε σὴς <u>οὔτε βρῶσις</u> ἀφανίζει	<u>ἐν</u> <u>τοῖς οὐρανοῖς,</u> ὅπου κλέπτης οὐκ ἐγγίζει	ЄϤMHN ЄBOΛ ΠMA ЄMAPЄ ΧOOΛЄC T2NO Є2OYN ЄMAY ЄOYΩM	<u>τὴν μένουσαν</u> εἰς ζωὴν αἰώνιον,
καὶ ὅπου κλέπται οὐ διορύσσουσιν οὐδὲ κλέπτουσιν·	καὶ ὅπου κλέπται οὐ διορύσσουσιν οὐδὲ κλέπτουσιν·	οὐδὲ σὴς διαφθείρει·	OYΔЄ MAPЄ {ϥ}ϤN̄T TAKO.[17]	

17. The Coptic text is taken from Layton, "The Gospel According to Thomas," in *Nag Hammadi Codex II,2-7*, 80. It will be argued below that the Greek text behind Coptic GTh 76:3 is best translated as follows: ζητεῖτε καὶ ὑμεῖς τὸν θησαυρὸν αὐτοῦ μὴ τὸν ἀπολλύμενον τὸν μένοντα, ὅπου οὐ σὴς εἰς βρῶσιν ἐγγίζει οὐδὲ σκώληξ ἀφανίζει. In conversation, James Robinson has suggested the possibility of ἐκλειπόμενον for ἀπολλύμενον.

will argue has happened with John independent of Matthew).¹⁸ John is similar to Luke and Thomas in the use of two object qualifiers pertaining to the contrast between perishability and non-perishability. Like Thomas, John understands this saying to be metaphorical. In Thomas, one is told to seek the treasure, but one is not told what the treasure is. GTh 76:3 is prefaced with images of selling cargo and buying a pearl (GTh 76:1–2), but the imagery is embedded in a parable, and thus is not to be understood concretely. The parabolic form leaves one to divine or discover just what the treasure is that is to be sought. John, on the other hand, spends most of the rest of chapter six unpacking the metaphorical images of 6:27—"work" is belief in the Christ, and the "food which endures" is his body, the "bread from heaven," which gives eternal life to those who spiritually or sacramentally eat of it.

Key parallels in vocabulary can also be discerned. John and Thomas both have two object qualifiers that are circumstantial constructions using the words "perish" and "abide." Similarly, Luke uses the adjective ἀνέκλειπτος ("unfailing") alongside of the modified Q phrase "in heaven." John and Matthew both use the word βρῶσις, though in drastically different ways. Thomas likewise refers to eating in its first adversity clause, in a way consistent with the use of βρῶσις elsewhere.¹⁹

The abundance of similarities between Q 12:33, its redacted versions in Matthew and Luke, GTh 76:3, and John 6:27 are simply too numerous to dismiss as coincidence: John 6:27 is a modified version of the Treasure in Heaven saying.

That βρῶσις is used in John in a manner different from Matthew or Thomas is partly understandable when it is recognized that the author of John found "food" to be more valuable than "treasure" as the object of one's striving when the author developed the Bread of Life Discourse

---

18. The implicit contrast is found in the Lukan and Thomasine versions as well. The IQP has voted the negative imperative into Q. Luke then changed this negative demand, "do not store up treasures," to a positive demand, "sell your possessions and give alms." Cf. Col 3:1–2 for a concept similar to the gospel versions, but with little common vocabulary (ζητεῖτε [GTh 76:3]; ἐπὶ τῆς γῆς [Matt 6:19]).

19. Numerous examples exist for the expression εἰς βρῶσιν ("for eating," or "for food"), especially in the LXX and medical writings. See also Sophocles *Frag.* 181.2; Strabo *Geog.* 16.1.7.4; Josephus *Ap.* 2.82.6; *Ant.* 3.230.4; Philo *Spec. leg.* 1.256.3; and 2 Cor 9:10. Moulton and Milligan cite P. London 1223.9 (*Vocabulary*, 118). Christian era usage is usually conditioned by the LXX and New Testament writings. See below, pp. 73–74, n. 45, for further discussion of εἰς βρῶσιν.

and its introduction around this saying. It served the author's purposes as a bridge between the Feeding of the 5,000 (John 6:1–14) and the Bread of Life Discourse and it provided a connection to John 6's sister passage, the Woman at the Well Discourse in John 4, with its initiatory "Give me a drink!" command and its subsequent discussion about "living waters." That John 6:27 uses the imperative form but lacks the two adversity clauses of the other versions is understandable if John wanted to focus on the imperative, its object, and their interpretation, which is precisely what John does in 6:28–58. John replaced the adversity clauses in 6:27 with the assurance "which the son of humanity will give to you. For it is on him that God the Father has set his seal."[20] This addition also assures the observant reader that subsequent interpretation of this saying will focus specifically on Jesus. Yet, if βρῶσις originally belonged in the first adversity clause of this saying, then its presence in John 6:27 is evidence that John knew of a fuller version of the saying and chose to abbreviate it.

Even with these changes made to the form and content of the saying in John, both the basic concept behind the Treasure in Heaven saying and significant vocabulary (βρῶσις and unperishing, abiding objects) and motifs shared with other versions are clearly identifiable in John 6:27.

One other issue should be addressed: Why would the author risk modifying the saying so much as to make it virtually unrecognizable in order to fit it into the author's larger theological schema? Part of this answer is simply that the author felt the freedom to alter sources when necessary. Even by conservative standards of judgment, the author of John regularly altered the text of the LXX when referring to it.[21] As observed above with John 12:25, it is the case that every generally known and accepted traditional saying of Jesus in John (that is, ones that have synoptic parallels) has been modified to fit the Johannine pericope into which it is embedded. Koester has found this to be true when trying to identify non-canonical parallels as well.[22] But this may not be the final

20. Υἱὸς τοῦ ἀνθρώπου is a technical term that is usually translated in English scholarship as "son of man," but is better translated today as "son of humanity" or "son of humankind" to reflect the generic meaning of ἄνθρωπος over against the exclusively masculine ἀνήρ.

21. See, e.g., Ensor, *Jesus and His 'Works,'* 58–82.

22. In attempting to identify a sayings source behind John 8:12–59 that is different in nature from synoptic sources, Koester achieved varying degrees of success in different parts of John 8, and two of his concluding comments explain why: "In most of the gnostic texts traditional sayings are already embedded in dialogue and discourse. It is difficult to

answer to the question. John may also be consciously modifying the saying away from its implied meaning or interpretation in John's source, or from its expressed interpretation in tradent communities that the author is in contact with.

What remains to be uncovered is the source for John's version of the Treasure in Heaven saying.

Thomas 76:3

The Gospel of Thomas has the Treasure saying attached to the Parable of the Pearl (76:1–2).[23] GTh 76:3 serves as a summary admonition: "So you also, seek his treasure."[24] The many verbal similarities between GTh 76:3 and the canonical gospel versions of the Treasure in Heaven saying have led to a number of proposals (often contradictory) concerning the relationship between these texts; these proposals are briefly summarized below.[25]

Lucien Cerfaux was first to suggest that the Thomas version of the Treasure saying was in fact a composite text constructed from the canonical gospels—a composition derived primarily from Matt 6:20 and John 6:27, with "worm" (σκώληξ) taken from Mark 9:48.[26] Specifically, he understood the construction ⲈⲘⲀϤⲰϪⲚ̅ ⲈϤⲘⲎⲚ ⲈⲂⲞⲖ ("which does not perish, which abides") to come from John, with the bulk of the rest of the saying being taken up from Matthew. Robert McL. Wilson suggested that the "most obvious explanation here is free quotation by an author familiar with all four Gospels."[27] Wolfgang Schrage focused on the Lukan

---

isolate them, and the exegete's eyes are not sufficiently trained for this task." And, in John, "there seems to be little respect for the original 'form' of a saying; i.e., basic formulations ('There is light within a man of light, and he lights up the whole world') can be transformed into I-sayings ('I am the light of the world')" (Koester, "Gnostic Sayings," 109).

23. Cf. Matt 13:45–46's Parable of the Pearl Dealer.

24. Ron Cameron observes that this use of a traditional saying to interpret a parable is unique in the Gospel of Thomas and therefore argues that it not be considered the product of the author but of an earlier stage of the tradition (Cameron, "Parable and Interpretation," 15).

25. Similarities include: "treasure" (Q, Matt, Luke); "which does not perish"/ "unfailing" (Luke, John); "which abides" (John); "where" (Q, Matt, Luke); "moth" (Q, Matt, Luke); "approaches" (Luke); reference to eating or food, probably with βρῶσι– (Q, Matt, John); "destroy" (Q, Matt, Luke).

26. Cerfaux and Garitte, "Les paraboles du royaume," 312–13.

27. Wilson, *Studies*, 92. However, his statement continues: "But as already noted this

parallels and argued that Thomas' singular "treasure" and its characterization as "that which does not perish" are derived from Luke.²⁸ Klyne Snodgrass went beyond Schrage to argue that Thomas' ⲦⲰⲚⲞ ⲈⲢⲞⲨⲚ ("approach") is taken from Luke's ἐγγίζει, Thomas' ⲈⲞⲨⲰⲘ ("to eat") comes from Matthew's ἀφανίζει, and Thomas' ⲦⲀⲔⲞ ("destroy") comes from Luke's διαφθείρει.²⁹ Some scholars who have addressed this saying have assumed that Thomas' ϥⲚⲦ ("worm") is a translation of βρῶσις, whether it was derived from Matthew or not.³⁰ In short, with a little perseverance, one can identify a canonical gospel source or sources for every word in GTh 76:3.

This perspective on the Treasure saying has not gone unchallenged. John Sieber questioned Schrage's redactional analysis and found Lukan redactional elements to be lacking in GTh 76:3.³¹ Ron Cameron, John Dominic Crossan, and Stephen Patterson took the approach of arguing that GTh 76:3 represents a stream of tradition that developed independent of canonical traditions.³² Alone, however, these observations do

---

does not seem to account for the phenomena presented by the gospel as a whole. It may be that we must reckon with the possibility that the several sayings are of diverse origin: some perhaps from genuine early tradition, others based on our Gospels directly, others again the result of free quotation and harmonization, and still others merely tendentious inventions." Elsewhere, in the context of discussing GTh 9, 76 and 109, Wilson argues that "independent access to a cycle of tradition similar to that of the Synoptics is surely a simpler and more probable explanation than random selection of sayings from all three" (Wilson, "'Thomas,'" 240).

28. Schrage, Verhältnis, 159.

29. Snodgrass, "The Gospel of Thomas," 36.

30. E.g., Schrage (Verhältnis, 160), who sees it deriving from Matthew indirectly from manuscripts of Tatian; Crossan, In Fragments, 130–31; Snodgrass, "The Gospel of Thomas," 36; Sieber, who sees no evidence of Thomas' dependence on the canonical gospels ("Redactional Analysis," 57, 60). But cf. Grant and Freedman, who translate βρῶσις as "rust," but suggest that "Thomas takes brōsis very literally to mean 'eating,' and therefore adds a word about worms" (Grant and Freedman, Secret Sayings, 177). Gundry correctly argues that βρῶσις seems not to mean 'rust' or 'corrosion,' but 'eating'" (Gundry, Matthew, 112). Charles rightly translates βρῶσις in Matt 6:19–20 as "devourer" (APOT, 1:601).

31. Sieber's comment that "the only certain editorial trait in the whole passage, Luke's βαλλάντια, is not found in Saying 76b," must be corrected in light of the work of the IQP ("A Redactional Analysis," 59). Specifically, there are several redactional elements in Luke's version of Q that are also found in Thomas: ἐγγίζω; the singular "treasure"; two qualifiers of the object of the imperative; and a verb of destruction in the second adversity clause.

32. Cameron claims that the saying "has no vestige of a distinctive language or style

not address the many similarities between GTh 76:3 and three different canonical gospel versions of the Treasure saying. A closer analysis is needed to clarify the relationship of the Thomas version to the canonical versions.

I will address this issue on several fronts. Ordinarily, Matthean, Lukan, or Johannine redactional elements found in Thomas would be considered evidence of Thomas' use of these versions. In the case of this saying, however, certain problems attend such a conclusion. In the case of Thomas' ⲉⲙⲁϥⲱϫⲛ̄ ("which does not perish"), does it come from Luke's redactional ἀνέκλειπτος ("unfailing"—Schrage) or John's μὴ . . . τὴν ἀπολλυμένην ("not . . . for that which perishes"—Cerfaux)?[33] The attributive clause ⲉⲙⲁϥⲱϫⲛ̄ is closer to John's phrasing than to Luke's adjective, though most Greek retranslations of Thomas use ἀνέκλειπτος to translate ⲉⲙⲁϥⲱϫⲛ̄![34] At the same time, the form of ἀπόλλυμι is not particularly Johannine in this instance, and may come from John's source for the saying.[35] Cerfaux also maintains that Thomas' ⲉϥⲙⲏⲛ ⲉⲃⲟⲗ ("which abides") is Johannine. However, the use of μένω in John 6:27 has likewise been shown to be non-Johannine. The one significant Johannine addition

---

attributable to the author of this gospel" and that it "is a version of an independent unit of tradition" (Cameron, "Parable and Interpretation," 15). Crossan argues for an independent tradition by implication: "I imagine an original saying of Jesus put negatively against earthly possessions. . . . That was changed into a positive version in Gospel of Thomas 76:2[3], developed into a parallel negative and positive or earthly and heavenly dyad as Matthew 6:19-20 accepted the Sayings Gospel Q version, and finally changed into a positive admonition to almsgiving as Luke 12:33 rewrote the Sayings Gospel Q version" (Crossan, *Historical Jesus*, 275-76). According to Patterson, "the Matthean and Thomas versions of this parable [of the Pearl] have traveled along different routes in the early history of their oral transmission. . . . On the Thomas side, a different tradition-history is evident in the secondary appending of Thom 76:3, itself originally an independent *mashal*, as an hortatory conclusion" (Patterson, *Gospel of Thomas*, 59).

33. Luke's ἀνέκλειπτος is redactional. See above, Chapter 2, p. 42, on Q 12:33[8].

34. See Kasser, *Thomas*, 98; Huck, *Synopse*, 38; Bethge et al., "Evangelium Thomae copticum," 538. Sellew notes the problem usually raised by such retroversions: "I have . . . quoted Greeven's Greek retroversions as though they were the original *Thomas* readings—which they could well be in many cases, though in doing that work there seems to have been a natural tendency to be influenced in both vocabulary and word order by the familiar NT parallels" (Sellew, "Reconstruction of Q 12:33-59," 618). Arguing that Thomas' Greek *Vorlage* had ἀνέκλειπτος ignores the Coptic construction of GTh 76:3 and finds little support in Crum (Sahidic Luke translates ἀνέκλειπτος with the adjective ⲁⲧⲱϫⲛ̄, not ⲉⲙⲁϥⲱϫⲛ̄—Crum, 540a).

35. See above, p. 59-60.

to John 6:27a, εἰς ζωὴν αἰώνιον, is missing from GTh 76:3, though the idea of eternal life is popular in the Gospel of Thomas (e.g., GTh 1, 18, 19, 85, 111). In short, there is no evidence of Johannine redactional material in Thomas.

Since the original form of John's Treasure saying has yet to be determined, it seems presumptuous to argue for Thomas' use of John without addressing alternative possibilities.

Another problem with the redactional argument concerns Lukan creativity vis-à-vis the use of sources. As seen in chapter 2, Luke has thoroughly modified the Q version of the saying. But how much of this can be determined to come from Luke's own genius? In fact, Luke 12:33a is clearly an adaptation of *another* source added to the saying (Mark 10:21, possibly replacing Q/Matt 6:19), giving a reading that is closely congruent with Lukan ethics. Likewise, Luke's replacement of Q's ἀφανίζω with διαφθέρω did not likely come out of creative thin air—the verb bears a reminiscence of Q's διορύσσω in the second adversity clause, which is precisely where διαφθέρω now stands in Luke 12:33.[36] Therefore, when we come to parts of the saying that are paralleled in Thomas, such as with the use of the word ἐγγίζω or the singular of "treasure," we cannot readily assume Thomas' use of Lukan redactional material. Other information must be assessed before one can arrive at such a conclusion.

Furthermore, a deconstruction of Thomas' text into numerous sources raises more questions than it answers. For example, *why* would the composer of GTh 76:3 go to such trouble picking out individual words here and there from *three*, or even *all four* canonical gospels? Do *any* of the individual words or phrases have especial meaning in the Gospel of Thomas? In fact, outside of the general concept of seeking, there are no elements of the saying that have any clearly identifiable theological relevance particular to the Gospel of Thomas, and a redactional rationale is lacking for almost every compositional maneuver one can suggest.

On the contrary, several points argue against canonical derivation. For example, the image of the "thief" as an adversary appears to be a

36. Concerning ἀφανίζω, it does not mean "to eat" and therefore is not the basis for Thomas' ⲉⲟⲩⲱⲙ (cf. Snodgrass, "A Secondary Gospel," 36). For that matter, βρῶσις does not mean "rust" or "worm" and is never used with either specific meaning in Greek literature prior to the New Testament. Sieber provides Hebrew and Latin evidence for the translation "eating thing"—or, as he translates אכל and *comestura*, "devourer"—though he decides for "worm" in opposition to "rust" ("A Redactional Analysis," 57, 59; see also *APOT*, 1:601).

popular image in the Gospel of Thomas (GTh 21, 103;[37] cf. also GTh 35, 39), and it would seem particularly appropriate following the Parable of the Merchant (GTh 76:1–2). Yet, Q's "thief" clause is missing in Thomas and a "worm" clause is found in its place.[38]

For what reason would Thomas use Matthew's order of adversities ("moth" and "eating thing" before "thief") but Luke's verbs ("approach," "destroy" [Snodgrass]) and verb order ("approach" in first clause, "destroy" in second) in the adversity clauses?[39] Such a careful and refined conflation of sources should suggest some theological or stylistic intentionality. Yet, Thomas' supposed addition of Luke's redactional ἐγγίζω would seem unnecessary: "Where moths eat and worms destroy" would make for a simpler, more concise saying. The second object qualifier, ЄϥМНN ЄΒΟΛ ("which abides"), argued by Cerfaux and Schrage to be Johannine and Lukan, respectively, also could be considered a stylistically redundant addition. On the other hand, as seen in Chapter 2, it is with *Luke* that we can identify clear rationales for making theological and stylistic changes to the Q version of the saying. Which conclusion, then, is more likely: Thomas conflates three sources with sophistication but without any apparent theological or stylistic rationale; or Luke, the commonly recognized collector and adapter of sources, has used elements of a third source in the wholesale recomposition of the Q saying? Without a rationale for a cut and paste theory of redaction, it seems more reasonable to assume that GTh 76:3 is not dependent upon the synoptic gospels for its text.

Recourse to a theory of "secondary orality" as postulated by Risto Uro is not satisfactory.[40] Uro provides one potential instance where independent transmission of a version of a saying of Jesus found only in Matthew (Matt 15:11), and possibly one from Q or Luke (Luke 10:8–9), have found their way into the text of Thomas (GTh 14:4, 5). In the

---

37. GTh 21:5 uses the Coptic construction ПРЄϥΧΙΟΥЄ ("one who steals") for thief, while 21:7 and 103 use the Greek loan-word ΛΗCΤΗC (λῃστής: "bandit," "brigand," "highwayman," "robber").

38. See GTh 9:4 for the only other use of worm. The "worm" clause in GTh 76 provides a better example of Semitic synonymous parallelism than Q's "thief" clause. See below, p. 74, n. 46.

39. As Sieber puts it, "if we suppose that Thomas used our Gospels as his sources, we also have to suppose that he switched back and forth between the Matthean and Lukan parallels for no apparent reason" ("Redactional Analysis," 58).

40. Uro, "'Secondary Orality.'" See above, chapter 1, pp. 8–9.

Treasure in Heaven saying, it would necessarily be a case of three different versions of this saying either being transmitted independently and conflated by Thomas, or being conflated in the process of oral transmission. While this kind of conflation is conceivable with Matt 6:20 and Luke 12:33, where the object "treasure(s)" and the adversity clauses are found, it is not apparent why John 6:27—though having the same theme and some common vocabulary—would have been drawn into the orbit of this process of secondary orality, especially considering how John has greatly modified the saying, placed it in an entirely different literary context, and given it a different hermeneutic.[41]

A different set of questions is raised by the coincidence of Luke 12:33 and John 6:27 each having two qualifiers that describe the permanence of the object of the imperative. Luke's first qualifier, ἀνέκλειπτον ("unfailing"), is a redactional addition to Q. But John has a similar qualifier in the first position, the attributive clause τὴν ἀπολλυμένην ("which perishes").[42] Does John reflect knowledge of the *redacted* Lukan version of this saying, though using Johannine terminology for Luke's ἀνέκλειπτος and replacing "in heaven" with "which abides"? If one argues for this point of view, it remains to be asked where Luke got the idea of doubling the qualifiers for the object "treasure" in the first place (inserting "unfailing" before "in the heavens").[43] And then there is John's βρῶσις, which is found in Matthew with a very different meaning, but which is not found in Luke. Is it likely that the author used *both* Luke's *and* Matthew's version of the

---

41. Based on a sample of texts from the second and third centuries CE, it can be said that rarely do early Christian authors conflate Matt 6:19–20 and Luke 12:33. The one clear exception that I have come across so far is Clement, *Strom.* 4.33, which uses Matthew's prohibition, then Luke's admonition, but uses Matthew's ἐν οὐρανῷ in place of Luke's ἐν τοῖς οὐρανοῖς. So far, I have found *no* cases of John 6:27 being conflated with Matt 6:19–20 or Luke 12:33 in extant early Christian writings to the end of the third century CE. Uro does not make the claim that different versions of individual NT sayings tend to be blended as they develop an orally transmitted life of their own.

42. The clause is part of a contrast of food which perishes and food which abides, implying that abiding food is food "which does not perish." The different sentence constructions in John and Luke may be due to the different use of their sources, as I will return to below.

43. As I argued in Chapter 2, Luke probably saw fit to create an appositive parallelism of "purses which do not wear out, a treasure unfailing" (Sellew, "Reconstruction of Q 12:33–59," 626), and by inserting the adjective ἀνέκλειπτος and reversing the order of adversity clauses created a word-play with κλέπτης (Anderson, quoted in Johnson, Q 12:33–34, 155). But such a redactional analysis still does not answer the question of where Luke first got the idea of doubling the qualifiers for the object "treasure."

saying in creating a version substantially different from either of the two? The jump from "eating thing" in Matthew to "food" in John is difficult to explain. John's use of the word would be better explained by use of a version of the Treasure in Heaven saying that looks like the synoptic versions but uses βρῶσις in a construction that has the implication of "food." If such a source is known to exist, then it is more plausible to assume that John used this source for the Treasure in Heaven saying—a version differing from both Matthew and Luke, but containing both βρῶσις and two object qualifiers.

There is a very simple solution to the questions just raised: *both* John *and* Luke used a source that itself had two qualifiers for the object of the imperative. To be more specific, while it is quite certain that Luke used Q 12:33 as the basis for the Lukan version of the saying, Luke was influenced by another tradition of this saying, the same or a similar one used as the basis for John 6:27. The only other version we know of that has two object qualifiers is GTh 76:3. Figure 3 highlights the similarities between the three texts:

Figure 3: Luke, Thomas (Coptic), and John Similarities

Luke:	θησαυρὸν	ἀνέκλειπτον	ἐν τοῖς οὐρανοῖς
Thomas:	ⲡⲉϥⲉϩⲟ	ⲉⲙⲁϥⲱϫⲛ̄	ⲉϥⲙⲏⲛ ⲉⲃⲟⲗ
John:	μὴ τὴν βρῶσις	τὴν ἀπολλυμένην...	τὴν μένουσαν

A Greek translation of Thomas that respects the Coptic relative constructions would look something like what is found in Figure 4:

Figure 4: Luke, Thomas (Greek), and John Similarities

Luke:	θησαυρὸν	ἀνέκλειπτον ἐν	τοῖς οὐρανοῖς
Thomas:	τὸν θησαυρὸν...	μὴ τὸν ἀπολλύμενον,	τὸν μένοντα
John:	μὴ τὴν βρῶσις	τὴν ἀπολλυμένην...	τὴν μένουσαν[44]

If one assumes, not that GTh 76:3 is a conflation of canonical texts, but that Luke and John are influenced by a Thomas-like version of the Treasure in Heaven saying, a number of questions are answered. First,

---

44. Against the translation of ⲉⲙⲁϥⲱϫⲛ̄ with ἀνέκλειπτος, see above, 63 n. 17; 68 n. 34.

one can see where Luke first got the idea for a qualifier of "treasure" ("unfailing") that parallels Luke's qualifier of "purses" ("which do not wear out"—all of the "purse" clause being of Lukan creation) *and* precedes the Q qualifier "in the heavens." Such an apposition of two qualifiers referring to the permanence of the object "treasure" was suggested by the Thomas version ("which does not perish, which abides").

Second, one can see how Luke, by using better Greek style, simplified the Thomas version of the first object qualifier (ἀνέκλειπτον replaces μὴ τὸν ἀπολλύμενον) when adding it to the Q version of the saying, employing a terser phraseology in this clause that parallels the redactionally-added "purse" clause. The grammar of Luke's redactional "purse" clause (βαλλάντια *μὴ παλαιούμενα*) is itself reminiscent of Thomas' pre-Coptic construction of the treasure clause and may have been occasioned by it.

Third, one can now see where Luke got the idea for several other modifications of the Q text. Figure 5 presents the Q and Lukan versions of the two adversity clauses, with a proposed original Greek text of Thomas:

Figure 5: Q, Luke, and Thomas Adversity Clauses

Q:	ὅπου οὔτε καὶ ὅπου	σὴς κλέπται	οὔτε βρῶσις οὐ	ἀφανίζει διορύσσουσιν οὐδὲ κλέπτουσιν.
Luke:	ὅπου οὐδὲ	κλέπτης σὴς	οὐκ διαφθείρει.	ἐγγίζει
Thomas:	ὅπου οὐ οὐδὲ	σὴς σκώληξ	εἰς βρῶσιν ἀφανίζει.[45]	ἐγγίζει

45. One has the choice of reconstructing the first clause of the Greek *Vorlage* either as I have above, or with Q's οὔτε βρῶσις, or with a more literal translation of the Coptic structure: ὅπου οὐ σὴς ἐγγίζει βιβρώσκειν (or φαγεῖν). As Tjitze Baarda rightly pointed out in response to an earlier version of this chapter given at the AAR/SBL, November 21, 1995, the latter alternative would imply that John changed the infinitive βιβρώσκειν to the substantive βρῶσις, coincidentally using the same Greek word that Matthew used, but with an altogether different meaning. From a transmission-history point of view, this is very unlikely. Φαγεῖν, while a more common synonym for "to eat," ignores the tradition history of the text regardless of one's theory of transmission. The translation of Thomas included above is superior for other reasons as well. (1) It explains the Coptic translator's attempt to retain a verbal force for βρῶσις—εἰς βρῶσιν can be translated "for eating" or "to eat" (for the latter, cf. esp. LXX Lev 25:7; 2 Sam 16:2). (2) The close affinity between the Thomas and Q versions is highlighted, indicating few differences in oral transmission for the first clause (significantly, οὔτε *vis.* εἰς and ἀφανίζει versus

So, for example, Luke retained Q's "thieves," changing it to the singular, but used Thomas' ἐγγίζει (ϮⲚⲞ ⲈϮⲞⲨⲚ) in the first clause in order to abbreviate Q's διορύσσουσιν οὐδὲ κλέπτουσιν.⁴⁶ This assisted Luke's creation of a tight, metrical pair of clauses. It also created the possible though not quite as likely image of a κλέπτης that approaches someone who is carrying a "treasure" in a purse (usually the role of a λῃστής?). The change to the singular subject "thief" to go with the third singular ἐγγίζει would have been consistent with the previous change from the plural to the singular "treasure (unfailing)," itself a change perhaps prompted by the adoption and adaptation of Thomas' singular "treasure which does not perish." Furthermore, one can now see that Thomas' agreement with Luke's order of verbs is actually due to Luke's use of Thomas' verb in the first clause when reversing the order of Q clauses in order to create the ἀνέκλειπτον–κλέπτης word-play that more closely connects the adversity clauses with the "purse" and "treasure" clauses.

ἐγγίζει). Placing the predicate accusative (εἰς βρῶσιν) before the verb is a more difficult reading, but the resulting emphasis on the verb makes better sense of Luke's retention of Thomas' ἐγγίζω in the first clause, though with a different subject. Hans-Martin Schenke suggested that a Coptic translator would have reversed the order of verb and predicate accusative out of grammatical necessity (personal conversation). (3) John's divergent use of βρῶσις is better understood—certainly in the LXX βρῶσις is usually best translated as "food," and εἰς βρῶσιν as "for food" or "for eating" (Gen 1:29, 30; 2:9; 3:6; 9:3; 47:24; etc.; for other Greek literature, see above, p. 64, n. 19). (4) Such a translation, which hints at Semitic influence (BDF §157(5)) and could represent one of several different Semitic constructions, might also point to the Aramaic *Vorlage* of the saying of Jesus (Matthew's use of βρῶσις as an active agent is rare, with one likely case in the LXX—Mal 3:11).

46. Based on a possible Aramaic paronomasia underlying the Greek text (קְרַב for ἐγγίζω ["approach"] and רְקַב ["rot"] for διαφθείρω ["destroy" or "spoil"]), Gundry argues that Luke's adversity clauses are original to Q (*Matthew*, 112). However, this observation would apply to a Semitic *Vorlage* behind the Coptic GTh 76:3 as well (ϮⲚⲞ ⲈϮⲞⲨⲚ and ⲦⲀⲔⲞ). Davies' and Allison's speculation that assonance in a Semitic *Vorlage* could have extended to "moth" and "worm" can only support the priority of the Thomas version (Davies and Allison, *Matthew*, 631). See also Black, *Aramaic Approach*, 135. What is more important is that, while numerous observers have noted the parallelism of the adversity clauses in Matthew, Luke, and Q, it is Thomas that provides the best instance of Semitic synonymous parallelism in the pairing of "moth" and "worm" (cf. Job 25:6; Isa 14:11; 51:8 [עָשׁ is paired with סָס, and רִמָּה with תּוֹלֵעָה. In each case in the MT, synonyms of either "worm" or "moth" are paired, but cf. the LXX of Job 25:6 [σαπρία and σκώληξ] and Isa 14:11 [σῆψις and σκώληξ], where רִמָּה has been rendered with cognates of σής [best translated "decay"]). See also Prov 25:20 (LXX): ὥσπερ σὴς ἱματίῳ καὶ σκώληξ ξύλῳ.

Fourth, one finally sees what John's source for this saying looked like. Consequently, we can describe the process of Johannine modification of this source with greater confidence and clarity. Figure #6 charts this modification:

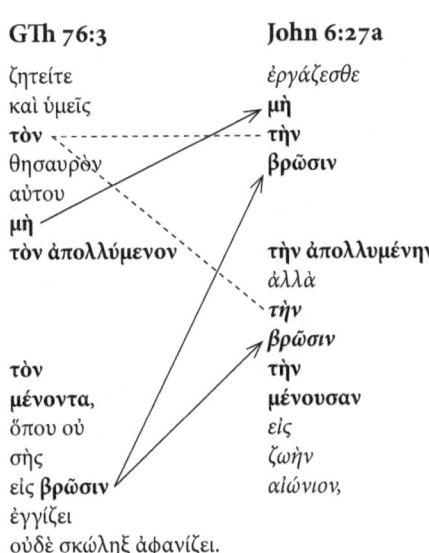

Figure 6: John's Use of Thomas

In focusing only on the imperative of the saying, John split the qualifiers of the object of the imperative into two separate clauses, creating negative and positive imperatives (with implied verb in the second clause).[47] John achieved this simply by moving the negative μὴ in front of the object of the imperative, adding the adversative conjunction ἀλλά and duplicating the object of the imperative in the new second clause. John's object, βρῶσις, would have come from Thomas' εἰς βρῶσιν in the first adversary clause, understanding Thomas' βρῶσις as a substantive.[48] John found the relative expression "which abides" already in the tradition and attached the Johannine "into eternal life" to the end of the traditional saying.[49]

---

47. Hence, John creates an incidental agreement with Matthew (or Q) in using antithetical parallelism.

48. As mentioned above, εἰς βρῶσιν in the LXX is often to be translated "for eating" or "for food." GTh 76:3 is therefore a more likely source for John 6:27 than Matt 6:19-20.

49. See above, p. 60. Cf. the use of μένω in John 6:52-58 (esp. 6:56), where John

As I have argued, apart from βρῶσις being used as the object of the imperative, John jettisoned the adversity clauses of the Treasure saying in order to focus subsequent interpretation on the terms used in the admonition proper. However, another element of Thomas' adversity clauses may have suggested the use of this saying at the beginning of John's Bread of Life Discourse, a discourse which contrasts the perishable manna in the wilderness with the abiding "true bread from heaven." According to Exod 16:19–24, the problem with manna is that it lasts no more than one night. More specifically, *worm*-infestation is cited as the cause of its putrefaction. Compare Thomas' second adversity clause, "nor worms which destroy."

It should be emphasized that such a solution as I have outlined above requires that only one of the five gospel versions of the saying be reliant on more than one source—Luke recomposed Q 12:33 with the aide of Mark 10:21 and GTh 76:3. Other solutions require that three of the five versions, Thomas, Luke and John, relied on a *minimum* of two sources *each* for their versions of this saying, or that two versions (Thomas and Luke) relied on at least two sources while the form, content and provenance of the source for John's version was similar to Thomas but remains unknown.

Thomas, Luke, and John

The relationship between Luke and Thomas in regard to the Treasure in Heaven saying is in some ways easier to understand than the relationship between Thomas and John. It is almost a commonplace in scholarship that the author of Luke was a collector and adapter of sources. This is made abundantly clear in the prologue to the gospel and has been demonstrated time and again in synoptic studies. In the case of the Treasure saying, while Luke's primary source was Q, aspects of the Thomas version were integrated in the process of redacting Q. The Lukan focus in this operation appears to have been less a concern for correcting the interpretation of the Thomas version and more a concern for focusing the interpretation of the Q version on specific, concrete Lukan concerns regarding wealth and almsgiving—hence the influence of Mark 10:21. In

---

returns to identifying βρῶσις as Jesus' flesh, forming an inclusio to Jesus' entire discourse of 6:25–59. Likewise, John returns to the use of μένω with the preposition ἐν in order more clearly to express his sense of a divine abiding presence.

other words, at least in this case, the author of Luke does not appear to have had a particular bone to pick with the tradition represented by GTh 76:3.[50]

The case is different with John, which has used only the Thomas version of this saying, but in so doing has greatly modified it and then reinterpreted it through subsequent discourse material. I would argue, furthermore, that the author of John may have known how the interpretive potential of the saying was actualized in the Thomas communities that transmitted the saying, and so altered the form and content of the saying in order to steer its interpretation in another direction.

If viewed from this anti-Thomasine perspective, the specific changes that John made to the saying become even more informative. For example, the imperative "seek" is replaced by the imperative "work for," which is then defined in 6:29 as "*believing* into him whom (God) has sent"; that is, believing into the Christ. Jesus is understood as the *means* of salvation and the *focus* of the admonition, not just the *transmitter* of the saying. Hence, a verb that was likely understood in the sense of a religious search for enlightenment is replaced by another imperative which is interpreted in a manner quite foreign, even odious, to Thomasine "Christians."[51] Yet, ζητέω is not eliminated by John. Rather, in connecting John 6:27 to the previous Feeding of the 5,000, John has Jesus saying in 6:26: "You *seek* me, not because you saw signs, but because you ate your fill of the loaves." The relocation of ζητέω at this point in particular creates a contrast be-

---

50. Previous studies suggest that this instance of Lukan use of the Thomas tradition is not an isolated case. Patterson's analysis of GTh 31 strongly suggests that Luke has used the pair of Thomas sayings in this logion in the construction of Luke 4:23–24, though reversing their order and substituting Thomas' physician proverb with another (Patterson, *Gospel of Thomas*, 31–32). Note that Luke has Jesus himself stating that this is a common proverb and therefore probably not an original saying of Jesus. Mark 6:4–5 is probably an expansion and narratization of this two-proverb cluster: Wendling, *Entstehung*, 54; Bultmann, *Geschichte*, 30–31. Riley has demonstrated Luke's addition of GTh 47 to the Patches and Wineskins sayings of Mark 2:21–22 and Luke's use of GTh 72's "divider" saying in creating Luke 12:13–14 (Riley, "Influence," 229–35). Riley argues that these two sayings have "passed through Thomas Christianity before being used by Luke" (230). Luke "conflates the two readings and produces the canonical text" (232). This kind of conflation of traditions is similar to what Luke has accomplished with Q, Thomas, and Mark in the creation of Luke 12:33.

51. Riley uses the terminology of "enlightenment" and "faith" to express, I think helpfully, the different soteriological foundations of the texts in question (*Resurrection Reconsidered*, 119–23).

tween "seeking" and "working for" (that is, "seeking" vs. "believing") that is surely intentional.[52]

In the same way, the object "treasure," which in GTh 76:3 is left undefined, but which may best be understood as wisdom, gnosis, or truth, is changed to "food," which is then defined in John 6:32 as the "true bread from heaven" and in 6:53–58 as Jesus' flesh. Then, after attaching the typically Johannine phrase "into eternal life" to the end of what is left of the traditional saying in 6:27, John also adds the clause "which the son of humanity will give to you." This final clause makes certain that Jesus is the focus of the admonition, not some ineffable experience of enlightenment.

It appears, then, that we not only have a positive rationale for Johannine redaction of the Thomas saying, introducing the Bread of Life Discourse with its meditation on Jesus as the source of life-giving food, but a second reason as well—the reworking of the Thomas saying to stress a Johannine, *anti-Thomasine* soteriology based on "faith" over against "enlightenment."[53]

This kind of intentional reformulation in the Gospel of John of a dominical saying popular in Thomasine communities is probably not an isolated phenomenon, but rather one example of the author of John's recasting of sayings of Jesus which embody theological concepts that are central for Thomasine groups.[54]

---

52. John 6:26–27 also sets up the contrast of manna and "true bread" of John 6:31–34, 48–50.

53. In chapter 4, I will present evidence that suggests that the author of Colossians used a sayings collection that most likely already had GTh 77:1 immediately following 76:3. If the sayings tradition that John used also had these two sayings together, it might explain John's motives with a less conflictual model. It is clear from the Prologue of John that the author knew of and adapted Wisdom traditions, transferring the qualities of personified Wisdom to Jesus. If the author of John saw GTh 77:1 as being related to 76:3, then the treasure sought in 76:3 would have been understood by John as personified Wisdom, or Jesus himself. Understanding the "seeking" of Jesus as a mostly negative action, the author of John modified the saying, replacing ζητέω with ἐργάζομαι and subsequently interpreting the verb as meaning "to believe" in Jesus.

54. A brief analysis of Thomas 1 and John 8:51–52, which provides another example of this phenomenon, is found in my article, "The *Gospel of Thomas* 76:3 and Canonical Parallels," 322–24. Ismo Dunderberg has argued against the position taken there, pointing out that the expression "taste death" is not unique to Thomas and John, but is found elsewhere, including Mark 9:1 par. and Heb 2:9 (see Dunderberg, "From Thomas to Valentinus," 234 n. 53). While it is true that the expression "taste death" is not unique to Thomas and John (see Chilton, "'Not to Taste Death,'" [esp. p. 31]), *only* in Thomas 1 and

Summary

The notions that dialogue and debate took place between Johannine and Thomasine communities and that the author of John intentionally attacked Thomasine hermeneutics are not new. The analysis of this chapter has suggested, however, that the author of John may have gone as far in this debate as to alter an individual saying transmitted by Thomas communities in an effort to combat their enlightenment soteriology and correlative lack of emphasis on the figure of Jesus as the means to salvation.

The use of the Thomas sayings tradition by Luke suggests that it had attained some degree of authoritative status in parts of the Mediterranean outside of specifically Thomasine communities late in the first or early in the second century CE. At the same time, John's use and alteration of the Thomas tradition indicates that a developing enlightenment-oriented form of Jesus religion had already begun to blossom by the time of John's writing. It also indicates the lengths to which some late first-/early second-century writers would go to counteract the perceived errors and misunderstandings of rival communities in the service of evangelism/recruitment or community teaching, and the liberties they could take with authoritative sayings traditions in this effort.

John 8:52 is the expression "*not* taste death" specifically identified as *a positive result of one's treatment of the teachings of Jesus*. In other words, this is the same saying of Jesus, but in different forms. Dunderberg argues elsewhere "that what is misunderstood by the Jews in John 8:51–52 is not the *wording* of Jesus' promise but his *authority* to make this promise" ("Thomas' I-Sayings and the Gospel of John," 47 n. 1; idem, *The Beloved Disciple in Conflict*, 29–30). Certainly he is correct—Jesus' authority *is* the issue of the immediate literary context in which this misunderstanding is embedded (John 8:12–59). This observation, however, still sidesteps the more contemporary (to the Johannine community) issue of *apostolic* authority by failing to explain the one curious difference in the two Johannine versions of Jesus' saying and the closer similarity of the *opponents*' version (8:52) to Thomas 1.

CHAPTER 4 | James and Colossians

INTRODUCTION

The previous chapters have provided examples of how the Treasure in Heaven saying developed in early sayings collections and were then adapted to the narrative gospel genre. The Letter of James and the Letter to the Colossians provide examples of how the Treasure saying has been adapted in the epistolary genre as well. The epistolary versions of the saying are not presented in the form of a saying of Jesus, which obviously makes the identification of the respective verses as versions of this saying more difficult. Nevertheless, not only do both of the passages to be dealt with here exhibit important verbal and conceptual similarities to the Treasure saying, but in each case characteristics of the wider literary contexts in which they are embedded support the conclusion that the authors of these letters have adapted this saying of Jesus in exhorting their readers. For this reason, an analysis of the Treasure saying in James must be preceded by a more general discussion of James' relationship to the synoptic sayings of Jesus tradition.

JAMES AND THE SYNOPTIC TRADITION

There is little debate today that the author of James knew a tradition or traditions of sayings of Jesus.[1] What is most commonly debated is the

---

1. But cf., e.g., Spitta, *Jakobus*, 155–83 (who explains all similarities to Synoptic material by reference to pre-Christian Jewish literature); and Massebieau, "L'Épitre de Jacques." Spitta and Massebieau considered the epistle to be a Jewish document and references to Christ in Jas 1:1 and 2:1 to be Christian interpolations. Most commentators on James recognize close connections to Jewish wisdom literature in James, but do not go this far.

nature of the source or sources behind the epistle.² Some commentators, most recently James Adamson, argue that this source is the mind and memory of James, the brother of Jesus, himself. But this thesis is pure speculation and is not supported by Adamson's data.³ Massey Shepherd suggested that the author of James knew the Gospel of Matthew through the repetition of readings in the liturgy, but did not have the actual gospel at hand. The author of the epistle alludes to sayings of Jesus found in Matthew but does not demonstrate verbatim recall—hence, no text of James is exactly like Matthew.⁴ Unfortunately, his study ignores too many instances where Luke gives a closer parallel to James than Matthew.⁵

   2. The issue usually revolves around the influence of Jewish wisdom literature on the author of James and the extent to which sayings of Jesus are used in the epistle. For an excellent summary of many of the positions held, see Deppe, *Sayings of Jesus,* 12–28.

   3. While James' authorship has been argued more cogently elsewhere on the basis of the similarities to Jesus' teachings (cf., e.g., Mayor, *James,* xlii–xliv, who notices the especially abundant similarities to Matthew's Sermon on the Mount), Adamson turns to the colorful romantic Ernst Renan for support of his thesis, which at times is itself a delightful demonstration of romantic inspiration (Adamson, *James,* esp. 186–94). In fact, Adamson's most recent study in James is hopelessly confused. At one point he argues that "the two [James and Matthew] . . . appear to be tapping—each in his own way—a primitive precanonical Gospel source" (189). Elsewhere he concludes that "the material has almost vivid Jewish coloring and, we believe, came straight from James the Lord's brother, one of the greatest men of early Christianity, who stood in the stream of preliterary tradition as the guardian of the *ipsissima verba* of Jesus" (193). Adamson begins his study with a charting of words found only in one synoptic gospel over against the other two (Luke-Acts is grouped together). His statistical results overwhelmingly demonstrate that James' vocabulary is closer to Luke-Acts than to Matthew or Mark (174–78). This presumably supports his later statement, with regard to the sayings of Jesus, that "as F. C. Grant thinks, the Lucan version is literally nearer to the word of Jesus than that of Matthew; and it is clear that in this field [social teaching on wealth and poverty] the Epistle of James is linked in the closest possible fashion with Luke" (190–91; Frederick C. Grant, "Method," 264). However, a look at Adamson's vocabulary comparison charts reveals that of the sixty instances of words that are peculiar to James and Luke-Acts, only two of these occurrences are found in material commonly recognized as sayings material (γέλως, Jas 4:9/γελάω, Luke 6:21, 25; μήνας, Jas 5:17/μήνας, Luke 4:25—for a list of "The Twenty-five Most Frequently Mentioned Parallels" between James and sayings of Jesus, see Deppe, *Sayings of Jesus,* 237–38). This finding suggests that the author of James had a Greek style and vocabulary more similar to the author of Luke, not that James and Luke best reflect the *ipsissima verba* of Jesus. Adamson does accept that the epistle in its final form was not written by James himself (186–87; following G. C. Martin, "Epistle of St. James"), but this leaves his argument of direct Jacobian influence on the content of the letter somewhat speculative.

   4. Shepherd, "Epistle of James."

   5. Shepherd promptly dismisses, perhaps correctly, the similarity between Jas 5:17 and Luke 4:25, but the parallels Jas 2:5/Q/Luke 6:20 and Jas 4:9/Luke 6:25b are more

The more widely held theory is that James knew of a pre-synoptic gospel sayings tradition or traditions. Martin Dibelius has perhaps been most influential in arguing that James made use of sayings of Jesus traditions, but not by way of a canonical gospel like Matthew. He proposed that many such sayings traditions reached James through the orbit of collected community paraenesis, teaching that did not always quote Jesus explicitly.[6] This explained for him why James knew sayings of Jesus traditions but never cited Jesus. The following summarizes what to him were the advantages for seeing James as an example of the paraenetic genre:

> For Dibelius the particular genre explained the lack of continuity and structure in the book (p. 5), the pervasive eclecticism of various sources by the author (p. 2), the repetition of identical motifs in different places within the writing (p. 11), the combination of Jewish and Hellenistic material (p. 26), the lack of explicit quotation formulas (p. 29), the relationship to 1 Peter (p. 30), Hermas, 1 Clement, and Hebrews (p. 32), the lack of Christology and specific Christian references (p. 46), our inability to determine the geographical localization of James (p. 47), its late and gradual dissemination into the canon (p. 53), and finally also the problem we are chiefly concerned with, the relationship between the Synoptic traditions and the Epistle of James (p. 17).[7]

Even if he overstated his case, Dibelius moved scholarship in the right direction by highlighting the importance of community paraenesis for understanding the genre of James.

At the same time, his examination of sources for James lacked a detailed examination of the similarities that exist between James and sayings of Jesus traditions. Consideration of sayings-source issues consists mostly of denying any derivation from the gospels. Dibelius seems to have assumed (and so occasionally argued) that if sayings of Jesus were used in James, then they must represent an independent source.[8] But few

---

substantial ("Epistle of James," 43–44). He overlooks the parallel between Jas 2:13 and Q/Luke 6:36–37—Matthew's parallels (5:7; 7:1) are more distant and split up—and the fact that Jas 3:12 reads "figs" and "grapevines" in the same order as Q/Luke 6:44b's "figs" and "grapes" (cf. Matt's "grapes" and "figs"), though retaining Q/Matt's rhetorical question form. James 2:2–3 and 4:13–14 are conceptually similar to Luke 14:8–10 and 12:16–20 respectively (Luke 12:16–20 has been voted out of Q by the IQP, though many have argued for its presence in Q). Luke 14:8–10 is connected to Q 14:11 in Luke and Q 14:11 is very similar to Jas 4:10.

6. Dibelius, *James*, 28–29.

7. Deppe, *Sayings of Jesus*, 24. Page numbers in parentheses refer to Dibelius, *James*.

8. For Jas 5:12, see Dibelius, *James*, 250–51. James 3:12 is explained by reference to

similarities are actually addressed in his commentary. Nowhere in his work is there consideration of sayings sources apart from "community paraenesis," though he asserts that "the sayings of Jesus were collected for a paraenetic purpose, and community paraenesis made use of such sayings, although frequently without identifying them by means of explicit quotation."[9] Dibelius also assumes a continuity, without distinction, between James and its sources—James shows itself to be community paraenesis by its lack of citation while Dibelius assumes James' sources to be community paraenesis as well: "Whoever taught the paraenesis of the Christian communities passed on to these communities the sayings of Jesus whether he was aware of it or not."[10]

This all fits with Dibelius' larger thesis of a developmental process of oral tradition that is represented especially in paraenetic sections of epistolary texts, such as Romans 12-14; 1 Peter; Didache 1-2, etc. He considers this tradition to be wholly distinct from narrative developments of tradition—developments represented, for example, by the canonical gospels.[11] However, his thesis is too strict and synthetic to be maintained. Paul quotes Jesus in argumentative texts that are not paraenetic in nature, but Dibelius does not indicate the nature of the "collection" these sayings come from. The very fact that paraenetic texts like James cite scriptures and other texts for authority or use everyday maxims and aphorisms from Greek philosophy requires at least the consideration of sayings sources that quote Jesus explicitly.

Two recent dissertations have addressed in some detail the issue of James' use of sayings of Jesus traditions.[12] Both Dean Deppe and Patrick Hartin support Dibelius' identification of James as a paraenetic text, but choose to focus their attention on the area of neglect mentioned above—the sayings of Jesus in James—to which Dibelius gives little more than a token discussion.

Deppe undertakes an exhaustive compilation and analysis of similarities between James and known sayings of Jesus in an effort to deter-

---

Stoic or other parallels (204–5). Mostly, similarities between James and sayings of Jesus in the synoptic tradition are noted without much comment.

9. Ibid., 28–29.
10. Ibid., 29.
11. See Dibelius, *From Tradition to Gospel*, 238–44.
12. Deppe, *Sayings of Jesus*, from Free University of Amsterdam, 1989; Hartin, *James and the Q Sayings of Jesus*, from the University of South Africa (Pretoria), 1988.

mine the extent of James' use of sayings of Jesus traditions.[13] He then examines the evidence for a relationship to specific canonical gospels and finds none.[14] As to the reason for the form of the sayings material in James, Deppe compares a variety of suggested genres for James and finds that the genre of paraenesis best explains especially the lack of citation formulae (as compared to James' occasional reference to scripture).[15] Deppe concludes by categorizing the sayings of Jesus according to allusions (8x), parallels in content and wording (6x), parallels in content alone (9x), parallels in wording alone (12x), and one case of a common textual source (Lev 19:18b for Jas 2:8 and Matt 22:39–40).

For Deppe, the essential difference between allusions and the other categories is intentionality. Allusions are meant to remind the reader/hearer of a known saying of Jesus while the other categories represent themes of Jesus' teaching that are taken up in community paraenesis and developed according to the dictates of the context and authorial intention (Deppe rightly corrects Dibelius' claim that there is no theology inherent in paraenesis).[16] With regard to sources, Deppe concludes that "the author was transmitting the paraenetic tradition of the church which included both specific sayings of Jesus as well as ethical themes extracted from Jesus' preaching."[17]

One problem with Deppe's analysis is that he seems to make the same assumption of generic continuity between James and its sources that mars the work of Dibelius (simply put, all is paraenesis). Like Dibelius, Deppe allows that community paraenesis could transmit sayings of Jesus with citation; but then one must question the basic differentiation of sayings forms and their functions that he sees existing between the genres of gospel and community paraenesis.[18] If James and passages like Romans 12–13; 1 Thessalonians 5; and *Did* 1:3–2:1 do not cite Jesus as the authoritative voice, why should community paraenesis ever cite Jesus as the authoritative voice?

Part of the problem may reside in the fact that Deppe lists only two genre forms that function to transmit sayings of Jesus in the first cen-

13. Deppe, *Sayings of Jesus*, 55–149. His synthesis of sixty different commentators' suggested sayings parallels listed by author and verse (Appendix I: 231–38) is an invaluable scholarly resource.

14. Ibid., 150–66.

15. Ibid., 167–88. Regarding James' citation of scripture, see 31–54.

16. Ibid., 219–30.

17. Ibid., 222.

18. Ibid., 225.

tury—the gospel and community paraenesis.¹⁹ The primary difference in the form that sayings take in these genres is that gospels tend to cite Jesus as the authoritative speaker of the sayings while paraenesis alludes to sayings without actually quoting or citing Jesus. This is partly seen as a result of different purposes: the primary purpose of gospels is to rehearse Jesus' words and deeds, while in community paraenesis the sayings function only as raw material that provide themes and vocabulary for addressing new social and ethical situations. For this reason, Deppe sees a greater degree of flexibility in the handling and adapting of sayings of Jesus in the context of community paraenesis than in the context of gospel development. It also suggests that intentional allusions to known sayings are likely to be the exception rather than the rule.

Deppe's distinctions are not without problems, however. First, the handling of Q sayings in Matthew and Luke shows a great degree of freedom depending upon the social context in which the gospels are written and the literary context in which the sayings are imbedded. They sometimes demonstrate as great a variability from Q as James does (as will be shown below). Second, both synoptic gospel authors have clearly adapted sayings of Jesus for the purpose of community instruction—Matthew has even been described as a "manual of church order"—and their treatment of Q reflects this.²⁰ Third, Deppe leaves a third genre out of consideration—the sayings collection. This is not irrelevant if James was written at a time when sayings gospels like Q existed.²¹ Similar to James, Q is mostly ethical and eschatological instruction. On the other hand, much like a gospel, Q quotes Jesus explicitly and authoritatively. For Dibelius, Q has no place in the discussion and so is completely ignored in his commentary.²² Yet, Q can easily be recognized as a potential source both for

19. Ibid., 225–27.

20. The Treasure in Heaven saying is but one excellent example—see above, Chapter 2. Both Dibelius and Deppe recognize this—Deppe argues that the paraenesis of the Sermon on the Mount is an important reason for its popularity in early Christianity—but it betrays Dibelius' theory of distinct, independent traditions of sayings development and undercuts Deppe's rather bald statement that "the primary purpose [of the gospel genre] is to rehearse what Jesus said and did" (*Sayings of Jesus*, 225).

21. Deppe tentatively dates James to the sixth decade of the first century under the authorship of Jesus' brother (218), but he is not at all certain of his decision on this point. He appears to be suggesting that James the brother of Jesus did not remember Jesus' words, but was strictly reliant upon community paraenesis (222). Even if one settles on a later date—Deppe suggests 80 CE as a possibility—one must still reckon with the existence of sayings gospels like Q (and possibly Thomas).

22. See *James*, 251, for Dibelius' one mention of Q as belonging to a "completely dif-

the gospels *and* for further paraenetic development, such as we find in James. The lack of citation would be due to the genre of James, not to the genre of its source.

Deppe does not ignore Q as a potential source for material used in James. Rather, he notes particular problems with seeing Q as a source.[23] Some problems he observes are mitigated by the reconstruction of Q, but other problems remain.[24] Indeed, he does not mention this, but the mere fact that the similarities between James and Q do not reflect the Q order of sayings can be used as an argument against the sustained use of a written Q source.

One other significant difficulty of Deppe's dissertation comes from his categories of similarities to sayings traditions. Whereas his three types of "parallels" seem to represent quantitative distinctions, his category of "allusions" appears to be a qualitative distinction. The three categories of parallels represent degrees of thematic development in the paraenetic tradition or in the redactional work of the author, while the category of allusions suggests a conscious and intentional reference to a known saying. Apparently, Deppe sees the fundamental difference being the presence of a common context.[25] It seems to me, however, that while common context can be an important determinant of whether a saying of Jesus is being used, it should not be a determining factor for indicating a different type of use, especially if the social context of James is different from that of its sources. Furthermore, I simply do not see an inherent, qualitative difference between Deppe's categories. What he calls allusions are simply the best and most clearly demonstrable cases of James' use of sayings of Jesus traditions. Or, to put it another way, they represent the material that is least adapted by the author for the instructional needs of the community. He is surely correct that James sometimes consciously alludes to the common knowledge of a saying, as in Jas 2:5, but that is not clear in some of his allusions.[26] In summary, while I don't always agree with his decisions or categories, I think his careful and thoroughgoing analysis is very

---

ferent process in the history of early Christian paraenesis." He seems to consider it a form of paraenesis in *From Tradition to Gospel*, 233–65, esp. 243, 246, 259.

23. Deppe, *Sayings of Jesus*, 224.

24. E.g., the IQP has determined that Luke 6:20 and Matt 6:20 are closer to Q than Matt 5:3 and Luke 12:33, but Luke 6:25 (cf. Jas 4:9) has been determined to come from the hand of Luke.

25. Deppe, *Sayings of Jesus*, 219.

26. Ibid., 90–91.

helpful in placing individual sayings parallels on a continuum of plausibility with regard to their derivation from sayings of Jesus traditions.

While Deppe focuses on a determination of what constitutes use of a sayings tradition, Hartin argues that one sayings tradition in particular, Q, is a significant source for the practical, ethical material of James. According to the preface of his book, the focus of Hartin's dissertation is "an investigation into the relationship of the Epistle of James to the traditions of early Christianity, namely the wisdom tradition and the Jesus tradition known as the Q source."[27] The first part of the book concerns the mutual use of the wisdom genre and wisdom themes in Q and James.[28] The second part compares the extensive textual similarities that Hartin sees between James and Q.[29] The third part attempts to locate James in the history of early Christianity.[30]

Hartin does not provide a detailed Deppe-like analysis of individual similarities in his Part II. Rather, he focuses on the vast number of "correspondences" between James and the Q tradition.[31] Hartin observes that synoptic sayings of Jesus similar in theme and content to paraenetic material in James are mostly also found in the synoptic sayings source, Q. More specifically, this material in James parallels especially the practical, ethical dimension of wisdom found in the Q Sermon and Matthew's Sermon on the Mount—much of the latter consisting of the Q Sermon combined with practical, ethical material found elsewhere in Q.[32] Furthermore, just

27. Hartin, *James*, 7.

28. Ibid., 12–37. Independent of Deppe, Hartin also argues that the genre of James is paraenesis, but that this is a development of the wisdom genre, practical wisdom ideas and forms being used and incorporated by Jesus and early Christian communities (44–80; cf. Deppe, *Sayings of Jesus*, 182–83).

29. Hartin, *James*, 140–217.

30. Ibid., 220–44.

31. Ibid., esp. 140–48.

32. Ibid., 140–72, 173–98. On the similarities of James to Matthew's Sermon on the Mount, the bibliography is extensive. See, e.g., Mayor: "Another marked feature of our Epistle is the close connexion between it and the Sermon on the Mount" (*St. James*, xliii). W. D. Davies lists numerous similarities between James and Matthew's Sermon but, strangely, argues that few of those are parallels to Q, though almost all of the Matthean texts he lists are Q texts (*Setting*, 402–3). Martin Klein argues, however, that if James is not using Matthew directly or indirectly, then the parallels specifically to Matthew's sermon are insignificant since Matthew has created the Sermon from wider Q materials (Klein, "Ein vollkommenes Werk"). Hence, he argues that the parallels are to Q. A few cases where James is similar to Sermon on the Mount material not found in Q lessens the impact of his argument and requires a more sophisticated hypothesis that recognizes the development of the tradition that comes to be Matthew's sermon. Essentially, however,

as similarities to the Q tradition extend throughout the epistle, so also do similarities to James extend throughout the practical, ethical material of Q.[33] Hartin concludes that "no example or detail on its own is conclusive. All such examples are to be judged not as individual items, but on the basis of coherence." In other words, "James is steeped in the tradition of the sayings of Jesus," but, like Q, is also steeped in the wisdom tradition as well. This allows Hartin to include many more James passages as sayings parallels than Deppe.

Several problems weaken Hartin's thesis. One is that he has to rely on a complicated theory of the development of Q—including QMt and QLk texts that existed prior to their redaction by Matthew and Luke—in order to make his case that James used the Q tradition. Added to this is the impression Hartin gives that a written text of Q was known to the author of James, even though he cannot prove textual dependence—the lack of extensive parallels makes that impossible. Yet it is almost an assured conclusion of biblical scholarship that a written text of Q was used by Matthew and Luke. Therefore, the nature of the Q tradition used by James must remain an open question.

Hartin also goes too far in concluding that "the Jesus traditions evident in Q and the development of Q within the Matthean community form the basis for all James's instructions."[34] Such a facile dismissal of the abundant Jewish and Greek parallels catalogued by, among others, Dibelius and Deppe, is not acceptable. Hartin is aware that James uses a variety of sources, including especially Jewish scriptures, and one can immediately point to Jas 2:14—3:11 as a substantial block of teaching that bears no evidence of a sayings of Jesus tradition behind it.

Nevertheless, recognition of James' rather free adaptation of Jesus traditions for the sake of contextual paraenesis allows us to expand the scope of possible correspondences to sayings traditions beyond Deppe's eight allusions. His thorough analysis of parallels and placing of similarities on a continuum of plausible relationship must be kept in mind, but one should also take stock of the vast number of Q parallels in Deppe's inventory. Five of his eight "allusions" are to Q sayings, five of his six "parallels of both content and wording" are to Q sayings, and five of his

---

most parallels are to Q. The distinction between Q and Matthean sermons is widely accepted among Q scholars.

33. Hartin, *James*, 186–87. Parallels between the two texts extend from Q 6:20 to Q 17:3, and from Jas 1:2 to Jas 5:19–20.

34. Hartin, *James*, 215.

twelve "parallels of content" are to Q sayings. Also significant to Hartin's thesis, one of Deppe's remaining three "allusions" is to a Matthean saying, seven of the nine "parallels of terminology" are to Matthean sayings, and five of the "parallels of content" are to Matthean sayings.[35] Therefore, it seems that the Q tradition, especially as it may have developed in or near a "proto-Matthean" community, must be taken very seriously as a source of sayings material for the paraenesis of James.

The following table is a list of what I consider to be significant parallels between James and Q (based on the IQP reconstruction of Q):

Figure 7: James / Q Parallels

	James	Matthew	Luke
Joy in Persecution	1:2	5:11–12	6:22–23
Ask and It Will Be Given You	1:5	7:7	11:9
Gifts from the Father	1:17	7:11	11:13
Hearing and Doing the Word	1:22–23	7:24, 26	6:46–49
The Poor and the Kingdom	2:5	[5:3]	6:20
Keeping the Whole Law	2:10	5:18–19	16:17
Mercy vs. Judgment	2:13	[5:7; 7:1]	6:36–37
Grapes and Figs	3:12	7:16	6:44
Ask and Receive	4:3	7:8	11:10
God vs. the World	4:4	6:24	16:13
The Humble Exalted	4:10	23:12	14:11
Judging Others	4:11–12	7:1	6:37
Laying Up Treasures	5:2–3	6:19–20	12:33
Persecution of the Prophets	5:10	5:11–12	6:23
Guiding a Sinner	5:19–20	18:15	17:3

In each case there are key conceptual similarities and usually significant (though rarely extensive) verbal parallels; there are often formal similarities as well. While the differences are usually substantial, if there was a source relationship between James and a Q tradition, then many of the differences between these passages would be attributable to the different genres of the texts (sayings collection vs. paraenetic epistle), the different authors' ethical positions and preferences regarding rhetorical and

---

35. Deppe, *Sayings of Jesus*, 219.

sapiential forms, different intended audiences (and their different social and historical contexts), and the different intent of the respective parallel passages.³⁶ The following two pairs of texts are representative examples of the strong similarities between James and Q, taken from the beginning and end of the Q Sermon. First, compare Jas 2:5 and the initial beatitude of the Q Sermon, Q 6:20:³⁷

Figure 8: Jas 2:5 and Q 6:20

Jas 2:5	Q 6:20
Ἀκούσατε, ἀδελφοί μου ἀγαπητοί·	Καὶ ἐπάρας τοὺς ὀφθαλμοὺς αὐτοῦ εἰς τοὺς μαθητὰς αὐτοῦ <εἶπεν>·
οὐχ ὁ **θεὸς** ἐξελέξατο **τοὺς πτωχοὺς** τῷ κόσμῳ πλουσίους ἐν πίστει καὶ **κληρονόμους τῆς βασιλείας** ἧς ἐπηγγείλατο τοῖς ἀγαπῶσιν αὐτόν . . .	μακάριοι οἱ **πτωχοί**, ὅτι ὑμετέρα ἐστὶν ἡ βασιλεία τοῦ θεοῦ.
Listen my beloved brothers:	And raising his eyes to his disciples, he said,
Has not **God** chosen **the poor** of the world to be rich in faith and **heirs** of **the reign** which he promised to those who love him?	"Blessed are **the poor**, for the reign of God is for you."

The differences between these two texts are obvious and these texts alone would not make an argument for a source relationship between the

---

36. Surprisingly, Koester misses the importance of these differences when he observes the different forms between Jas 2:5 and Q 6:20, and Jas 4:9 and Q 6:21 (*Ancient Christian Gospels*, 71–75, esp. 73–74). When he accepts only Deppe's eight allusions (*Sayings of Jesus*, 237–38) as assumable parallels between James and Q, then tries to explain away half of those parallels as common stock material or with reference to possible other sources in early Christian paraenesis or Jewish writings, noting the different forms in three of these cases, he misses the cumulative force of the argument that the numerous parallels suggest. Indeed, even Deppe would agree that Koester's (and Spitta's) argument that Jas 5:2–3 is closer to *1 Enoch* 97:8–10 than to Matt 6:19–20 is plainly wrong (*Sayings of Jesus*, 126–27).

37. The Q text is adapted from *CEQ*, 46.

larger texts. If there is a relationship, however, part of the difference between these passages would be due to the different audiences and intent of the passages (chastisement of the status bigots [James] *contra* comfort for the poor [Q]), which would require different rhetorical or sapiential forms (rhetorical question [James] vs. beatitude [Q]).[38] It should be noted that the author of James has included "my beloved brothers" immediately preceding the above rhetorical question, just as the Q Sermon is prefaced with Jesus addressing the disciples. While undoubtedly this introduction in James was meant to fit into the rhetorical construction of the diatribe of Jas 2:1–12, it is quite plausible that its presence here was suggested by the presence of an introductory formula in the author's source for the verse in question.[39]

In another example, the content is somewhat different, but similar forms are used. Compare Jas 1:22–25 with the close of the Q Sermon, Q 6:46–49 in Figure 9 (on the following page).[40]

Once again, the differences are obvious: different parables, different order of comparison in the parables, and few (though significant) lexical parallels. For these reasons, some dismiss Jas 1:22–25 as a sayings parallel.[41] Yet, both texts begin with statements that specifically criticize hearers of "the word"/"my words" who are not also doers. These statements are followed by brief examples, in parabolic form, that contrast what doers and non-doers are like and what will happen to them. At the very

---

38. Despite the differences in form and intent between the parallels, Deppe includes this parallel as one of eight allusions to sayings of Jesus in James (*Sayings of Jesus*, 89–91).

39. Hence, Deppe is wrong to rule out the presence of an introductory formula to this verse; there is one, though it is not the same formula used to introduce OT quotations (*Sayings of Jesus*, 90). Martin argues that the formula "my brothers" or "my beloved brothers" is indicative in James, as elsewhere in early Christian literature, of the use of sayings material ("James as a Storehouse," 176–77). However, some of his parallels in James are questionable, and even more so in other canonical literature.

What is most important about this observation is that the presence of introductory formulae in both James and Q could be taken as indicative of James' use of a *written* sayings collection.

40. The Q text is adapted from *CEQ*, 94–100.

41. Deppe, *Sayings of Jesus*, 83–86. Deppe argues that "it is unlikely that James would allude to a gospel saying and then recreate the imagery so that it is totally unrecognizable" (86). Yet, the saying is the second most recognized sayings parallel in James by Deppe's count. Furthermore, the author would change the imagery if the new images better fit what the author was trying to express—this is especially true of Jas 1:25.

Figure 9: Jas 1:22–25 and Q 6:46–49

Jas 1:22–25	Q 6:46–49
Γίνεσθε δὲ **ποιηταὶ λόγου** καὶ μὴ μόνον ἀκροαταὶ παραλογιζόμενοι ἑαυτούς. ὅτι εἴ τις **ἀκροατὴς λόγου** ἐστὶν **καὶ οὐ ποιητής**, <u>οὗτος ἔοικεν ἀνδρὶ</u> κατανοοῦντι τὸ πρόσωπον τῆς γενέσεως αὐτοῦ ἐν ἐσόπτρῳ· κατενόησεν γὰρ ἑαυτὸν καὶ ἀπελήλυθεν καὶ εὐθέως ἐπελάθετο ὁποῖος ἦν. ὁ δὲ παρακύψας εἰς νόμον τέλειον τὸν τῆς ἐλευθερίας καὶ παραμείνας, οὐκ **ἀκροατὴς** ἐπιλησμονῆς γενόμενος ἀλλὰ **ποιητὴς** ἔργου, οὗτος μακάριος ἐν τῇ ποιήσει αὐτοῦ ἔσται.	τίς με καλεῖτε· κύριε κύριε, καὶ οὐ **ποιεῖτε** ἃ **λέγω**; πᾶς ὁ **ἀκούων** μου τ.. λόγ.. **καὶ ποιῶν** αὐτούς, <u>ὅμοιός ἐστιν ἀνθρώπῳ</u>, ὃς ᾠκοδόμησεν αὐτοῦ τὴν οἰκίαν ἐπὶ τὴν πέτραν· καὶ κατέβη ἡ βροχὴ καὶ ἦλθον οἱ ποταμοὶ καὶ ἔπνευσαν οἱ ἄνεμοι καὶ προσέπεσαν τῇ οἰκίᾳ ἐκείνῃ, καὶ οὐκ ἔπεσεν τεθεμελίωτο γὰρ ἐπὶ τὴν πέτραν. καὶ πᾶς ὁ **ἀκούων** μου τοὺς **λόγους καὶ μὴ ποιῶν** αὐτοὺς ὅμοιός ἐστιν ἀνθρώπῳ ὃς ᾠκοδόμησεν αὐτοῦ τὴν οἰκίαν ἐπὶ τὴν ἄμμον· καὶ κατέβη ἡ βροχὴ καὶ ἦλθον οἱ ποταμοὶ καὶ ἔπνευσαν οἱ ἄνεμοι καὶ προσέκοψαν τῇ οἰκίᾳ ἐκείνῃ, καὶ εὐθὺς ἔπεσεν καὶ ἦν ἡ πτῶσις αὐτῆς μεγάλη.
But be **doers of the word**, and not only hearers who deceive themselves. For if any are **hearers of the word and not doers**, they are like those who look at themselves in a mirror; for they look at themselves and, on going away, immediately forget what they were like. But **those** who look into the perfect law, the law of liberty, and persevere, being not **hearers** who forget but **doers** who act—they will be blessed in their doing.	Why do you call me "Lord, Lord" and do not **do** what I **say**? Everyone **who hears** my words **and does** them is like a person who built one's house on bedrock; And the rain poured down and the flash-floods came, and the winds blew and pounded that house, and it did not collapse, for it was founded on bedrock. And everyone **who** hears my **words** and **does not do** them is like a person who built one's house on the sand; And the rain poured down and flash-floods came, and the winds blew and battered that house, and promptly it collapsed, and its fall was devastating.

least, the common vocabulary *and* the combination of common forms suggests the possibility of a tradition of Jesus' sayings such as Q being used by the author of James, with the author exercising the freedom to replace the Q parable with a briefer metaphor and shifting to a declaratory statement when stressing the importance of observing the law and blessing the doers.

The similarities between James and the Q sayings of Jesus are not limited to similarities in theme and content. In his discussion of literary relationships to James, Dibelius observed that James, like known sayings of Jesus traditions, predominates in typical paraenetic forms such as the "short, pointed imperative."[42] Include typical sapiential and rhetorical forms such as maxims, aphorisms, rhetorical questions, etc., and James looks increasingly like Q, the main exception being the difference in genre (and, hence, a significant reason for the difference in the way the sayings of Jesus are handled). Even here, James is not very different from the authors of Matthew and Luke in their treatment of Q. The work of the International Q Project has demonstrated repeatedly and decisively that the Matthean and Lukan redactors of Q have consistently shaped the sayings of Jesus in accordance with, among other influences, their own writing styles, purposes for writing, and/or theological and ideological interests. One example of this intentional shaping is the change in form that a Q saying sometimes takes when adapted by the author of Matthew or Luke. For instance, the Q pericope Free from Anxiety like Ravens and Lilies (Matt 6:25–33; Luke 12:22–31) begins with the imperative "do not be anxious about . . . ." However, the following motive clause in Matthew is a rhetorical question ("Is not the soul more than food, and the body more than clothing?"), while in Luke it is an aphorism ("For the soul is more than food, and the body more than clothing."). In the sayings on The Lamp and the Eye (Q 11:33–35), Matt 6:22–23 ends with an aphoristic statement ("If then the light in you is darkness, how great is the darkness!"), while the parallel in Luke 11:35 is an admonition ("Therefore watch lest the light in you be darkness."). In the Q Sermon, Luke 6:44b is an aphorism ("For figs are not gathered from thorns, nor are grapes picked from a bramble bush."). The Matthean parallel in 7:16b is a rhetorical question ("Are grapes gathered from thorns, or figs from thistles?").

---

42. Dibelius, *James*, 28.

Just as Matthew shows a preference for (and usually retains from Q) the rhetorical question form, and Luke prefers the aphorism over the rhetorical question, so James shows a preference for the imperative form. Figure #10 provides an example:

Figure 10: Q 14:11 (Matt 23:12) and Jas 4:10

Q 14:11 (Matt 23:12)[43]	Jas 4:10
πᾶς ὁ ὑψῶν ἑαυτὸν ταπεινωθήσεται, καὶ ὁ **ταπεινῶν ἑαυτὸν ὑψωθήσεται.**	**ταπεινώθητε** ἐνώπιον κυρίου, καὶ **ὑψώσει ὑμᾶς.**
Everyone who exalts oneself will be humbled, and the one who **humbles oneself will be exalted.**	**Humble yourself** before the Lord, and [the Lord] **will exalt you.**

The behavior that Q 14:11 (Matt 23:12) encourages indirectly in the form of a maxim, Jas 4:10 encourages directly in the form of an admonition with motive clause. Sometimes the form in James is the same as the form in Q, but the content differs, even if the meaning or intent is the same. Figure #11 provides an example of this by comparison of Jas 3:12 to synoptic parallels noted previously (see the following page).[44]

Matthew retained Q's rhetorical question form, while Luke retained Q's fruits and plants in Q order. Both Matthew and Luke therefore show variation from a common written text either in form or in content. Like Matthew, James retains the rhetorical question form but varies the content of the Q saying and surrounds it with further metaphors to establish the point. James keeps Q's order of figs and grapes, as found in Luke, but changes "figs" to "fig tree" and "grapes" to "grapevine" to make the point that different fruits do not come from the same tree.[45] A look at the wider

---

43. The Q text is from *CEQ*, 430.

44. The Q text is from *CEQ*, 88.

45. Deppe argues that the Q version would better fit the context created by Jas 3:9–11, and so was probably not available to the author (*Sayings of Jesus*, 100). However, while Jas 3:12 lacks the contrast of good fruits and bad bushes found in Q, the images of 3:11–12 all make the same point that two different products do not come from the same source.

Figure 11: Figs and Grapes in James and the Synoptics

Jas 3:11-12	Matt 7:16b	Q 6:44b	Luke 6:44b
μήτι ἡ πηγὴ ἐκ τῆς αὐτῆς ὀπῆς βρύει τὸ γλυκὺ καὶ τὸ πικρόν; μὴ δύναται… **συκῆ** ἐλαίας ποιῆσαι ἢ **ἄμπελος** σῦκα; οὔτε ἁλυκὸν γλυκὺ ποιῆσαι ὕδωρ.	μήτι συλλέγουσιν ἀπὸ ἀκανθῶν **σταφυλὰς** ἢ ἀπὸ τριβόλων **σῦκα**;	μήτι συλλέγουσιν ἐκ ἀκανθῶν **σῦκα** ἢ ἐκ τριβόλων **σταφυλάς**;	οὐ γὰρ ἐξ ἀκανθῶν συλλέγουσιν **σῦκα** οὐδὲ ἐκ βάτου **σταφυλὴν** τρυγῶσιν.
Does a spring pour forth from the same opening both fresh and brackish water? Can a fig tree … yield olives, or a grapevine figs? No more can salt water yield fresh.	Are grapes gathered from thorns, or figs from thistles?	Are figs gathered from thorns, or grapes from thistles?	For figs are not gathered from thorns, nor are grapes picked from a bramble bush.

literary context of the above parallels shows that James exhibits similarities to Matthew and Luke by embedding the saying in a cluster of sayings that argue for wise and proper speech, or in Matthew's case, the discernment of good speech. Matthew reconfigures the Q cluster (represented by Luke 6:43–45) in order to instruct members of the *ekklesia* to watch for false prophets who are wolves in sheep's clothing. Matthew introduces the cluster with the direct warning, then frames the cluster with the statement that "you will know them [prophets, not trees] by their fruits."

This point is not as obvious in the Q version and would have been changed had James used the Q tradition as a source.

James uses a cluster of aphorisms and rhetorical questions, including the figs and grapes question, to argue that wise and foolish speech should not come from the same mouth.

All of this is not to say that the author of James was dependent solely upon one sayings source, or on a fixed form of Q. James may have used a written text of Q—this does not seem provable—but the development of oral tradition does not end when the material of the sayings tradition is put to paper.[46] Continuing development of the tradition is likely to have occurred as Q was adopted by different communities, or as communities themselves changed and created new needs and contexts for instruction. Hartin has argued that a developing tradition would account, on the one hand, for instances where James has used Sermon traditions that have developed in a Matthean community (modifications to Q sayings not reflected in Luke's version of the Q Sermon), while on the other hand, Lukan readings of Q found in James, which are fewer, would argue for this Q tradition being used prior to its adoption and modification by the Matthean redactor. Such a theory, if substantiated, would help in dating the letter of James, since it would put it somewhere in the period of 65–85 CE (after whatever substantial expansions of the Q tradition had taken place and before Matthew was written).

Use of other community paraenetic traditions is probable, as evidenced by the non-Q parable in Jas 1:23 and the additional metaphors in 3:11–12. This would account for James knowing of teachings or parables similar to those otherwise found only in Luke, such as Jesus' instructions on humility and seating in public places and his parabolic teaching about the good life and what tomorrow holds.[47] Clearly James adapts and modifies the Q tradition somewhat freely in accordance with the particular issues the author wishes to address. What is most important to recognize,

---

46. Koester has devoted a career to demonstrating this very point: see esp. *Synoptische Überlieferung*; idem, *Ancient Christian Gospels*.

47. James 2:2–3/Luke 14:8–10 and Jas 4:13–14/Luke 12:15–20. In the first pair of teachings, James directs the reader/hearer not to play favorites when seating others, especially distinguishing between rich and poor. Luke has Jesus directing the readers/hearers themselves not to take the best places, but to sit in a more humble position. This is essentially the same issue, but with a different audience. In the second pair, James is much briefer, but gets across the same point about money-making, living the good life, and not being prepared for an unknown future (cf. Sir 11:17–19). James does not appear to be using Luke, but rather teachings on wealth and attitudes toward the wealthy that also find their way into Luke.

however, is the preponderance of parallels to Q over against significantly fewer parallels to the rest of Matthew and Luke. This indicates that the author of James probably used a sayings of Jesus tradition that is reflected in the sayings source Q. To be more precise, I would argue that James has used the Q sayings tradition, if not adapting the sayings of an actual written version of the text of Q.[48]

JAMES 5:2–3 AND Q 12:33

Figure 12: Q 12:33 and Jas 5:2–3

Q 12:33	Jas 5:2–3
(μὴ θησαυρίζετε ὑμῖν θησαυροὺς ἐπὶ τῆς γῆς ὅπου σὴς καὶ βρῶσις ἀφανίζει καὶ ὅπου κλέπται διορύσσουσιν καὶ κλέπτουσιν.) θησαυρίζετε (δὲ) ὑμῖν θησαυροὺς ἐν οὐρανοῖς, ὅπου οὔτε σὴς οὔτε βρῶσις ἀφανίζει καὶ ὅπου κλέπται οὐ διορύσσουσιν οὐδὲ κλέπτουσιν.	ὁ πλοῦτος ὑμῶν σέσηπεν καὶ τὰ ἱμάτια ὑμῶν σητόβρωτα γέγονεν, ὁ χρυσὸς ὑμῶν καὶ ὁ ἄργυρος κατίωται καὶ ὁ ἰὸς αὐτῶν εἰς μαρτύριον ὑμῖν ἔσται καὶ φάγεται τὰς σάρκας ὑμῶν ὡς πῦρ. ἐθησαυρίσατε ἐν ἐσχάταις ἡμέραις.
(Do not treasure up treasures on the earth, where moth and eating thing destroy and where thieves dig through and steal.) (But) Treasure up for yourselves treasures in (the) heavens where neither moth nor eating thing destroys and where thieves do not dig through and steal.	Your riches have rotted and your garments have become moth-eaten. Your gold and silver have rusted and their rust will be a witness against you, and will eat your flesh like fire. You have stored up treasure for the last days.

---

48. According to Dibelius, the lack of any direct quotation of Jesus in James is due to the use of community paraenesis, which made use of sayings of Jesus without identifying them as such (*James*, 28–29). Gerhard Kittel says somewhat the same thing in reference to early Christian teaching and preaching ("Der geschichtliche Ort"). What Dibelius and Kittel say about Christian paraenesis may be true, but the lack of direct quotation in James may be due to the paraenetic intentions of the author and not to the lack of quotation formulae in the source.

Hartin rightly includes Jas 5:2–3 as an example of reflection on a Q-like sayings tradition as opposed to other potential sayings collections:

> The similarities in thought and vocabulary support the contention that James is operating in a world which is aware of the Q tradition of the sayings of Jesus. James is not quoting the Q tradition directly, but is using it according to his usual method of working it into his argument. In fact, one can say that this passage in James is a commentary upon the Q saying, reflecting upon it and showing its further implications.[49]

In this statement, Hartin provides a more specific explanation not only for the lack of extensive verbal similarity between James and Q, but also for the lack of direct quotation. His explanation is consistent with what has been highlighted in the previous section of this chapter—the author of James freely adapts the sayings tradition to a different social context, adding further images along the way and giving the saying a different hermeneutical focus. Hartin gives two reasons for considering Jas 5:2–3 to be a reworking of the Treasure in Heaven saying of Q 12:33 specifically (as opposed, for example, to Luke 6:24[50]):

> (a) Both passages have a similar reference to wealth. Q refers to moths and rust (σὴς καὶ βρῶσις) and their ability to destroy things by consuming them. James also refers to riches rotting and the garments being moth-eaten (σητόβρωτα), a form in which the two words in Q are now combined.
>
> (b) Both passages look beyond the present possession of earthly wealth to the hope of attaining heavenly wealth.[51]

In (b) Hartin recognizes the basic theme of the saying of Jesus in Q and James, and in (a) he identifies the verbal content distinctive of the two versions of the saying (σὴς and βρῶσις). His analysis can be refined and expanded. While Jas 5:2 uses the non-Q word πλοῦτος ("riches") as

---

49. Hartin, *James*, 179–81, esp. 180. By focusing only on the differences between Matthew and Luke, Deppe argues for two different sources for this saying, Q and M (*Sayings of Jesus*, 123–24). See above, chapter 2, pp. 27–29, for a critique of this position. Nevertheless, he agrees that Jas 5:2–3 alludes to the saying of Jesus, recognizing that a difference in vocabulary is just as observable between Matthew and Luke (125–26). He further argues that "both Luke and James have combined the saying of Jesus with other paraenetic teaching of the church" (126).

50. Cf., e.g., Adamson, "James," 182.

51. Hartin, *James*, 180.

a general word for possessions or treasures, the verb used to indicate its process of destruction is a cognate of Q's noun σής (σέσηπεν). James understands Q's βρῶσις to refer to "eating," as opposed to "rust" or "worm," as shown by the use of the compound σητόβρωτα in reference to the moth-eating of garments.⁵² It is only when referring to precious metals in 5:3 that James uses non-Q words for "rust" (κατίωται, ἰός). Even then, however, James understands the basic form of destruction in the Q saying as that of "eating," as shown by the elaboration that the rust "will eat your flesh" (φάγεται).⁵³ James does not mention the threat of stealing in 5:2-3, focusing only on the first strophe of Q 12:33's parallelism. But Deppe suggests that "James omits the loss of wealth by stealing since he intends to save that description for the oppressor himself who in the next verse (5:4) is accused of stealing from the poor."⁵⁴ One is assured that we are speaking of a Q passage when James provides commentary that the rich have "stored up treasure for the last days" (ἐθησαυρίσατε ἐν ἐσχάταις ἡμέραις), using the first identifiable word of the Q version of the Treasure saying, θησαυρίζω.⁵⁵

In writing Jas 5:2-3 this way, the author moves from simple condemnation of earthly treasures in earthly terms (moth-eating and rust) to understanding the accumulation of wealth as a self-judgment at the end of time.⁵⁶ In other words, like Matthew's version of the saying, James

52. Contrary to Hartin (and LSJ ["βρῶσις," 332b], among others; Danker corrected BAGD ["βρῶσις," 158a] on this point in BDAG [184b-85a]), βρῶσις refers, not to "rust" (or even to "worm"), but to "food" or "eating," and the compound word form σητόβρωτα ("moth-eaten") in Jas 5:2 is indicative of this. See above, chapter 3, p. 64, n. 19; p. 73-74, n. 45. Charles rightly argues that in Mal 3:11, Ep Jer 13, and Matt 6:19-20, βρῶσις means "devourer" (APOT 2:601; cited by Deppe, Sayings of Jesus, 124-25).

53. Koester is right to see here close similarities to 1 Enoch 97:8-10 and Jewish wisdom writings on the perishability of wealth (Ancient Christian Gospels, 74; citing Dibelius, James, 236). This tells us about the author's literary and cultural world-view and perhaps explains why James has altered the Q saying to make it one of the few overtly eschatological passages in the letter. Koester is wrong to conclude that, overall, Jas 5:2-3 is closer to 1 Enoch and not reliant on the Q saying.

54. Deppe, Sayings of Jesus, 125-26.

55. Cf. Hartin, who follows Polag here when opting for Luke's verb ποιέω in Q (Hartin, James, 179; Polag, Fragmenta Q, 62-63). But Luke's ποιέω fits better with its subsequent redactional phrasing—"make for yourselves purses which do not wear out"—and should be considered redactional. See above, chapter 2, pp. 37-38, on Q 12:33³. The IQP has voted with certainty for θησαυρίζω (Moreland and Robinson, "Work Sessions 1994," 481; CEQ, 328).

56. In this way, James goes beyond the sapiential observation that riches cannot be

moves from earthly to eschatological concerns.⁵⁷ But James applies this prophetic warning to a specific, end-of-the-age judgment (anticipating the "coming of the Lord"—Jas 5:7, 8). In this way, James takes the Q tradition of the saying in a different direction from Matthew by providing the saying with even stronger eschatological content and interpreting its ramifications in this light. This move may be likened to Mark's use of 10:21(-25) in that they both use the saying to address a particular cross-section of society, though James is much more condemnatory. The result is that, unlike the Q version, which is focused on the positive admonition to "store up treasures in the heavens," James shades the saying toward the negative, judgmental side of apocalyptic expectation.

If there is a common thread that connects James with Q, Matthew, Mark, and Luke, it is the understanding that the Treasure saying actually addresses the issue of wealth and its maintenance in this lifetime. This is true despite the diverse ways these texts use and interpret the saying. Indeed, it is remarkable considering the many possibilities for using the imagery of wealth in the wisdom tradition.

Problems in the Interpretation of Colossians 3:1–11

The beginning of the third chapter of Colossians is commonly seen as signaling a transition in the letter from teaching to exhortation. Col 3:1–4, specifically, is usually recognized as the beginning of a substantial paraenetic section that extends to Col 4:6.⁵⁸ This is not to say that Col 3:1–4 is understood to be disconnected from what goes before it. On the contrary, Col 3:1a ("so, if you have been raised with Christ") is commonly seen as hearkening back to Col 2:12–13 ("when you were buried with him in baptism, you were also raised with him") and 2:20 ("if with Christ you died . . ."").⁵⁹ Colossians 2:12–15 speaks of the empowering transformation that has come to the Colossians from identifying with Christ's resurrection in their baptism. Col 2:20–23 chastises the Colossians for not living as though they have been so empowered and Col 3:1a, also

---

kept after one dies—Sir 11:18–19; *Ps-Phoc* 110; GTh 63; Luke 12:16–20 (cf. Luke 12:21); Jas 4:13–14.

57. The contrast is implicit in Q even if Matthew 6:19 is not included in Q.

58. E.g., Grässer, "Kol 3,1–4 als Beispiel," 146; R. P. Martin, *Colossians and Philemon*, 100; Schweizer, *Kolosser*, 130; Aletti, *Colossiens*, 215.

59. E.g., Lähnemann, *Der Kolosserbrief*, 31; Martin, *Colossians and Philemon*, 100; Harris, *Colossians and Philemon*, 100.

recalling 2:12, introduces a series of positive exhortations that are based upon the confidence that they should have in their ritual identification with the dying and rising Christ.

In closer analyses of the text, Col 3:2's τὰ ἄνω φρονεῖτε, μὴ τὰ ἐπὶ τῆς γῆς ("set your mind on the things above, not on things of the earth") is seen to interpret the imperative of 3:1b (ζητέω) and begin the contrast between living according to the passions (3:5–8; the vices of 3:5 are called "things of the earth") and living a life of Christ-like virtue (3:12–17).[60] φρονεῖτε defines the pious lifestyle, one of self-controlled focus on right attitude and action toward fellow believers.

Just as Col 3:1 reminds the readers/hearers of the *kerygma* that they have been taught—that of Christ's resurrection and exaltation to heaven—Col 3:3–4 points to the future Parousia, at which time the new life will be more fully revealed.[61]

In Col 3:5–8, the believer is exhorted to "put to death" or "put away" the vices associated with living according to the passions. Commentators recognize the ubiquity of vice lists in antiquity, especially in the philosophical schools.[62] Closer parallels are found in other contemporary Jewish circles—this is observed particularly in the common mention of πορνεία or εἰδωλολατρία in Jewish vice lists as compared to non-Jewish lists.[63] Col 3:9a, μὴ ψεύδεσθε εἰς ἀλλήλους ("do not lie to one another") is often seen as "rounding off" or summarizing the vices of 3:8 (or 3:5–8), though the prohibition is grammatically connected to what follows in Col 3:9b–11.[64] The paraenesis of 3:1–17 as a whole is largely considered to be post-baptismal exhortation that explicitly (cf. 2:12) or implicitly

---

60. E.g., Martin, *Colossians and Philemon*, 101; Bratcher and Nida, *Handbook*, 74–75; Lindemann, *Kolosserbrief*, 53; Petr Pokorny, *Colossians*, 160; Dunn, *Colossians and Philemon*, 205. Ernst Lohmeyer is one of the very few commentators to emphasize the first verb (ζητέω) over the second (φρονέω) in his or her analysis, and one of the few to explicitly associate the virtues of Col 3:12–14 with the τὰ ἄνω of 3:1 (Lohmeyer, *Kolosser und Philemon*, 131–33, 134, 144).

61. E.g., Schweizer, *Kolosser*, 130.

62. For extensive discussion of the vice lists, see, e.g., Pokorny, *Colossians*, 162–65; or Lohse, *Colossians and Philemon*, 137–39.

63. Pokorny, *Colossians*, 164; Dunn, *Colossians and Philemon*, 213. On the ubiquity of πορνεία and εἰδωλολατρία in Jewish lists, see Cannon, *Use*, 59.

64. Joüon, "Note"; Lohmeyer, *Kolosser*, 139; Lindemann, *Kolosserbrief*, 55, 57; Martin, *Colossians and Philemon*, 104–5; Pokorny, *Colossians*, 168; Lohse, *Colossians and Philemon*, 140. Cf. Eph 4:22–32.

recalls the believers' pre-baptismal instruction. Col 3:9b–11 is just such an implicit reminder of their having "put off" their old person—one dominated by the "things of the earth"—and "put on" a new person.[65] In this new humanity, baptismal initiates are no longer to understand themselves according to common social distinctions, such as Jew or Greek, slave or free. Colossians 3:11 ends with a summary statement about the pervasive presence of Christ ("Christ is [the] all and is in all"), and commentators often see in this an epitome of the high Christology of the letter as a whole.[66]

With regard to sources behind the text, most commentators see a connection between Col 3:2 and Phil 3:17–21—in particular, Phil 3:19–20—where Paul contrasts οἱ τὰ ἐπίγεια φρονοῦντες with the Philippians, whose "citizenship is ἐν οὐρανοῖς.[67] Philippians 3:21 continues with Paul's reminder that "it is from there that we are expecting a Savior, the Lord Jesus Christ, who will transform our humble bodies"; this reference to the future could have inspired the reference to the Parousia in Col 3:3–4. Murray Harris points to Rom 8:5 as a parallel to Col 3:2, with its contrast of "things of the spirit" vs. "things of the flesh."[68] Reference to "where Christ is, sitting at the right hand of God," is commonly recognized as an allusion to Ps 110:1, though at this time it was already appropriated in the *kerygma*.[69] There is very nearly a consensus that Col 3:5–8 and 3:9b–11 use traditional material, though the vice lists of 3:5–8 may simply reflect a common Jewish and Greek ethical topos. Almost all scholars recognize Col 3:9b–11 to be a variation of the baptismal creedal formula found in Gal 3:28, whether Col 3:9b–11 be a Pauline adaptation of a pre-Pauline baptismal formula or a post-Pauline adaptation of Gal 3:28. Many commentators discussing the final statement of Col 3:11 (3:11b) note the similar statement about God in 1 Cor 15:28 and some further suggest that Col 3:11 is meant to recall the Christ Hymn of Col 1:15–20.[70]

---

65. On the liturgical elements of Col 3:9b–11a, see Betz, *Galatians*, 181–85.

66. E.g., Lightfoot, *Colossians and Philemon*, 217; Aletti, *Colossiens*, 234.

67. E.g., Sanders, "Literary Dependence," 44; Martin, *Colossians and Philemon*, 101; Pokorny, *Colossians*, 159–60; Aletti, *Colossiens*, 221. Günther Bornkamm disagrees with this connection (Bornkamm, "Hoffnung," 61).

68. Harris, *Colossians and Philemon*, 138.

69. E.g., Schweizer, *Kolosser*, 132; Martin, *Colossians and Philemon*, 100; Dunn, *Colossians and Philemon*, 203; Pokorny, *Colossians*, 160.

70. On 1 Cor 15:28, see Sanders, "Literary Dependence," 42–43. On Col 1:15–20, see

There are, however, problems and gaps in the literature on Col 3:1–11. For example, while it is commonly recognized that φρονέω in Col 3:2 complements or further defines ζητέω in 3:1b, no one questions why the author includes 3:1b in the first place. As used here, ζητέω is so general as to be somewhat meaningless without φρονέω or subsequent interpretation. This is implicitly recognized in the fact that many commentators skip over the first imperative in order to discuss the meaning of the second.[71] Likewise, what the τὰ ἄνω are cannot be understood without further explanation. How does one "seek" the "things above" if one does not even know what they are? In short, why did the author not begin with Col 3:1a and move directly to 3:2? Instead, "seek the things above" is used as the keynote imperative for the paraenetic section of Col 3:1–4:6. Unlike Col 3:3–4, 3:1–2 is not particularly well structured; hence 3:1b most likely would not have been included for stylistic reasons.

Another problem attends the interpretation of μὴ ψεύδεσθε in Col 3:9a. Most commentators see it as continuing or summarizing the vice lists of 3:5–8, especially the last two vices (βλασφημία; αἰσχρολογίαν) in 3:8.[72] Grammatically speaking, however, it is unconnected to what

---

e.g., Dunn, *Colossians and Philemon*, 200.

71. E.g., Schweizer, *Kolosser*, 130–34; Moulton, *Colossians, Philemon and Ephesians*, 42–43. See also Radford, *Colossians and Philemon*, 256–57; Bratcher and Nida, *Handbook*, 74. Cf. Lohmeyer, *Kolosser*, 131–34.

72. E.g., Joüon, "Note," 185–89; Carson, *Colossians and Philemon*, 84; Lohse, *Colossians and Philemon*, 140; Martin, *Colossians and Philemon*, 104–5; Pokorny, *Colossians*, 168; Dunn, *Colossians and Philemon*, 220.
Ernst Lohmeyer (*Kolosser*, 139), Joachim Gnilka (*Kolosserbrief*, 185), and others have argued that the vice lists are evidence of catechetical reflection on the Decalogue. Lohmeyer and Gnilka look to Matt 5:21–30 as an example of a generalizing commentary on specific commandments of the Torah. Lohmeyer sees all of Col 3:5–6 as an exposition on the commandment against adultery, and all of Col 3:7–8 as an exposition on the commandment against murder. Gnilka associates Col 3:5 with the commandments against adultery and stealing, apparently connecting evil desire and greed (Col 3:5) with stealing (but not covetousness!), and seeing sexual immorality, impurity, and passion as an extension of the commandment against adultery, similar to Matt 5:27–30. Gnilka also associates Col 3:8 with the commandments against murder and bearing false witness, seeing the list as going beyond Matt 5:22–26's elaboration on the commandment against murder to include an expansion on the commandment against false witness (presumably with the vices of slander and foul language). Gnilka sees the inclusion of the prohibition against lying as confirmation that the author is reflecting upon the Decalogue. However, Aletti (*Colossiens*) is correct in disputing these connections to the Decalogue. There is almost no verbal kinship between Col 3:5, 8 and the LXX (Exod 20:1–17; Deut 5:6–21). In fact, there are only two verbal parallels—parallels not even mentioned by

goes before it and is explicitly justified by what comes after it.[73] The context of Galatians 3 does not help explain the presence of this isolated prohibition. Galatians 3:28 is immediately preceded by Paul's statement that "we are longer subject to a disciplinarian." Yet, in Col 3:9–11, the baptismal material is used to justify a specific prohibition of social behavior. Furthermore, contrary to some commentators, Col 3:9a does not "summarize" the vice lists: only two of the vices specifically address the misuse of the tongue. Even further, this prohibition stands out as one of the few prohibitions of the entire letter. Considering the fact that 3:5 and 3:8 are admonitions that function to prohibit behavior, it is notable that, formally speaking, 3:9a is a prohibition and thus is a distinctive element in this paraenetic section.

If the author understood lying to be just another vice, it is not clear why it was not more closely linked with Col 3:8. Instead, it is grammatically set apart as its own prohibition and further supported by the baptismal creedal material. The compositional peculiarity in the manner of

---

Gnilka (ἐπιθυμ–: Col 3:5//Exod 20:17 par.; εἴδωλα + λατρ–: Col 3:5//Exod 20:4, 5 par.). Even here, ἐπιθυμέω ("covet") and ἐπιθυμία ("passion") have very different meanings in their respective contexts (228), the Decalogue being focused on the desire to possess another's property, while Col 3:5 is concerned with lack of sexual self-control. Likewise, the words εἴδωλα ("idols") and εἰδωλατρία ("idolatry") do not have the same function in the Decalogue, which prohibits the cult of idols, and in Col 3:5, where greed is idolatry (228, n. 37).

With so few verbal connections, one would at least hope for stronger thematic connections between the Decalogue and the Colossian vice lists; but this is not the case. Gnilka apparently connects evil desire and greed (Col 3:5) with stealing, but not with covetousness, though most commentators consider the latter two vices to be related to the sexual immorality of the first three. Only with the inclusion of Col 3:9a does Gnilka make his case in associating slander and foul language with bearing false witness. Yet, lying is not part of the second list. Furthermore, if the vice lists were, in fact, expansions on prohibitions in the Decalogue, who would have been responsible for this association? If the author of Colossians is responsible for the creation of the lists, then why is idol-worship *tacked onto* the first list as a synonym of greed, and why is lying not included in the lists at all? If, on the other hand, the author used a source for the lists, we still do not have a plausible explanation for the inclusion of the prohibition after the lists, since it does not clarify a connection with the Decalogue (a reference back to Col 2:8?).

73. E.g., Bratcher and Nida, *Handbook*, 74. Cf. Radford, *Colossians*, 265. Joüon sees Col 3:9a as nothing more than a final sin in the second vice list, but grammatically unconnected to what comes before it, and therefore nothing more than a parenthetical addition to the main verb ἀπόθεσθε in 3:8 ("Note," 185–89). What is notable is his recognition that, grammatically, 3:9a does indeed stand out from that which comes before it (186).

3:9a's inclusion in the text, and its importance relative to 3:5, 8, seems inexplicable at first glance.

Yet another problem with the literature on Col 3:1–11 lies in the interpretation of 3:11b. As noted above, this statement is variously interpreted as (1) an adaptation of the summary statements of Gal 3:28 and/or 1 Cor 12:13; (2) the All-predication of 1 Cor 15:28 reinterpreted to refer to Christ; or (3) a summary statement derived from the Christ Hymn, especially Col 1:17. Some commentators have no problem in seeing the influence of all three texts on Col 3:11b.[74] Each of these positions needs to be addressed.

First, it is obvious that Col 3:9b–11a derives from a baptismal creed that is adapted for use by Paul in Gal 3:28 and 1 Cor 12:13. This is beyond dispute. However, Col 3:11b differs significantly from both summary statements and it is not at all obvious that the All-predication here was suggested by those statements. Specifically, πᾶς has a different referent in Gal 3:28 and 1 Cor 12:13, both of which are considered to be older Pauline adaptations of the creed.

>
> Gal 3:28: πάντες γὰρ ὑμεῖς εἷς ἐστε ἐν Χριστῷ
> for all of you are one in Christ
>
> 1 Cor 12:13: καὶ πάντες ἓν πνεῦμα ἐποτίσθημεν
> and all of us were made to drink of one spirit
>
> Col 3:11: ἀλλὰ [τὰ] πάντα καὶ ἐν πᾶσιν Χριστός
> but Christ is the All and is in all

In Galatians, the referent for πᾶς is the reader/hearers; in 1 Corinthians it is the author and reader/hearers. But in Colossians, the referent for πᾶς is the Christ and πᾶς serves, not in its usual adjectival sense (as in Gal 3:28 and 1 Cor 12:13), but as a predication defining the nature of Christ (and in this substantive sense is similar to τὰ πάντα in Col 1:16–17 and several places in the undisputed Pauline corpus).

Second, it is problematic to argue the influence of 1 Cor 15:28 on Col 3:11b. While the form used in both statements is similar, the differences

---

74. Lohse, *Colossians and Philemon*, 145. See also Sanders, "Literary Dependence," 42–43.

are perhaps even more significant.[75] In 1 Cor 15:28b, the son is subjected under God along with the All, and so is put on the same level as (though not equated with) the All. However, God does not appear to be equated with the All in 1 Cor 15:28. In 15:28c, τὰ πάντα does not appear to refer specifically to the cosmic All of 15:28ab, but makes better sense interpreted as the more abstract "all things"—hence, "that God may be all in all."[76] In Col 3:11b, Christ is expressly identified with the All. The second half of 3:11b is perhaps even more significant than the first, as it places Christ (in Col 3:11b) on a level with God (in 1 Cor 15:28): both are "in all things" (ἐν πᾶσιν). Therefore, even if one argues for the meaning of τὰ πάντα as "all things" instead of "the All" in Col 11b, one is still faced with significant differences between this statement and 1 Cor 15:28, where the focus is primarily on Christ's subjection under God. Furthermore, to limit one's view of similar material to the prior letters of Paul is to ignore the abundance of All-predications in the wider literary context, including Stoic and Jewish wisdom literature.[77] If the author of Colossians sees Christ as representing God or Wisdom—and Col 1:15–20 would seem to indicate this—then wisdom literature might be a better place to look for parallels.[78]

Third, it does not follow from the inclusion or creation of the Christ Hymn by the author of Colossians that Col 3:11b would have been created from the Christ Hymn. Colossians 3:11b expressly identifies Christ as τὰ πάντα, but Col 1:15–20 does not. While Col 1:15–20 is very consistent with wisdom literature with regard to Wisdom's (Jesus') role in creation and relationship to τὰ πάντα, Col 3:11b is closer to Jesus' identification

---

75. 1 Cor 15:28:   ἵνα ᾖ ὁ θεὸς [τὰ] πάντα ἐν πᾶσιν
that God may be [the] all in all

Col 3:11:   ἀλλὰ [τὰ] πάντα καὶ ἐν πᾶσιν Χριστός
but Christ is [the] All and is in all

76. The manuscript evidence concerning the τά in 1 Cor 15:28 roughly parallels that of τά in Col 3:11 (0 † A B D* 0243. 6. 33. 81. 1241^S. pc ¦ txt ℵ D² F G Ψ 075. 1881 𝔐; cf. below, p. 110, n. 90). Internal arguments are somewhat equally weighted. Τά may have been added by scribes due to its presence in 15:28ab. On the other hand, it may have been excluded by some scribes specifically because πάντα does not have the same meaning in 15:28c as it does in 15:28ab.

77. See, e.g., Norden, *Agnostos Theos*, 240–50; Pöhlmann, "All-Prädikationen."

78. For Wisdom's relationship to τὰ πάντα, see esp. Wis 1:14; 7:24–27; 8:1, 5; 9:1–2; 15:1.

with God, from whom Wisdom proceeds.⁷⁹ Explicitly identifying Christ as the All is different than saying that the All is held together in Christ.

One other problem with the text should be noted. Colossians 3:3–4 is a well-constructed text that expresses the believer's past, present, and future status with God in two sentences.⁸⁰ Occasionally, commentators on Colossians have observed that κρύπτω is a term that is never used by Paul.⁸¹ In Romans 8, Paul speaks of the glory that is about to be revealed. There, however, Paul does not speak of the first half of the hidden/revealed duality, that which is now "hidden." Cognates and synonyms of κρύπτω are occasionally used by Paul, but rarely in relation to upcoming revelation.⁸² Colossians 3:3–4, however, spells out the status of the believer as presently being hidden, but soon to be revealed. Hence, while Col 3:3–4 as a whole can be seen as an expression of Pauline eschatology as found in Rom 8:18–25, expressing the duality of hiddenness and revelation in explicit terms is due to the author of Colossians. It is also possible that the explicit duality was suggested to the author from a source other than Paul's letters or Paul himself.

The four problems discussed above have one thing in common: they can be explained as the result of the author's incorporation of authoritative source material in the composition of the paraenesis of 3:1–11. Ironically, few commentators have ever tried to uncover traditional elements in Col 3:1–4, 9a, and 11b.⁸³ The inclusion of Col 3:1b would make sense, however, if 3:1b was source material that the author recognized as authoritative and adapted for use here. The further expansion upon the imperative with 3:2 would then make a great deal of sense. What was a known wisdom admonition was adapted for use as the keynote imperative of the entire hortatory section of Col 3:1–17. Colossians 3:2 and φρονέω were then used to define ζητέω more specifically to fit with the subsequent paraenesis. The inclusion of the prohibition in Col 3:9a at the beginning of 3:9–11, disconnected from the vice lists of 3:5–8, also

---

79. Cf., e.g., Sir 43:27.
80. Dunn, *Colossians and Philemon*, 209.
81. E.g., Dunn, *Colossians and Philemon*, 207.
82. Cf., e.g., 1 Cor 4:5.
83. George Cannon's comment is perhaps indicative of the present state of research on the subject: "Colossians 2:16–3:4 is the only passage in the 'main argument' [Col 1:24–4:6] which does not allude to or cite traditional materials" (*Use*, 170).

makes sense if the author recognized it as an authoritative teaching coming from source material.[84] Other (Pauline) sources having been considered, the idea of Col 3:11b appears to come either from the author's own conceptuality or from a source that identifies Christ, Wisdom, or God with the All. It is also possible that the explicit duality was suggested by a somewhat abstract aphorism commonly known in early Jesus communities: what is hidden will be revealed.

If source material was used in Col 3:1-4, 9a, 11b, the nature of this source remains to be identified. Considering the strong sapiential orientation of Colossians—in particular the Wisdom identification of Christ in 1:15-20—popular Jewish wisdom literature would be a good place to start. One can find most of the concepts discussed above in various sapiential and apocalyptic texts. For example, in popular sapiential texts, the following themes can be identified: seeking Wisdom (Sir 4:11-12; 6:27; 24:34; 50:13-22; Wis 6:12; 8:18 [cf. Prov 2:4-6; 8:17]);[85] Wisdom revealing what was hidden (Sir 4:18; Wis 6:12; 7:21-22); the immorality of lying (Sir 7:12-13; 20:24-26; Wis 14:28; *Ps-Phoc* 7 [cf. Prov 24:28; 30:8]); the relationship of God or Wisdom to the All (Sir 18:1; 43:26-27; Wis 1:14; 7:24-27; 8:1, 5; 9:1-2; 15:1 [note esp. Sir 43:27: "and let the final words be: He is the All"—τὸ πᾶν ἐστιν αὐτός]).[86] One could therefore say that the ideas were in the air, even if the texts noted above refer to God and God's Sophia, and not to Jesus Christ.

While looking to sapiential topoi might help to explain the presence of these themes in Colossians 3, it does not explain their particular usage, especially with regard to Col 3:1b, 3:9a and 3:11b. The significant position that these three passages hold in the paraenesis suggests the use of a source or sources that the author saw as particularly authoritative. One place to look for such an authoritative voice in the first century CE would be a sayings of Jesus tradition. In fact, isolated cases of concepts or expressions common to Colossians and the gospel tradition, but foreign

---

84. Martin recognizes the possibility that "this challenge belongs to tradition, which is used to round off the list in verse 8" (*Colossians and Philemon*, 105).

85. See also 4Q185 2.10-12 and 4Q525 2.2.2-4.

86. The themes of hiddenness revealed, seeking the eternal, and lying can be found in a number of apocalyptic texts, though they are far more scattered—much has been made of the similarities in Col 3:1-5 and the Syriac *Apocalypse of Baruch* in particular. See Levison, "2 *Apoc Bar* 48:42—52:7."

to Paul—such as the expression "forgiveness of sins" in Col 1:14 (τὴν ἄφεσιν τῶν ἁμαρτιῶν)—have been observed before.[87] However, these similarities are few and far between. On the other hand, there does exist a sayings of Jesus collection that contains material such as that which underlies Col 3:1–2, 3–4, 9a, 11b: the Gospel of Thomas.

Colossians 3:1–11 and the Gospel of Thomas

Isolated similarities in Colossians to the Gospel of Thomas have been noted before.[88] However, parallels to Col 3:1–11 in particular can be found in two sections of the Gospel of Thomas, in sayings of Jesus that are found side-by-side in the text. Figure #13 illustrates these parallels:

---

87. See, e.g., Houlden, *Paul's Letters From Prison,* 154–55. The text references in the outer margins of NA²⁷ are to scattered and isolated themes throughout the four gospels (523–31).

88. Craig Evans, Robert Webb, and Richard Wiebe gathered together all of the potential canonical parallels to the Nag Hammadi Library mentioned in the secondary literature and inventoried them according to the categories of (1) "reasonable *probability* that there is some form of influence between the text of Scripture and the text of the Nag Hammadi tractates" due to "*close* verbal and/or conceptual correspondence"; and (2) "only a *possibility* of some form of influence between the biblical text and the Nag Hammadi text" due to "*vague* verbal and/or conceptual correspondence" (Evans, Webb, and Wiebe, eds., *Nag Hammadi Texts and the Bible,* xviii). For the Gospel of Thomas and Colossians, they found no close correspondences suggesting probable influence. Under vague correspondences, they included the following: GTh 6≈Col 3:9; GTh 19≈Col 1:17–18; GTh 53≈Col 2:11; GTh 61≈Col 1:17–18; GTh 77≈Col 3:11, 1:16–17 (88–144; cf., e.g., Kasser, *Thomas,* 37, 81; Guillaumont et al., *The Gospel according to Thomas,* 59–60; Doresse, *Thomas,* 189). Parallels between GTh 19, 61 and Col 1:17–18 are dubious, and Col 2:11 may come from acquaintance with Rom 2:29. However, the following parallel is ignored in the secondary literature:

Col 1:16, 17:   ὅτι ἐν αὐτῷ ἐκτίσθη τὰ πάντα . . . καὶ τὰ πάντα ἐν αὐτῷ συνέστηκεν
         for in him the All was created . . . and in him the All has held together

GTh 77:1c: ⲚⲦⲀ ⲠⲦⲎⲢϤ ⲈⲒ ⲈⲂⲞⲖ Ⲛ̄ⲚϨⲎⲦ ⲀⲨⲰ Ⲛ̄ⲦⲀ ⲠⲦⲎⲢϤ ⲠⲰϨ ϢⲀⲢⲞⲈⲒ
         from me the All came forth, and to me the All attained

89. Where the Coptic reads ⲦⲠⲈ ("heaven"), P. Oxy. 654.38 reads ἀληθ[ε]ίας ("truth"). The Berliner Arbeitskreis has recommended emending ⲦⲠⲈ with Ⲧ<Ⲙ>Ⲉ ("truth"): H.-G. Bethge et al., "Evangelium Thomae copticum," 520. GTh 5 contains a doublet about the revealing of that which is hidden:

Jesus said, "Know what is in front your face,
    and what is hidden from you will be revealed to you.
For there is nothing hidden which will not be made known." (NHC 33.10–14)

Figure 13: Colossians / Thomas Parallels

	Colossians	Gospel of Thomas
a)	**3:1–2** ¹ So if you have been raised with Christ, <u>seek the things that are above,</u> <u>where Christ is,</u> seated at the right hand of God. ² Set your minds on things above, not on things that are on earth.	**76:3** "You also, <u>seek the treasure that does not</u> <u>perish, that abides,</u> where no moth comes to eat and no worm destroys."
b)	**3:3–4** ³ For (γάρ) you have died and <u>your life has been hidden</u> with Christ in God. ⁴ When Christ who is your life is revealed, then <u>you also</u> <u>will be revealed</u> with him in glory.	**6:4–5** ⁴ "... since all things are revealed before heaven. ⁵ For (γάρ) <u>there is nothing hidden</u> <u>that will not be revealed</u> ... "[89]
c)	**3:9** <u>Do not lie to one another,</u> seeing that you have stripped off the old person with its practices ...	**6:2–3** ² Jesus said, "<u>Do not lie,</u> ³ and do not do what you hate, ... "
d)	**3:11b** but <u>Christ is [the] All*</u> and is in all.	**77:1** Jesus said, "I am the light that is over all. I am the All*: from me the All came forth, and to me the All attained."
	* (or "all things"—[τὰ][90] πάντα)	* (or "everything"—ⲠⲦⲎⲢϤ)

90. The editors of *GNT⁴* include τά with brackets, owing to the somewhat balanced evidence for inclusion or exclusion (692). External evidence weighs only slightly in favor of the inclusion of τά in 3:11, the corrector of ℵ agreeing with B, D, and the Byzantine text over against ℵ, A, C, a few important minuscules, and Clement (cf. NA²⁷: 0 † ℵ* A C 33. 81. 1241ˢ *pc*; Cl ¦ *txt* ℵ² B D F G Ψ 075. 0278. 1739. 1881 𝔐). Likewise, internal issues

Individually, these similarities might be dismissed as coincidental. For example, the concept of what is or has been hidden being revealed is a common topos in Jewish wisdom and apocalyptic literature.[91] However, such a *concentration* of thematic and material parallels to the Gospel of Thomas in one section of Colossians is significant and must be explained. Coincidence due to the mutual use of common wisdom topoi should be ruled out for at least two important reasons.

First, on the surface, there is little or nothing that thematically links (a) the seeking of heavenly things over against earthly things with (b) the future revealing of what is presently hidden, (c) the importance of not lying to others, and (d) the concept of the Christ being the All (or "all things" in a universal sense). Yet, the author of Colossians collects and or-

---

seem to favor inclusion, but not strongly. Against τά, (a) the lack of an article in Col 3:11 could be indicated by the lack of an article in Gal 3:28 and 1 Cor 12:13 (but πάντα has a different referent in those two texts and does not have the cosmic or universal meaning it has in Col 3:11), and either (b) the τά was accidentally included due to the influence of Col 3:8 (but again, the use of πάντα is different there), or (c) scribes were influenced by Col 1:16, 17. In favor of τά, (d) the use of τὰ πάντα in Col 1:16, 17 (and Phil 3:21; 1 Cor 8:5-6; 15:28; etc.) could be an indication of the author's preference for τά in the cosmic/universalistic use of πάντα (so also Eph 1:23; 3:9; 4:10), and either (e) τά was later omitted for doctrinal reasons (because of Gnostic use of "the All"—but why then does ℵ² restore it; to preserve the reading of the exemplar?) or (f) it was omitted due to haplography (ΑΛΛΑΤΑΠΑΝΤΑ).

91. On Wisdom revealing what was hidden, see, e.g., Sir 4:18; Wis 6:12; 7:21-22. It is particularly striking, and unfortunate, that older literature devoted to Thomas virtually ignores Jewish wisdom literature when considering the interpretive background of GTh 77, highlighting instead its supposedly pantheistic or "panchristic" gnostic hermeneutic. Cf. Fitzmyer, "Oxyrhynchus *Logoi*," 540; Grant and Freedman, *Secret Sayings,* 69-72. Geraint Jones not only overlooks the wisdom background to Thomas and Colossians, but he also demonstrates an obvious canonical bias in dealing with GTh 77: "It is a kind of parable of the omnipresence of Christ, which is hardly to be distinguished from pantheism, for according to the preceding clauses Jesus is the source and end of all, but in a different sense from Col. 1.15 ff, though the 'panchristicism' of the latter is *dangerously* near to that of Thomas" [emphasis mine] (Jones, "Parables," 236). How Col 1:16-17 differs conceptually from GTh 77 escapes me. Such a narrow focus on pantheism may have been acceptable following Eduard Norden's work on the Stoic understanding of τὰ πάντα (though no one mentioned above cites him), but certainly not after Pöhlmann's study on the adaptation of Greek philosophical concepts in Jewish wisdom literature (particularly on the All-predications) as it pertains to the background of Col 1:15-20, and James M. Robinson's study of the genre "words of the wise," especially as it pertains to the Gospel of Thomas. See Norden, *Agnostos Theos,* esp. 240-50; Pöhlmann, "All-Prädikationen," 53-74; Robinson, "LOGOI SOPHON." The ignoring of Jewish wisdom in studies of Thomas is slowly being corrected. See, e.g., S. L. Davies, *Gospel of Thomas.*

ganizes all of these concepts in Col 3:1–11 for the purpose of kerygmatic, post-baptismal instruction, while these *four* concepts are also found side-by-side in only *two* sections of Thomas, GTh 6:2–6 and 76:3—77:1.

Second, not only is the underlying concept the same in each pair of similarities, but three of the four parallel texts are similar *in form*: (a) GTh 76:3 and Col 3:1–2 are admonitions; (c) GTh 6:2 and Col 3:9 are negative imperatives, or prohibitions; and (d) GTh 77:1 and Col 3:11b are sentences on Jesus'/the Christ's cosmic identity. In (b), GTh 6:5's simple aphoristic form is not found in the two sentences of Col 3:3–4, but both GTh 6:4–6 and Col 3:3–4 function in their respective texts as motives for previous admonitions. Given the variability in the form and function of Jesus' teachings in literary redaction and oral tradition, the similarity of forms exhibited in these two texts—a collection of sometimes elaborate sayings clusters (Thomas) and the exhortatory section of a letter (Colossians)—argues for a source relationship.

For these reasons, coincidental use of common topoi is unlikely and a plausible explanation should be found for these formal, conceptual and verbal parallels. I see several possibilities.

1. The two documents reflect use of a common baptismal creedal tradition.
2. Both documents quote from a lost Jewish wisdom or apocalyptic book.
3. Sayings of Jesus in Thomas were constructed from the teachings of Colossians.
4. The two texts reflect the use of a common source of sayings of Jesus.
5. The author of Colossians constructed 3:1–11 using sayings of Jesus found in the Gospel of Thomas.

A Common Creedal Tradition

A common baptismal creedal tradition is not likely because it does not explain the diversity of elements used in such close proximity in both Colossians and Thomas. Furthermore, the All-predication of Col 3:11b must be explained, since πᾶς has a different referent in Gal 3:28 and 1 Cor 12:13, both of which are considered to be older Pauline adaptations of the creed.

A Lost Jewish Wisdom and/or Apocalyptic Book

Postulating a lost Jewish wisdom or apocalyptic text is problematic for the first reason given above: the diversity of content in close proximity within larger texts.[92] Also, it does not explain the specific prohibition against lying being isolated in Colossians 3 from potentially tens or hundreds of negative admonitions that are found in such sapiential documents as Proverbs, Wisdom of Ben Sira, Wisdom of Solomon, or Q. Though improper speech is a common topos in wisdom literature, specific types of improper speech are manifold (gossip, foolish talk, wordiness, verbal abuse, belittling, loudness, quarreling, ill-timed talk, habitual oath-taking, slander, course language, etc.[93]). More decisively, comparison with the synoptic tradition suggests that GTh 6:5–6 and 76:3, and the forms they take, are based on a sayings of Jesus tradition, not a hypothetical lost wisdom text.[94]

Thomas' Use of Colossians

It might be assumed, because Colossians and Thomas both have prohibitions against lying and an All-predication referring to Jesus—both of which are virtually unknown elsewhere in the New Testament—that Thomas has read and borrowed from Colossians. Because GTh 6:5–6 and 76:3 are derived from a sayings tradition, however, it is less likely that the Thomas parallels are sayings of Jesus constructed from the teachings of Colossians. One must assume that Thomas strips the material in Colossians of much of its kerygmatic content in the construction of more esoteric sayings using primarily this one, particularly kerygma-laden passage in Colossians and virtually ignoring the rest of the letter with its many references to the *gnosis, epignosis,* and *mysterion* of God (as well

---

92. The closest combinations of themes I have found are the following in the Wisdom of Solomon:

Wisdom as a "treasure":	7:13–14	Wisdom and the All:	8:1, 5
Wisdom revealing what is hidden:	7:21–22	Wisdom as "wealth":	8:5, 18
Wisdom and the All:	7:24–27	Seeking Wisdom:	8:18

93. The last two are found in the vice list of Col 3:8.

94. For a brief discussion of the different versions of GTh 6:5–6, see Funk et al., *Five Gospels,* 475–77. The Jesus Seminar voted for GTh 6:5 as an authentic saying of Jesus, but was divided on 6:6. The idea of God revealing what is hidden may be common enough, but the form of the statement is not. On the forms of GTh 5 and 6, see Johnson, "The Hidden/Revealed Saying."

as its popular philosophical and potentially gnostic concepts such as the *Pleroma*, the *Stoicheia*, and the visible *image* of the *invisible (unknown) God)*. None of this latter material in Colossians is found in Thomas.[95] A viable alternative, that the composer of Col 3:1–11 took more general sayings tradition material and incorporated it into a structured paraenesis focused around kerygmatic, baptismal teaching, seems to me to be much more plausible from the perspective of tradition history. It also makes sense of the problems discussed in the previous section of this study.[96]

A Common Sayings Source

I see two viable options remaining: either Thomas and Colossians represent the use of a common sayings tradition, or the author of Colossians used the Gospel of Thomas. Deciding between these options with any degree of certainty would be impossible.

The main difficulty with a common source for the two texts—its hypothetical nature—is mitigated by the generally accepted existence of numerous collections or traditions of Jesus' teachings that developed and circulated in the first century. Following standard New Testament historical criticism, a number of no longer existing collections have been identified in the gospels, including but not limited to Q, Matthew's parable source, Luke's parable source, and collections used in Mark 4 and Mark 12. As argued in Chapter 1, the undisputed letters of Paul also provide evidence of otherwise unknown oral or written sayings sources.

---

95. As noted above (p. 109, n. 88), the only other clear parallels between Colossians and Thomas are GTh 53//Col 2:11 (but cf. Rom 2:25–29) and GTh 77:1//Col 1:16, 17.

96. One could speculate that a redactor of Thomas read the Christ Hymn in Col 1:15–20, noticed the related identity statement of Col 3:11b, and combined Col 1:16–17 and 3:11b into GTh 77:1. Then the redactor noticed the prohibition against lying in Col 3:9 and observed the similar conceptuality of Col 3:1–4 in GTh 6:5–6 and 76:3, and so got the idea to expand the brief chreia elaboration of GTh 6:2–6 with the prohibition against lying, perhaps complimenting an already existing prohibition against doing what one does not like, and then attached the new logion about Jesus' identity to Thomas 76. This speculative reconstruction has a couple of problems associated with it, however. First, why would the composer of Thomas place 77:1 after 76:3—to interpret the treasure as Jesus himself? The author of John may have interpreted the close association of sayings in this way, but juxtaposing the two texts with this in mind conflicts with the rest of the Gospel of Thomas, which clearly does not advocate seeking *Jesus*. Second, the expansion of GTh 6:2–6 only makes sense if the prohibition of 6:3 already existed there—and we don't know this.

Nevertheless, the hypothesis of a common sayings source is akin to the Q hypothesis, and that makes it problematic. The Q hypothesis is based on the comparison of texts of like genre—the synoptic gospels. The material of Q is primarily identified, in both Matthew and Luke, as sayings of Jesus. There is a substantial amount of material to work from, and if their use of Mark is indicative, Matthew and Luke arguably use most of Q as well. Thomas and Colossians are of different genres, even though the parallel material is found in the exhortatory section of Colossians. The material for comparison is only identified as sayings material in Thomas—the teachings of Colossians are ostensibly Pauline. And there are only four parallels available for comparison. Presumably, a common sayings source would have significantly more material to work from, but this is not in evidence when comparing Thomas and Colossians. Of course, a number of sayings from a common source could have been taken up in one or the other of the texts—this surely happened in Matthew and Luke with regard to Q. But without a substantial hypothetical document like Q to serve as a backdrop, such an assumption cannot be made when arguing for a common source.

Colossians' Use of Thomas

If the studies reviewed in the first chapter of this dissertation accurately reflect the transmission and redaction history of some of the sayings of Jesus found in the Gospel of Thomas, then had the author of Colossians used a text or tradition reflected in Thomas, it is surely the case that this source differed to some degree from the gospel found in the Nag Hammadi codices. What the shape and extent of a Thomas text or tradition may have looked like in the first century remains mostly unknown at this stage in biblical scholarship. Therefore, it is impossible to claim outright that the author of Colossians used the "Gospel of Thomas" as we know it. Rather, one can only suggest that the author may have used a text or sayings tradition like or akin in form to the extant gospel.

At the same time, if an early compiler or composer of Thomas is responsible for the sayings cluster in GTh 6:2–6 and the contiguity of sayings in GTh 76:3—77:1, and these associations are not a random result of the collection and transmission of otherwise disparate materials, then one has evidence of a primitive Thomasine sayings collection. In other words, these clusterings point to a sayings tradition that has grouped sayings material in a manner reflected only in the Gospel of Thomas among early Christian documents. There is certainly not enough evidence in these few sayings to suggest a collection that reflects a distinctively Thomasine theology or hermeneutic. There is, on the other hand, enough evidence to at least suggest a Jewish wisdom orientation to the collection as a whole.[97]

The differences between the fourth and fifth options are perhaps semantic. If Colossians and Thomas represent use of a common sayings source, then it is a collection that has already begun to develop along the lines of the extant Gospel of Thomas. If one speaks of Colossians reflecting use of Thomas, then it must be clarified that the "Gospel of Thomas" so used was a more primitive version of what currently is known to exist. In neither case can one definitively argue that the author of Colossians made use of either a written text or oral tradition.

That Colossians has made use of such a sayings collection, however, is supported by further analysis. Figure 14 presents two known versions of the Treasure in Heaven saying of Jesus alongside of Col 3:1–2 (see the following page).

At first glance it might appear that Col 3:1–2 is similar to the Treasure in Heaven saying in concept alone—the instruction to seek what is heavenly and abiding over against what is earthly and temporal. There are few verbal parallels to the gospel versions, the exceptions being the parallel to GTh 76:3 with the imperative "to seek" (ζητεῖτε; ϢΙΝΕ ⲚⲤⲀ), the parallel to Matt 6:19 with "upon the earth" (ἐπὶ τῆς γῆς), and the adverbs of location in all three texts, ὅπου, οὗ, and ⲠⲘⲀ, translated "where." However, certain of these verbal parallels become more significant with the observation that all three texts include a further locative qualification to the "treasure(s)" or the "things above" (Colossians—"where Christ is, seated at the right hand of God"; Thomas and Q—adversity clauses). Taken together with the admonitory nature and conceptual similarity of the three texts, it appears that the author of Colossians has incorporated the Treasure saying into the paraenetic section of the letter.

---

97. It would, therefore, not be coincidence that this orientation toward the Jewish wisdom tradition is shared by the author of Colossians, especially as both texts reflect a Middle Platonic cosmology as well.

Figure 14: Col 3:1-2; GTh 76:3; and Q 12:33

Col 3:1-2	GTh 76:3	Q 12:33 (IQP, 1995)
Εἰ οὖν συνηγέρθητε τῷ Χριστῷ, τὰ ἄνω ζητεῖτε, οὗ ὁ Χριστός ἐστιν ἐν δεξιᾷ τοῦ θεοῦ καθήμενος· ² τὰ ἄνω φρονεῖτε, μὴ τὰ ἐπὶ τῆς γῆς.	ⲚⲦⲰⲦⲚ ϨⲰⲦ ⲐⲎⲨⲦⲚ ϢⲒⲚⲈ ⲚⲤⲀ Ⲡ{Ⲉϥ}ⲈϨⲞ ⲈⲘⲀϤⲰⲬⲚ ⲈϤⲘⲎⲚ ⲈⲂⲞⲖ ⲠⲘⲀ ⲈⲘⲀⲢⲈ ϪⲞⲞⲖⲈⲤ ⲦϨⲚⲞ ⲈϨⲞⲨⲚ ⲈⲘⲀⲨ ⲈⲞⲨⲰⲘ ⲞⲨⲆⲈ ⲘⲀⲢⲈ {ϥ}ϤⲚⲦ ⲦⲀⲔⲞ.	(μὴ θησαυρίζετε ὑμῖν θησαυροὺς ἐπὶ τῆς γῆς, ὅπου σὴς καὶ βρῶσις ἀφανίζει καὶ ὅπου κλέπται διορύσσουσιν καὶ κλέπτουσιν.) θησαυρίζετε ὑμῖν θησαυροὺς ἐν οὐρανοῖς, ὅπου οὔτε σὴς οὔτε βρῶσις ἀφανίζει καὶ ὅπου κλέπται οὐ διορύσσουσιν οὐδὲ κλέπτουσιν.
¹ So if you have been raised with Christ, seek the things that are above, where Christ is, seated at the right hand of God. ² Set your minds on things above, not on things that are on earth.	You also, seek the treasure that does not perish, that abides, where no moth comes to eat and no worm destroys.	(Do not treasure up treasures on the earth, where moth and eating thing destroy and where thieves dig through and steal.) But treasure up treasures for yourselves in (the) heavens, where neither moth nor eating thing destroys and where thieves do not dig through and steal.

If the construction of Col 3:1–11 is analyzed with the Thomas parallels in mind, one can see how sayings material was used by the author. Colossians 3:1–4 would have consisted of two basic elements—sayings of Jesus akin to GTh 76:3 and 6:4–6, and an elaboration of Pauline thought concerning the relationship between baptism and kerygma. Figure 15 underlines this mixing of materials:

Figure 15: Tradition and Redaction in Col 3:1–4

Kerygmatic Additions and Reformulations	Traditional Sayings Reformulated
¹ So if you have been raised with Christ (Col 2:12; cf. Rom 6:4),	
	seek the things that are above, where
Christ is, seated at the right hand of God (Ps 110:1). ² Set your minds on things that are above, not on things that are on earth (Phil 3:19–20), ³ for you have died (Col 2:20) and your life	
	[what] has been hidden
with Christ in God. ⁴ When Christ who is your life is revealed, then you also	
	will be revealed
with him in glory (Rom 8:18–23).	

In Col 3:1a, the author explicitly roots the motive for seeking the higher things in the kerygmatic soteriology of being raised with Christ, employing a conditional if-then construction. The author later returns to this baptismal motive in 3:3 with the use of a γάρ clause. While the author replaces the Thomasine "treasure" with τὰ ἄνω, omits Thomas' two asyndetic qualifiers ("which does not perish, which abides"), and omits reference to the earthly agents of destruction (moths and worms), one can still detect the influence of the asyndeton and the locative reference of the Thomas saying in Figure 16 (see the following page).

The overall three-part qualification of Thomas' treasure is roughly retained, if not in the same form, then in Colossians' repeated reference to the location of the things to be sought—"things that are above," "where Christ is," and "seated at the right hand of God." Thomas' reference to earthly agents appears to be replaced by Colossians' "things that are upon the earth."

Figure 16: Col 3:1-2 and GTh 76:3

Col 3:1-2	GTh 76:3
¹ So if you have been raised with Christ, seek the things (τά) that are above (ἄνω), where Christ is, seated at the right hand of God. ² Set your minds on things that are above, not on things that are on earth.	So also with you, seek the treasure which is unfailing, which remains, where no moth comes to eat and no worm destroys.

Colossians 3:2 is a restatement of the traditional saying, further defining ζητέω through φρονέω and adding an earthly counterpart to τὰ ἄνω. If Colossians is post-Pauline, then one can also see the influence of Phil 3:19–20 in this verse, though the vocabulary is unique to Colossians.[98]

The saying behind Col 3:3–4 is less obvious, since it is embedded in two different sentences, the first being the motive clause for 3:2 and the second continuing the thought of the first while interpreting the relevance of the Parousia. With this expansion, Colossians explicates what remains enigmatic in the saying of Jesus and unspoken in Romans 8—it also prevents esoteric interpretation of the saying of Jesus by focusing on the kerygma.

The nature of τὰ ἐπὶ τῆς γῆς in Col 3:2 is then interpreted in Col 3:5–8. The earthly "members" are defined by standard vice lists in 3:5 and 3:8, and these lists are separated by even more eschatological elaboration in 3:6–7. Each vice list follows an imperative cast in a positive form—that is, without μή ("put to death" and "put away")—that derives from the *implied* negative imperative of 3:2. It is not until Col 3:9 that the author exhorts the hearers with a single, explicit negative imperative (μὴ ψεύδεσθε εἰς ἀλλήλους). The prohibition form in Col 3:9a sets it apart as distinctive teaching from the admonitions that precede the vice lists, even though the goal of 3:5–8 is to prohibit certain behavior and the list of Col 3:8 ends with slander and obscene language. The prohibition is supported

---

98. Sanders argues that the use of ἐπὶ τῆς γῆς, ἐν τοῖς οὐρανοῖς, and ἄνω as substantives with the article τά is distinctive of Colossians ("Literary Dependence," 36–37, nn. 15, 16; 44 n. 31).

by yet another motive clause in 3:9b–10, a metaphorical reference to the different nature of the post-baptismal life. While the kerygma is lacking in Thomas, the two imperatives in Thomas (76:3; 6:2) paralleled in Colossians (3:1, 9a) are both supported in Colossians by motive clauses grounded in the author's eschatology (3:3–4) and theology of baptism (3:9b–10).

The passage as a whole—and the reference of Col 3:11a to communal unification in baptism in particular—is summed up in the christological statement "Christ is the All (τὰ πάντα) and is in all (ἐν πᾶσιν)." This final statement not only epitomizes the high Christology of the entire letter, but also provides legitimation to the claim of 3:11a and serves as a linchpin to the subsequent positive admonitions of 3:12–17.

Yet, interpretation of the sayings material is not yet complete. If τὰ ἐπὶ τῆς γῆς is interpreted by the vice lists in Col 3:5 and 3:8, then the nature of τὰ ἄνω is interpreted by the virtue list of 3:12 and the subsequent exhortations of 3:13–17. These are the things that one should seek; or to be more specific, these are the things that one should set one's mind on.

A result of this analysis is the observation that while *all four* of the Thomas parallels in Colossians are integrated into a kerygma-based, post-baptismal exhortation, three of these parallels still stand out as distinctive and critical elements in the construction of the passage. The first is the keynote imperative to the hortatory half of the letter. The third stands out as the sole negative imperative of Col 3:5–17, and one of only six in the entire letter. The fourth expresses, even more summarily than the so-called Christ Hymn of 1:15–20, the author's understanding of the pervasive influence of the Christ in the cosmos. Ironically, the sections of Col 3:1–11 that scholars have poured over and sought out cultural and literary sources for (3:5, 8, 9b–11a) turn out to contain merely supportive material for the previously unidentified sayings of Jesus material. The vice and virtue lists are used to interpret "earthly things" and the "things above," while the baptismal formula of 3:9b–10 is used as a rationale for why one should not lie.

Colossians 3:1–2 and Thomas 76:3

From the foregoing analysis, several preliminary inferences can be made. First, since the author of Colossians appears to have used GTh 76:3 for the construction of 3:1–11, then Colossians' use of ζητέω in 3:1 argues for the antiquity of the Thomas version of the Treasure in Heaven saying relative to the synoptic tradition (as represented by Q 12:33). There is no good reason to assume that Colossians was not written sometime soon after the death of Paul and the destruction of Colossae (the latter dated to 60–61 CE). Certainly, it had to be written before Ephesians, which uses Colossians extensively, and a generation before the Pastoral Epistles, which exhibit substantial differences in theology and developments in ecclesial polity. This dates the Thomas version of the Treasure saying comfortably in the 60s or 70s.[99]

Second, the presence of the phrase ἐπὶ τῆς γῆς in an implied prohibition in Col 3:2, a phrase also found in the prohibition of Matt 6:19, could be an indication that a prohibition existed in Colossians' source, and at some later point was replaced in Thomas with the Parable of the Pearl. However, it would need to be established that Matthew's prohibition came from Q and not from Matthean redaction. Furthermore, the heavenly or abiding focus of the saying leaves an earthly, temporal contrast implicit, and the moth/worm images of the traditional saying in Thomas further encourage an explicit contrast of the eternal vs. the ephemeral; so this conclusion cannot be certain.[100]

Third, it has been demonstrated in Chapters 2 and 3 that a saying of Jesus can be applied to a specific gospel narrative context, limiting the saying's range of hermeneutical possibilities (Mark 10:17–21; John 6:26–34). James 5:2–3 and Col 3:1–17 provide epistolary examples of how authoritative teachings can be adapted in paraenesis to specific theological points of view. With regard to Col 3:1–2, even more can be said. It is striking that the Treasure saying, relegated to an attachment to the Free from Anxiety like Ravens and Lilies pericope in Q, is used in modified form as the keynote saying both to John's Bread of Life Discourse *and* to Colossians' hortatory half of the letter. Furthermore, in both cases, the modified saying is further interpreted by subsequent elaboration. In the case of John, 6:28–34 explicates what is implicit in the

---

99. See Pokorny, *Colossians*, 10–21, for a discussion of the authorship and date of Colossians.

100. If Sanders is correct that the use of ἐπὶ τῆς γῆς, ἐν τοῖς οὐρανοῖς, and ἄνω as substantives with the article τά is distinctive of Colossians (see above, p. 119 n. 98), then this stylistic preference of the author provides a rationale for some of the differences between Col 3:1–2 and GTh 76:3. It is *not* likely an indication that ἐπὶ τῆς γῆς and ἐν τοῖς οὐρανοῖς existed in the source for Col 3:1–2, since there is no obvious reason for the author to have replaced ἐν τοῖς οὐρανοῖς with τὰ ἄνω.

language of 6:27—"working" is believing and the "food" is Jesus. In the case of Colossians, "seeking" is clarified as "setting one's mind upon," and "the things above," as opposed to the "things of the earth," are defined in 3:12–17 as virtuous attitudes and actions. Unlike the Gospel of John, however, I do not see in Colossians an attack on Thomasine soteriology. The soteriology of Colossians, being rooted in the kerygma, is no doubt different from Thomas. But the soteriology of Colossians is also a realized eschatology, and Colossians 1–2 is saturated with sapiential and, perhaps, "proto-gnostic" concepts and terminology. The Christ Hymn is only one example of this.

Fourth, all of the parallel Thomas-Colossians material we have observed finds a ready home in Jewish wisdom literature, and Colossians and Thomas both contain substantially more wisdom themes than the parallel texts in question. On the level of common generic and thematic materials, then, it makes sense that the author of Colossians could utilize and adapt elements of a Thomas-like sayings collection. Furthermore, if there is a common thread that connects Colossians with Thomas and, indirectly, with John, it is the wisdom tradition understanding of "treasure" as a metaphor not for wealth, but for something completely different. As shown in Chapter 3, GTh 76:3 sees the treasure as a metaphor for something hidden—perhaps wisdom, spiritual gnosis, or truth—which is to be sought in the here and now. The author of John, fully acquainted with the personified Wisdom tradition of interpretation and in accordance with a program of interpreting Wisdom as Jesus (if John's Prologue is an indication), reinterprets the Thomas version of the saying along these lines. Colossians reinterprets the Thomas saying by embedding it in a kerygmatic, post-baptismal instruction on how to live the spiritual life. In none of these cases is there even the hint that the saying addresses the individual's attitude and actions regarding earthly wealth.[101]

Summary

Both Jas 5:2–3 and Col 3:1–2 provide first-century CE examples of the Treasure in Heaven saying. By logical extension, this means that their sources were first-century sources as well. This has implications for the dating of the Thomas version especially. Both versions are developments

---

101. Even the fifth vice in Col 3:5, "greed," in the context of the other vices would seem to have a sexual content akin to "desiring someone else's spouse."

from more primitive sayings forms. James uses a version most similar to Q and Matthew. Colossians uses a version most similar to Thomas. Like Q and Matthew, James understands the saying as referring literally to the disposition of wealth. Like Thomas, Colossians interprets the saying metaphorically. Like John, the saying itself is greatly modified and further interpreted by subsequent text. Both epistolary versions, like their sources, develop a separate Jewish wisdom theme—this will be discussed in the next chapter.

CHAPTER 5 | Inferences and Reconstruction of an Archetype

Dating GTh 76:3 and Q 12:33

The findings of Chapter 3 indicate that the Thomas saying must have existed prior to the writing of Luke and John, which means that the saying can reasonably be dated to ca. 100 CE at the latest. If Paul did not write Colossians late in his career (which would put Colossians squarely in the early 60s at the latest), then it was probably written between 65 and 90 CE, after the death of Paul and the destruction of Colossae, and before the writing of Ephesians. If Colossians 3:1–11 is founded upon, among other sources, a pre-existing collection of sayings, then the Thomas form of the Treasure saying can reasonably be dated—*at the very latest*—to between 60 and 85 CE.

The adoption of Q into Matthew dates it as a written document prior to ≈80–90 CE. Further considerations (which can be found in most introductions to Q) place the Q document closer to 70 CE or earlier. However, most Q scholars agree that the document as we know it from Matthew and Luke expanded over time. Dating Q 12:33 is a difficult proposition. John Kloppenborg includes it in his earliest stratum of Q in conjunction with the Q pericope Free from Anxiety like Ravens and Lilies (Q 12:22–31). This would date the saying to perhaps 50–70 CE.[1] It is more closely related in theme to this speech than to what follows in Q 12:39–40. At the same time, it is not actually a part of the speech, and it may reflect a different social location for its implied audience.[2] Even if

---

1. Kloppenborg, *Formation*, 221–23.
2. Kloppenborg states that "there is no eschatological motivation to the saying. Its

Hartin is correct that James has used the Q tradition prior to Q's incorporation into Matthew, this does not help to date the Treasure saying. It is impossible to say with certainty whether James used a written or oral collection of sayings; sayings material from both of Kloppenborg's two main strata is represented in James. The best one can suggest for Q 12:33 is a date between 30 and 70 CE.

How Early a Written Thomas Collection?

Throughout this dissertation I have tried to be careful about how I have characterized the first century Gospel of Thomas—usually referring to it as a collection or tradition of sayings of Jesus. This has been intentional. Now is the time to address the question of its oral or literary existence by sifting what little circumstantial evidence can be gleaned from this study and presenting it in an orderly fashion.

The most important datum for the existence of a written collection comes from Luke. It is almost certain that Luke used two *written* versions of the Treasure saying (Q and Mark) in constructing Luke 12:33. Luke 1:1 indicates knowledge of "many . . . orderly accounts" that have been written. Luke does not appear to be countering another oral interpretive tradition (i.e., "community") when using GTh 76:3 to reconstruct Q 12:33. By implication, it seems plausible to suggest that Luke could have used a third written text as well—one that includes GTh 76:3. A second datum is the finding that the Thomas tradition of the Treasure saying was used by three different authors (Colossians, John, and Luke) in the composition of their texts. Unless a schema can be constructed to explain this phenomenon on the basis of oral transmission theory, it can be compared to the written text of Q 12:33 being used in at least two different texts

---

structure and argumentation as well as its immediate context identify it as sapiential" (*Formation*, 222; Kloppenborg cites Bultmann, *History*, 104; Percy, *Botschaft*, 91). Q 12:33 may be sapiential, but it is also eschatological, promising a future heavenly reward for present behavior. Wisdom literature, such as Tobit and Ben Sira, promises good things for those who act wisely, but the rewards are usually in this life. Also, whereas Q 12:22–31 does not presuppose access to or ability to accumulate wealth—it seems more concerned with elements of survival—Q 12:33 does. Arland Jacobson concludes: "The fact that it uses traditional language means that it is probably hazardous to propose that it reflects some special circumstance in the life of the community. In fact, there seems to be nothing in the saying which would help locate it within the compositional history of Q" (Jacobson, *First Gospel*, 193).

(Matthew and Luke). Secondary evidence comes from the use of sayings in Col 3:1–11 found side-by-side in two sections of Thomas.

There are several problems with this evidence. First, the Gospel of Thomas, even as it stands in the fourth century manuscript and despite its extensive use of the chreia rhetorical form, does not appear to be an "orderly account." Luke 1:2 reveals knowledge of pervasive oral traditions in addition to written sources. Second, the evidence above does not require a written source; it only suggests the possibility. Recourse to explanations for why the authors of Luke, John, and Colossians have altered GTh 76:3 apply equally to literary redaction and free use of oral tradition.

The most important evidence against the use of a written collection of sayings is the way in which Colossians and John have modified the saying. One of the two most important arguments for the existence of a written Q document is the extensive verbatim agreement between Matthean and Lukan versions of individual sayings, agreements that cover extensive sections of Q.[3] The versions of the saying in Colossians and John contain important verbal parallels to GTh 76:3, but not extensive ones. This is true for Col 3:3–4//GTh 6:4–6 as well. This is also the primary difficulty with assuming that James used a written text of Q.

Perhaps the best evidence for the use of oral traditions is John's apparent argument with a Thomasine soteriology that can be implied by the Treasure saying. I have argued that it is at least plausible that the author had an anti-Thomasine redactional interest as well as a positive Johannine interest in reworking the Thomas saying. Since the Treasure saying in Thomas does not require an enlightenment soteriology for its interpretation, John would likely be countering a known interpretation of a existing community. Second, there is a growing recognition in biblical scholarship that oral traditions were more authoritative in the first century than has been traditionally recognized. Third, while this study has uncovered some kind of a Thomasine sayings collection behind Col 3:1–11, other parallels between Thomas and John, and parallels between Thomas and Luke that cannot be explained by Luke's use of Q and Mark, are scattered throughout the two gospel texts. Even if one could establish that each of these parallels in Luke and John came from using Thomas (and recent studies noted in Chapter 1 show otherwise in isolated cases),

---

3. The other key argument is the substantial agreement in the order of sayings and clusters.

there is no apparent order to Lukan use of Thomas when Lukan parallels are compared to those found in the four extant manuscripts of Thomas. Luke substantially retains the order of Markan and Q material, but this would not be the case for the order of Thomas material.

As with arguments for a written version of GTh 76:3 in the first century, the arguments for an orally-transmitted collection are only circumstantial and suggestive. First, John's stand against a different tradition of interpretation does not preclude the existence of a written text known to the author. Second, oral traditions certainly could be authoritative, and were pervasive in the first century, but the notion of "oral traditions" can be used as a catch-all term for any sayings traditions or collections that cannot be proven to be literary. The notion that written sayings "lists" were pervasive seems equally plausible, as does the notion of small written sayings collections. Third, the ostensibly random nature of Thomas militates against Luke using even a written text in an orderly fashion. The Gospel of Mark forms the narrative base for the Gospel of Luke while Q provides a number of orderly pericopae that are fit into the Markan framework. The extant manuscripts of Thomas show no overall narrative framework and the internal coherence of individual logia is not often readily perceptible. Hence, random application of tradition is no sure argument that the Thomasine source for Luke was oral in nature. In the case of the Treasure saying, Luke is clearly using the Q text as a base—this is clear from the Q position of the saying. Therefore it tells us nothing of the nature of the Thomas sayings collection. On the contrary, the Sayings Gospel Q was a mid- to late-first century written sayings collection. Its probable existence as a written document is evidence for the plausibility of a contemporary written Gospel of Thomas as well.

To summarize, there is no decisive evidence for Luke, John, or Colossians using either a written text or an oral tradition of which GTh 76:3 was a part. Substantially more evidence is needed to make such a determination. In my opinion, it is extremely unlikely that the Gospel of Thomas was only first put to papyrus in the mid- to late-second century. By the end of the second century, it was known from Edessa (Book of Thomas, though the date of BTh is debated) to Rome (Hippolytus and the Naassenes) to Upper Egypt (Oxyrhynchus). I think it is safe to assume that a written collection was already widely circulating at the turn of the first century. On the basis of the evidence presented here, any earlier dating of a written text is necessarily conjectural, but not unlikely.

Practical Wisdom versus Esoteric Wisdom

All of the versions of the Treasure saying reflect a development in wisdom literature from the second century BCE forward, wherein future concerns for personal welfare extend beyond one's present existence. In Ben Sira and Tobit, for example, one still sees a present lifetime orientation. Wise and pious action will benefit the individual in *this* lifetime. The Wisdom of Solomon represents a significant change, however, in stressing the gift of individual immortality. A future, increasingly eschatological orientation comes to dominate wisdom literature. This future life perspective underlies the Treasure saying in all of its manifestations.

A significant finding of this study is the observation of two divergent topoi in the Jewish wisdom tradition operating in the transmission and interpretation of the Treasure saying. The first topos is that of the wise and pious treatment of wealth and the benefits of such action. The second topos concerns the search for divine Wisdom, who gives from her treasures and is herself a treasure. Both topoi are developed in different ways, depending on the text in which the Treasure saying is used.

The first topos is played out in the four synoptic versions and James. All of these versions address one's treatment of wealth and the heavenly reward (or punishment—James) that results. The attitude towards or disposition of wealth dominates each of the versions. This topos is especially evident in the Wisdom of Ben Sira and Tobit. In Ben Sira, for example, one is exhorted to gives alms to others: almsgiving atones for sins (3:30–31); it is rewarded by God (17:22); it rescues one from disaster (29:11–12). While, generally speaking, wealth is a good thing to have, storing up treasures and not spending them renders them useless. Ben Sira even asks the following question in two different places (20:30; 41:14): "Hidden wisdom and unseen treasure, of what value is either?" Tobit similarly argues:

> If you have many possessions, make your gift from them in proportion; if few, do not be afraid to give according to the little you have. So you will be laying up a good treasure for yourself against the day of necessity. For almsgiving delivers from death and keeps you from going into the Darkness. (Tob 4:8–10; NRSV)

Tobit 12:8–9 specifies in maxim form with motive clause that "it is better to give alms than to lay up gold. For almsgiving saves from death and purges away every sin." The ethic of helping others in need is certainly not unknown in the Hebrew Bible, even if almsgiving itself is never mentioned. Parallels in ethical perspective can also be found in Greek literature. Aristotle, for example, speaks of the value of liberality (ἐλευθεριότητος) over against the ethical Scylla and Charybdis of prodigality (ὑπερβολαί) and miserliness (ἐλλείψεις; *Eth. Nic.* IV).

Q 12:33 and Matt 6:19-20 argue against the storing up of earthly treasures in favor of storing up treasures in heaven. James 5:2-3 roundly condemns the rich with prophetic denunciation (see also 5:4-6). Mark 10:21 and Luke 12:33 go far beyond the ethic of liberal giving by requiring complete sacrifice of wealth on earth for the heavenly benefits to come.[4]

Common to GTh 76:3; John 6:27; and Col 3:1-2, in contrast to the synoptic versions and James, is the fact that none of them can be understood in their wider literary context as having anything to do with the disposition of earthly wealth.[5] Instead, the second wisdom topos is developed in these versions. Wisdom literature is replete with examples of this topos:

> If you seek [wisdom and understanding] like silver,
>> and search for it as for hidden treasures—
> then you will understand the fear of the LORD
>> and find the knowledge of God. (Prov 2:4; NRSV)

> I [Wisdom] love those who love me,
>> and those who seek me diligently find me.
> Riches and honor are with me,
>> enduring wealth and prosperity.
> My fruit is better than gold, even fine gold,
>> and my yield than choice silver. (Prov 8:17-19; NRSV)

> Wisdom teaches her children
>> and gives help to those who seek her. (Sir 4:11; NRSV)

---

4. Contemporary to these writings is 2 Esdr 7:76-77: "Do not include yourself with those who have shown scorn, or number yourself among those who are tormented. For you have a treasure of works stored up with the Most High, but it will not be shown to you until the last times."

5. This is especially ironic in the case of GTh 76, which has a parable about a merchant selling his cargo to buy a pearl preceding an admonition to seek after a treasure.

> Search out and seek,
>> and [Wisdom] will become known to you. (Sir 6:27; NRSV)

> Who has found [Wisdom's] place?
>> And who has entered her treasuries? (Bar 3:15; NRSV)

> Wisdom is radiant and unfading,
>> and she is easily discerned by those who love her,
>> and is found by those who seek her. (Wis 6:12; NRSV)

> I do not hide [Wisdom's] wealth,
>> for it is an unfailing treasure for people;
> those who get it obtain friendship with God . . . (Wis 7:13b–14b; NRSV)

> If riches are a desirable possession in life,
> what is richer than Wisdom,
>> the active cause of all things (τὰ πάντα)? (Wis 8:5; NRSV)

> Wisdom was given to Israel,
>> and He measures it out generously,
> and He redeems all His people,
>> but kills those who reject . . .
> nor should the braggarts say,
>> "Truly we have found it by ourselves."
> Seek it, and you will find it. (4Q185 2.10–12)

> Blessed are those who see [Torah/Wisdom] with pure hands,
>> and do not search for it with a deceitful heart.
> Blessed is the man who attains wisdom,
>> and walks in the law of the Most High. (4Q525 2.2.2–4)[6]

GTh 76:3 should be understood within this interpretive framework. The "treasure" in the Thomas saying is not specified, however, which leaves open the question of its nature. Thus far I have tried to avoid giving an opinion on the identification of the Thomasine treasure because I am

---

6. Dead Sea Scroll translations are from Wise et al., *The Dead Sea Scrolls: A New Translation*, 243, 424.

not sure where this saying lies on the historical and conceptual continuum between early Jewish wisdom literature and emerging (pro- or anti-) Jewish-Christian forms of gnostic esoterism, as influenced by popular philosophy. Indeed, interpretation of the "treasure" probably changed over time and differed between tradent communities.

John 6:27 appears to have understood GTh 76:3 as a (wrongly directed) call to search for personified Wisdom. Considering the use of both GTh 76:3 and 77:1 in Col 3:1–11, it is plausible that the author of John found the two side-by-side as they now stand in the Gospel of Thomas.[7] Though GTh 76:3 may not have been interpreted in the light of 77:1 *in a Thomasine community*, the contiguity of the sayings may have suggested to John the reformulation and reinterpretation of GTh 76:3 as an exhortation to believe in Jesus, who in the Gospel of John (especially in the Prologue) embodies many of the attributes of personified Wisdom.

Colossians 3:1–2 recasts the abiding treasure of GTh 76:3 as the "things from above" (τὰ ἄνω), which come to be interpreted as the attributes of compassion, kindness, humility, meekness, patience, and love (Col 3:12, 14). As the "things from above" are located where Christ is seated (3:1), so one should also let the peace of Christ rule in the heart and the word of Christ dwell richly within, and teach and admonish one another in all *wisdom* (Col 3:15–16).[8]

Reconstructing a Pre-Q, Pre-Thomas, Treasure in Heaven Saying

If this study has demonstrated a very early Thomas version of the Treasure in Heaven saying of Jesus, one contemporary with the Sayings Gospel Q, it seems fitting to try to look behind these two texts for an archetype. To do so, a couple of issues must be considered. First, there is the issue of

---

7. The provenance of the initial I-saying in GTh 77:1, "I am the light that is over the All" (ⲁⲛⲟⲕ ⲡⲉ ⲡⲟⲩⲟⲉⲓⲛ ⲡⲁⲉⲓ ⲉⲧϨⲓϪⲱⲟⲩ ⲧⲏⲣⲟⲩ), has not been adequately explored, though Dunderberg argues that there is no literary relationship between GTh 76:3 and John 8:12, 9:5 ("I am the light of the cosmos"). He attributes the similarity of the sayings to "a common background in Wisdom Christology" (Dunderberg, "Thomas and the Beloved Disciple," 81–84).

8. Tertullian understands the "things above" as specifically referring to wisdom, as indicated by his citation of Col 3:1–2 in *Carnis res.* 23.4.13: "If you have risen with Christ, seek those things which are above, where Christ is seated at the right hand of God; *have that wisdom which is above*, not that which is below. Thus he shows that it is in mind we rise again, since it is with mind alone that we can as yet touch heavenly things."

which version is more in accord with other known sayings of Jesus. A few passages in Q speak of the Wisdom of God in relation to Jesus and much of the document contains sapiential didactic sayings. However, rarely if ever does Jesus appear to call on people to search for Wisdom or the knowledge of God. On the other hand, practical and specifically financial concerns are found throughout Q. In the Gospel of Thomas, while numerous sayings are understandable within a hermeneutic of the search for Wisdom or divine knowledge that saves from death, many sayings can also be seen to have had a more practical, everyday application in life. Therefore, it seems more likely that the Q hermeneutic of dealing practically with wealth, with the promise of eternal reward, is the hermeneutic closest to the teaching of Jesus. However, in reconstructing a more primitive version of this saying, one should seek a text which makes understandable the development of *both* texts and their hermeneutics. The practical orientation and interest of instruction like Q 12:22–31 may have led to minor modifications of the Treasure saying in this direction just as only minor alterations may have been necessary to fit the saying into a Thomasine hermeneutic. It seems most prudent to seek a version that best explains both developments.

This consideration leads to a second issue. The differences between the two sayings are significant enough that the content of one or the other or both must have changed in the course of transmission. It is possible that both versions have metamorphosed in so many ways that the reconstruction of a common archetype is impossible. However, the International Q Project and I have reconstructed Q 12:33 from Matt 6:19–20 and Luke 12:33 with very minor disagreements, and Matt 6:19–20 and Luke 12:33 are far more dissimilar than Q 12:33 and GTh 76:3. Therefore, an attempt should be made to reconstruct a more primitive archetype from which both texts may have developed.

There are three important caveats to this task. First is the hypothetical nature of both texts. Q 12:33 is a reconstruction from two gospel texts and GTh 76:3 is a Greek translation of the Coptic Nag Hammadi text. Hence, like those who have divided the hypothetical Q into foundational and redactional strata, this task must be undertaken at a level once removed from extant manuscripts. Second, while Q 12:33 is clearly imbedded in a larger text, a similar text cannot be assumed for the first century CE collection of sayings I am calling the Gospel of Thomas. The point of this study has been to focus on the Treasure saying alone. To bring in the

Inferences and Reconstruction of an Archetype | 133

whole of the Coptic Gospel of Thomas at this point is anachronistic. The only other first century sayings in Thomas that have been discerned from this study are GTh 6:2; 6:4–6; and 77:1. Hence, reference to other Thomas sayings must be tentative. Third, just as there can be no certainty that Luke, John, and Colossians used an early written text of Thomas, then barring other evidence to the contrary, there must be even less certainty of a written text behind Q and Thomas. Therefore, redaction-critical methods should only be used with some reservation.

I have placed the two sayings side-by-side in IQP style in order to align, and thus highlight, the commonalties of the texts ("minimal archetype," to coin and adapt an IQP expression). In the interest of space and time, in a couple of places I have conflated what should be distinct variants. Archetype⁵ should be broken down into two variants, θησαυρούς vs. θησαυρόν and a preceding article or no. Archetype¹² should be split into two variants by making the addition of οὐδὲ κλέπτω a separate variant.

Figure 17: Q 12:33 and GTh 76:3 (Greek)

Q	Thomas
( )¹	[ ]¹
(θησαυρίζετε)²	[ζητεῖτε]²
(«δὲ»)³	[καὶ]³
ὑμ(ῖν)⁴	ὑμ[εῖς]⁴
( )⁵ θησαυρο(ὺς)⁵	[τὸν]⁵ θησαυρὸ[ν]⁵
(ἐν οὐρανοῖς)⁶	[μὴ]⁶ [τὸν]⁵ [ἀπολλύμενο[ν]⁵]⁶
( )⁷,	[τὸν]⁵ [μένοντα]⁵]⁷,
ὅπου οὔ(τε)⁸ σῆς (οὔτε)⁸ βρῶσι(ς)⁸	ὅπου οὐ[]⁸ σῆς [εἰς]⁸ βρῶσι[ν]⁸
⁹⌠ ἀφανίζει ⌡⁹	⁹⌠ [ἐγγίζει]¹² ⌡⁹
(καὶ ὅπου)¹⁰	[οὐδὲ]¹⁰
(κλέπται)¹¹ οὐ	[σκώληξ]¹¹
⁹⌠ (διορύσσουσιν	⁹⌠ ἀφανίζει ⌡⁹.
οὐδὲ κλέπτουσιν)¹² ⌡⁹.	

1. Did a prohibition exist before the exhortation?
2. Q's θησαυρίζετε or Thomas' ζητεῖτε
3. Q's «δέ» or Thomas' καί (I am undecided on the presence of δέ in Q)

4. Q's dative ὑμῖν or Thomas' nominative ὑμεῖς
5. Q's θησαυρούς or Thomas' τὸν θησαυρόν
6. Q's ἐν οὐρανοῖς or Thomas' μὴ ἀπολλύμενον
7. Thomas' μένοντα
8. Q's οὔτε . . . οὔτε βρῶσις or Thomas' οὐ . . . εἰς βρῶσιν
9. The position of ἀφανίζω in the adversity clauses
10. Q's καὶ ὅπου or Thomas' οὐδὲ
11. Q's κλέπται or Thomas' σκώληξ
12. Q's διορύσσουσιν οὐδὲ κλέπτουσιν or Thomas' ἐγγίζει[9]

Archetype[1]: Did a Prohibition Exist before the Exhortation?

A decision on this variant could also have the consequence of helping to establish a *terminus a quo* for the addition of GTh 76:1–2 to 76:3. If Colossians and John provide evidence of a prohibition in GTh 76:3, then the addition must necessarily postdate the writing of John. This would help provide a datum for understanding the history and development of the Gospel of Thomas as a whole.

Matthew 6:19 contains a prohibition that parallels the positive admonition of 6:20. Based largely on arguments concerning Matthew's redactional preferences, I could not decide with any degree of certainty whether or not Q contained a prohibition.[10] The IQP, on the other hand, has decided that it did.[11] James 5 may provide external evidence for a prohibition in Q. It is directed solely at those who have treasured up wealth on earth. If James used a source that had both prohibition and admonition, then 5:2–3 would seem to be commenting on the prohibition more than the admonition, though the eschatological nature of the admonition provides the idea of end time recompense for earthly deeds. In fact, a prohibition in the source is an unnecessary assumption, since condemnation of the rich is a theme of the epistle.

In the Coptic text, GTh 76:3 is preceded by the Parable of the Pearl. Surely the two were attached at some point in time in the development of the Thomas tradition. Two questions are of importance: when were

9. See the Appendix for a description of the formatting sigla used here.
10. See above, Chapter 2, pp. 33–37.
11. See the Appendix.

they attached and did GTh 76:1–2 replace something else that originally preceded the admonition? The first question is difficult to answer partly because John and Colossians demonstrate no knowledge of the parable and partly because there is no consensus on a source relationship between Thomas and Matthew.[12] As to the second question, Colossians and John may provide evidence that GTh 76:3 originally had a prohibition attached that condemned the seeking of earthly treasures, which would necessarily date the attachment of GTh 76:1–2 to 76:3 later than the composition of John. Both Colossians and John make a contrast: in Col 3:1–2, the things from above are contrasted with the things on earth, while in John 6:27 the food which perishes is contrasted with the food that abides. This could indicate an antithetical parallelism in their source, GTh 76:3.

It must be recognized, however, that the very nature of a saying that uses earthly imagery to speak of seeking heavenly or abiding things lends itself to expansion into a prohibition against seeking earthly or perishable things. Considering the metaphorical imagery of GTh 76:3, a preceding prohibition can only realistically be understood as a prohibition against seeking wealth. Yet, neither Colossians 3 nor John 6 shows any concern for the disposition of wealth. John 6:27 is about food, and by extension, Jesus; Col 3:12–17 is about the characteristics of virtuous and pious living.

I find no argument to be persuasive with regard to GTh 76:3. I do not see how a confident decision could be made in either direction. I recognize, however, that if one sees in Matt 6:19–20 (and Luke 12:21) evidence for a prohibition in Q being replaced by an admonition in Luke 12:33a, then one might also see the contrasts in Colossians and John and the parable in GTh 76:1–2 as evidence of a prior prohibition in 76:3. By logical extension, one should then see the date of the Gospel of John as the *terminus a quo* for the attachment of GTh 76:1–2 to 76:3.

Archetype²: Q's θησαυρίζετε or Thomas' ζητεῖτε

Colossians 3:1–2 has "seek" as its main verb, the key word for initially identifying 3:1–2 as an elaboration on the Thomas version of the say-

---

12. Cf. Cerfaux and Garitte, "Les paraboles du royaume," 312–13; Grant and Freedman, *Secret Sayings*, 177; Wilson, *Studies*, 53, 92; idem, "'Thomas,'" 235, 239–40; Gärtner, *Theology*, 37–38, 66; Montefiore, "Comparison," 227, 239–40; Schrage, *Verhältnis*, 155–60; Jeremias, *Parables*, 90–91, 199–200; Cameron, "Parable," 13–15; Koester, *Ancient Christian Gospels*, 103–6; Patterson, *Gospel of Thomas and Jesus*, 57–59; Baarda, "Logion 76."

ing. This means that Thomas' "seeking" is arguably contemporary with Q's "treasure up."[13] Additionally, John condemns wrongful seeking in the immediately prior verse, 6:26 ("you seek not because you saw signs, but because you ate your fill of the loaves"), possibly a reminiscence of ζητέω in John's source for 6:27.

Perhaps the strongest argument against Thomas' verb is simply the fact that it is the only word in GTh 76:3 that clearly fits into the larger theological schema of the Gospel of Thomas (cf. GTh 2; 38; 59; 92; 94; 107). Therefore, it is possible that at some point θησαυρίζω was replaced with ζητέω, ζητέω reflecting an enlightenment soteriology (cf., e.g., GTh 2, 92, 94).[14] This possibility is countered by the possibility that the presence of ζητέω in the saying may have been the reason for its inclusion in the collection in the first place. Other alterations to the saying would have

---

13. This depends, of course, upon the dating of Colossians.

14. It is possible but highly unlikely that the Parable of the Pearl originally had the merchant "seeking" the pearl (as in Matt 13:45) and that the redactor of GTh 76:3 replaced θησαυρίζω with the parable's verb ζητέω, bringing the admonition more in line with the enlightenment soteriology of the Gospel of Thomas.

What is not explained by this suggestion is why the redactor would have displaced the verb from the parable to the admonition, thereby creating a disjunction between the parable and the admonition. In Thomas' parable (76:1-2), the merchant happens upon the pearl. GTh 76:3 begins "you also, seek . . . ." This disjunction would not have occurred if the redactor had merely copied the verb from the parable. Admittedly, the combiner of 76:1-2 and 76:3 didn't help this disjunction by probably connecting the two elements with "you also." But the problem remains. Furthermore, transferring ζητέω from the parable to the admonition would break up the "seek and find" pairing of verbs in the parable—not likely in the Gospel of Thomas.

The usual explanation for why the parable and the admonition of GTh 76 were attached is that, in adopting Matt 13:44's Parable of the Pearl and Matt 13:45-46's Parable of the Treasure in the Field, the author of Thomas separated the two parables and, feeling the loss of the Treasure parable in connection with the Parable of the Pearl, replaced it with the Treasure saying. See Grant and Freedman, *The Secret Sayings of Jesus*, 177; Gärtner, *The Theology of the Gospel of Thomas*, 37-38, 66; Turner, "The Gospel of Thomas: Its History, Transmission and Sources," in Turner and Montefiore, *Thomas and the Evangelists*, 36; Schrage, *Das Verhältnis*, 155-60; Lindemann, "Gleichnisinterpretation," 220; Snodgrass, "Gospel of Thomas" 35; Koester, *Ancient Christian Gospels*, 103-6. Several questions are left unanswered by proponents of this idea. (1) Why would Thomas have "displaced" the Treasure in the Field parable? (2) Why would Thomas have "felt the need" to replace the Treasure parable with another treasure saying? As an explanation for the attachment of 76:1-2 and 76:3, this is ludicrous. (3) Why are Thomas' parables scattered throughout the gospel if most of them derive from Matthew 13 (So asks Wilson, "'Thomas' and the Growth of the Gospels," 235-40)? Until these questions can be satisfactorily answered, the thesis should be considered unlikely.

focused the interpretative range of ζητέω (see Archetype⁵ below) without replacement of the verb.

The best supportive evidence for Q's θησαυρίζω comes from its use in Jas 5:2-3. In fact, if it could be determined that James used not Q, but early community paraenesis, it might provide independent evidence for Q's verb. The date of James and its relationship to the Q tradition is, however, uncertain.

On the other hand, a closer look at the Q context might suggest Thomas' "seek" being original there. According to the IQP, the written text of Q 12:29-31, 33 originally read:

> ²⁹ Therefore do not be anxious, saying, What shall we eat? . . .
> ³⁰ For the Gentiles **seek** (ἐπιζητοῦσιν) all these things;
> for your Father knows that you need them.
> ³¹ But **seek** (ζητεῖτε) his kingdom, and these things shall be yours as well.
> ³³ Do not **lay up** (θησαυρίζετε) for yourselves treasures on earth . . .
> But **lay up** (θησαυρίζετε) for yourselves treasure .. in .. heavens . . . ¹⁵

Q 12:30-31 contrasts the seeking of earthly things with the seeking of God's kingdom. Q 12:33 contrasts treasuring up earthly treasures with treasuring up heavenly treasures (without the prohibition it does this implicitly). Though Q 12:29-30 concerns daily needs and 12:33 concerns treasures, the temporal-eternal contrast is similar. If one does not address Q's construction of the Free from Anxiety like Ravens and Lilies pericope, this alone could be considered a reason for the attachment of Q 12:33 to 12:31, especially if Matt 6:19's prohibition existed in Q (though this is uncertain).

However, as has been pointed out elsewhere, a number of scholars trying to identify the core of the pericope in Q 12:22-31 have rejected 12:31 as a secondary accretion attributable to Q.¹⁶ Furthermore, P. Oxy.

---

15. Moreland and Robinson, "Work Sessions 1992," 505; idem, "Work Sessions 1994," 481. The IQP and I disagree with the *CEQ* on the position of Q 12:33.

16. Robinson, "Pre-Q Text," esp. 756-66. Robinson cites Erich Klostermann, *Apokrypha II: Evangelien*, 20; Bultmann, *History*, 104; Minear, *Commands of Christ*, 139-40; Zeller, *Die weisheitlichen Mahnsprüche*, 87; Hoffmann, *Tradition und Situation*, 93-113. Cf. Merklein, *Gottesherrschaft*, 174-83; Luz, *Matthäus 1-7*, 365-66, 370-71; Gnilka, *Matthäusevangelium*, 245-52; Dillon, "Ravens," 605; Wischmeyer, "Matthäus 6,25-34 par."

655.1–17, which supports scholarly reconstructions of a pre-Q 12:22–31 core in several other places, could be evidence that all of Q 12:29–31 was added by the composer of Q.[17] In fact, Q 12:29–30 is recapitulative and Q 12:31 stands out as an additional admonition supported by the previous arguments, a typical exhortatory conclusion to an instructional chreia elaboration.

If the Treasure saying was included in Q at the initial stage of literary composition (i.e., at the time of the composition of Q 12:22–31) and contained ζητέω, it may have occasioned the use of ζητέω and ἐπιζητέω in Q 12:30, 31, especially in the creation of the kingdom saying of Q 12:31. The transfer of ζητέω to Q 12:30, 31 and its replacement with θησαυρίζω in Q 12:33 would make a better (than catchword) connection between Q 12:22–31 and 12:33 because the replacement of ζητέω with θησαυρίζω in Q 12:33 creates an admonition that is more consistent with the image of the crows who neither sow nor reap *nor gather into barns* (Q 12:24). If Q 12:33–34 was added at a redactional stage of Q, stylistic concerns could have come into play. Without changing the verbs, the text of Q would have read:

> ²⁹ Therefore do not be anxious, saying, What shall we eat? . . .
> ³⁰ For the Gentiles **seek** (ἐπιζητέω) all these things;
> for your Father knows that you need them.
> ³¹ But **seek** (ζητεῖτε) his kingdom, and these things shall be yours as well.
> ³³ Do not **seek** (ζητεῖτε) for yourselves treasures on earth . . .
> But **seek** (ζητεῖτε) for yourselves treasure .. in .. heavens.

If "seek" was originally a catchword that suggested the connection between 12:31 and 12:33, then it would have been eliminated in the second case for stylistic reasons: (a) to avoid a redundancy caused by the repetition of the verb in adjoining sentences; (b) to create a good Greek phrase that uses cognates for the verb and its accusative object, (μὴ) θησαυρίζετε ὑμῖν θησαυρούς ("treasure up for yourselves treasures").[18] As noted above,

---

17. Robinson, "Pre-Q Text." Secondary accretions to Q include the addition of Q 12:23; the modification of 12:25, replacing "food" and "clothing" with "life/soul" and "body"; and the scribal error of reading "grow" (αὐξάνω) for "not card" (οὐ ξαίνω).

18. Grammatical construction using the cognate accusative (or accusative of content)

θησαυρίζω would also improve the connection to Q 12:22–31 with the birds that do not sow, reap, or gather into barns.

Good rationales can be suggested for alteration of the verb in both texts. Both verbs were used in this saying in the second half of the first century. Neither verb fits well in the opposing context. The key is to ask which verb makes *better* sense in *both* contexts, and so would be the base from which alterations, be they through redaction or oral transmission, would have been made. As Luke 12:33 shows, minor alterations to other parts of the Q saying—in particular, the addition of an article before θησαυρός and the change of θησαυρός from plural to singular—do not greatly affect the hermeneutic of the saying. Only the additional change of the verb to ζητέω would effectively alter the hermeneutic, as GTh 76:3 would indicate. At the same time, ζητέω could have been spoken by Jesus or early tradents with the practical concern for not seeking earthly treasures, but seeking heavenly treasures instead. While changing ζητέω to θησαυρίζω would have been an improvement in the specific Q context and would have changed the meaning only from the active search for treasure to the storing of it, changing the hermeneutic of GTh 76:3 to accord with a search for wisdom topos could have been accomplished without changing the verb. Therefore, ζητέω makes better sense as the verb from which both Q 12:33 and GTh 76:3 sprang. Also, the presence of ἐπιζητέω in Q 12:30 and ζητέω in 12:31 strikes me as too much of a coincidence. Most likely, the composer or redactor of Q was responsible for changing the verb of the archetype, ζητέω, to θησαυρίζω.

Archetype³: Q's «δέ» or Thomas' καί

GTh 76:3's καί can be readily dismissed as an addition made in conjunction with the attachment of the Parable of the Pearl. Q's δέ could have existed with or without a preceding prohibition, but is likely occasioned by it in Matthew. As I am uncertain about the presence of δέ in Q, so I am undecided with regard to the archetype.

Archetype⁴: Q's dative ὑμῖν or Thomas' nominative ὑμεῖς

Thomas' nominative ὑμεῖς is occasioned by the attachment of the Parable of the Pearl. There is no good argument against Q's ὑμῖν being original.

---

is standard Greek. BDF observes that "a comparable idiom is found in both Hebrew and Aramaic" (§153 [1]).

It should be noted that the presence of the pronoun in this position in Thomas provides stronger evidence for Matthew's ὑμῖν being the Q reading, even though Thomas' ὑμεῖς operates differently in that version.

Archetype[5]: Q's θησαυρούς or Thomas' τὸν θησαυρόν

The admonition to "seek (the) treasures which do not perish/in heaven" by no means has to refer to the search for wisdom or gnosis, as is suggested by the saying in Thomas. In fact, it would only take a simple but subtle shift in wording to emphasize this meaning. At some point in the tradition, "seek (the) treasure*s* which *do* not perish/in heaven" could have become "seek the treasure which *does* not perish/in heaven," changing the emphasis of the passage with the change of the plural to the singular (and possibly the addition of the article). With the change, a more general view toward a future pleasant life in heaven for rewards sacrificed in the present can be understood as a search for Divine Wisdom or gnosis in the present, with eternal benefits. Hence, we have a good redactional rationale for an alteration in GTh 76:3.

The opposite could have taken place, but here we run into the question of which sapiential orientation is more original—the practical or the esoteric. If the saying goes back to Jesus, then the abundance of aphorisms and admonitions about practical everyday living in the sayings of Jesus traditions of the first century weigh heavily in favor of Q's "treasures." But this is not certain. The Jesus seminar is doubtful about the saying in any of its forms, finding little that distinguishes it from common wisdom themes, though recognizing that Jesus could have uttered the saying in some form.[19] Hence, the Thomas version could be more original, deriving from an enlightenment-oriented community, the Q version reflecting Q redaction away from a more esoteric search and towards a more practical application. Overall, modification of the archetype in the Thomas tradition seems more likely.

Using the same reasoning as above, the article focuses the Thomas version not on any treasure, but on *the* treasure, a possible sign of Thomasine redaction seen elsewhere (as in, perhaps, 76:1–2 and *the* pearl). The article could have already existed in the saying and been omitted by the composer or redactor of Q, but a strong rationale is lacking. Therefore, Thomas' articles would appear to be secondary.

19. Funk et al., *Five Gospels*, 90–91, 150–51, 340–41, 418, 515.

Archetype[6]: Q's ἐν οὐρανοῖς or Thomas' μὴ ἀπολλύμενον

The two concepts of Wisdom having imperishable treasures and of treasures awaiting the righteous in heaven are both found in Jewish literature known to or written in the first century.[20] Therefore, neither is unique to the Jesus tradition.

The expression "which does not perish" is not found elsewhere in the Gospel of Thomas, and so cannot readily be assumed to be a modification of the archetype in the Thomas tradition. "Heaven," understood as the domain of the "Father" and the "kingdom," is very common in Thomas, occurring there as often as it occurs in Q.[21] For this reason, while any comparison to the rest of Thomas must be tentative, it does not appear that "heaven" was avoided in the Thomas tradition. On the other hand, the concept of the "treasure which does not perish" is consistent with the rest of the imagery in the saying—it stands in metaphorical contrast to treasures that are eaten by moths and destroyed by worms. Therefore it is reasonable to assume that the attributive participle came from Thomas' source.

That Col 3:1–2 indirectly refers to heaven in τὰ ἄνω ... οὗ ὁ Χριστός ἐστιν suggests the possibility that the Thomas version of the saying contained "heaven" in it when it was used by the author of Colossians. Had "heaven" been in the source for Col 3:1–2, however, it is hard to see the author not using "things in heaven" to contrast "things on earth."[22] Instead, Colossians uses τὰ ἄνω. Furthermore, a locative reference is inherent in Thomas' ὅπου. The author of Colossians would have understood the locative reference of "where," along with references to "not perishing" and "abiding"—all of which may have suggested the "hiddenness" connection (Col 3:1–4)—to mean heaven, though without using the word.

Evidence for Q's expression is problematic. First, if Q does not use οὐρανός very often, it does at least once in a way that is relevant to Q 12:33. Q 6:23 reads "Rejoice and [[be glad]], for your pay is great in

---

20. For the former, see, e.g., Wis 7:14; 8:18. For the latter, see, e.g., 2 Esdr 7:77; 8:33.

21. In Thomas: 6; 12; 20; 44; 54; 114. Other occurrences of ⲡⲉ appear to refer to the sky and the heaven above it (the astral-planetary heaven)—3; 11; 20; 91; 111. In Q: 6:23; 10:15; 10:21; 11:13; 15:7. Other occurrences of οὐρανός appear to refer to the sky—9:58; 12:56; 13:19; 16:17. The occurrence in GTh 6 may be the result of a third or fourth century scribal correction. P. Oxy. 654.36–40 has "truth" where the Coptic has "heaven." See above, Chapter 4, p. 109, n. 89.

22. See Col 1:5; 1:16; 1:23; 4:1; esp. 1:20 (τὰ ἐπὶ τῆς γῆς εἴτε τὰ ἐν τοῖς οὐρανοῖς).

heaven (ἐν τῷ οὐρανῷ), for so they did to the prophets [[before you]]."²³ The presence in Q 6:23ab of ἐν τῷ οὐρανῷ as the location of a future reward for present suffering could be taken as evidence that ἐν οὐρανοῖς in 12:33 was also found in Q's source. But it might also be taken as evidence of Q's soteriology, and therefore Q redaction. Second, since the ὅπου that precedes the adversity clauses suggests a location for the treasure in the Q saying, the reference to a specific location could be considered an improvement. Colossians 3:1–2's replacement of Thomas' τὸν θησαυρόν with τὰ ἄνω κτλ. is evidence of this process taking place elsewhere in the transmission of this saying.

In summary, the Thomas version has more going for it as the archetype. A "treasure *which does not perish*" is not only consistent with the rest of the metaphor in the saying, it is also the expression that is more open to variable interpretation. In the redaction-historical development of sayings collections, the tendency is to clarify and narrow the interpretive range of a saying. The change to "in heaven" does just that.²⁴ The alternative, changing "in the heavens" to "which does not perish," lacks a transmission-historical rationale in the Thomas tradition—other Thomas sayings refer positively to the heaven of the Father's abode. That Q 6:23 imagines rewards being accumulated in heaven therefore supports Q modification in 12:33. The composer of Q appears to have changed the archetype's "treasure which does not perish" to "treasure in (the) heavens."

Archetype⁷: Thomas' μένοντα

Overlooked in the literature on the Gospel of Thomas is the fact that the presence of "which abides" in GTh 76:3 forms an abbreviated synonymous parallelism to what comes before it. While lacking a second parallel object, it still functions as the second stich of a synonymous parallelism is meant to function: as a progressive deepening of the meaning of the first stich. This perhaps would not be as noticeable if not for the clear and obvious synonymous parallelism in the adversity clauses that follow. This could be the result of conscious literary redaction, but it could also have been a result of the development of oral tradition under Septuagintal

---

23. Moreland and Robinson, "Work Sessions 1992," 502.

24. As another example of this process, whereas Thomas' qualifier of "treasure" is locatively unspecified, Luke makes it specific by pairing it with "in the heavens."

influence or could even be original to the saying of Jesus.²⁵ It was in the saying when it was taken over by the author of John 6:27, and the adjectival clauses that define τὰ ἄνω in Col 3:1–2 appear to confirm that this parallelism existed late in the second half of the first century.

Had μένοντα been in the archetype, Q probably would have omitted it as an unnecessary redundancy when μὴ ἀπολλύμενον was changed to ἐν οὐρανοῖς. Had it not been in the archetype, unless someone consciously added it in order to create the abbreviated synonymous parallelism that further defines the treasure, I find it difficult to see its theological or metaphorical value. The evidence presented points to μένοντα being in the archetype.

Archetype⁸: Q's οὔτε ... οὔτε βρῶσις or Thomas' οὐ ... εἰς βρῶσιν

This variant concerns the first adversity clause in Q and Thomas. I have argued in Chapters 2 and 3 that Q contained οὔτε βρῶσις and the Greek version of the Gospel of Thomas contained εἰς βρῶσιν. While both use the same somewhat uncommon word (βρῶσις), the very common words that precede it determine its meaning in the respective text. Q says that "moths and eating things (or 'devourers')" destroy, while Thomas says that moths approach "for eating" or "to eat."

The Thomasine construction is common in the LXX, perhaps suggesting its antiquity. However, the saying could have been modified (here and with the synonymous parallelism of the destructive worm) on the basis of Septuagintal usage. Εἰς βρῶσιν is a Septuagintal way of expressing the phrase "for food," "for eating," or "to eat."²⁶

With regard to the Q clause, the use of βρῶσις as a substantive for an active agent is rare—only one case is known to exist prior to the writing of Matthew (Mal 3:11; LXX). The usual meaning of βρῶσις without

---

25. Luke 12:33b provides evidence of synonymous parallelism created by the author:

ποιήσατε ἑαυτοῖς	Make for yourselves
βαλλάντια μὴ παλαιούμενα	purses which do not wear out
θησαυρὸν ἀνέκλειπτον	a treasure unfailing
ἐν τοῖς οὐρανοῖς	in the heavens

26. BDF considers εἰς βρῶσιν a Semitism (§145, 157[5]). It replaces several forms of אכל usually with ל prefix (e.g., Gen 1:29; 1:30; 2:9; 3:6; 9:3; 47:24; Isa 55:10; Jer 7:33; 15:3; 19:7; 41:20; Ezek 29:5; 47:12), sometimes replacing the infinitive construct, as in Lev 25:7 and 2 Sam 16:2, where the meaning is "to eat."

the preceding εἰς, and often even with the preposition, is "food," as in βρῶσις καὶ πόσις ("food and drink"); in other words, as something which is eaten, not something which eats.

Whence, then, came the change? The expression in Q is rare, and hence problematic, but the principle of *lectio difficilior* does not seem to apply here. Considering the descriptive imagery in the rest of this saying—be it Thomas' destructive worm or Q's digging and burgling thieves—it seems doubtful that Jesus or an early follower would have used a generalizing, abstract term alongside of a specific bug in describing agents of treasure destruction.[27] And had this saying been transmitted in Aramaic with two specified agents, it seems likely that Greek tradents would have had equivalent terms to translate them. For this reason, it seems more problematic to suggest that the clause took on a *more* Septuagintal meaning in the transmission of the saying, than that Q made the change on the level of the Greek version either somewhere in the oral transmission of the saying in Q communities or—more likely—at the point when the composer of Q modified the saying for inclusion in the Q text.[28] Therefore, the archetype probably read εἰς βρῶσιν and was changed by Q in the restructuring of the adversity clauses.

Archetype[9]: The Position of ἀφανίζω in the Adversity Clauses

A decision for this variant is tied to decisions on Archetypes[8], [11], and [12]. Based on decisions there, I would have to argue for Thomas' position of ἀφανίζω in the second clause as being the archetype reading.[29] When Q changed εἰς βρῶσιν to οὔτε βρῶσις, ἀφανίζω was moved to the first adversity clause to give the subjects, σής and βρῶσις, an appropriate verb of destruction. At the same time, Q replaced Thomas' ἐγγίζω with διορύσσω and κλέπτω in order to create a thief clause as the second adversity.

---

27. The only similar pairing of terms that comes to mind is the combination "sinners and tax collectors; but that pairing is not used by Jesus in such a metaphorical context. Moreover, those terms may have represented—for Jesus or early sayings tradents—two distinct spheres of social morality.

28. As Charles aptly points out (*APOT* 1:601), the one sure case in the LXX of βρῶσις being used as an eating thing—Mal 3:1—appears to be an instance of mistranslating the unpointed Hebrew text. In other words, it could only have occurred in written text translation, not in oral transmission.

29. The alternative reading, based on my decision for Archetype[8]—ὅπου οὐ σής εἰς βρῶσιν ἀφανίζει—does not make sense.

Archetype¹⁰: Q's καὶ ὅπου or Thomas' οὐδέ

Q's repetitive καὶ ὅπου is suggested by the multiple subjects in Q's first adversity clause. Thomas' οὐδέ indicates the simpler structure wherein the negatives are related to the single agents of adversity in each of the two clauses. Therefore, οὐδέ was probably in the archetype.

Archetype¹¹: Q's κλέπται or Thomas' σκώληξ

It was observed in Chapter 3 that GTh 76:3 presents good Semitic parallelism in the use of moths and worms as almost synonymous agents of destruction. Q's parallelism contains moths, devourers, and thieves. The question is, which parallelism is more original? Did Thomas eliminate the thieves and create a parallelism with two types of bugs, or did Q create the "thieves" clause and condense the two bug clauses into one, generalizing the worm as an "eating thing"?

GTh 76:3's closer parallelism could be a sign of redactional improvement. At the same time, as observed in Chapter 3, there is no good reason for Thomas to have replaced a "thieves" clause, at least based on the use of the metaphor elsewhere in the gospel.[30] Furthermore, I have never before come across any persuasive evidence of a Thomas redactor creating a text that is closer to LXX style than are parallels in the synoptic gospels or Q.[31]

Q 12:33 and 12:39 are connected by the catchwords "thief" and "dig through." If these words had been in Q 12:33 originally, they may have been the basis for the connection, though the coincidence of two pre-Q sayings of Jesus coincidentally containing the words "thief" and "dig through" seems remote.[32] On the other hand, Q could have replaced the source's second adversity clause with the thief clause, with Q 12:39 being attached by a later redactor on the basis of the catchword κλέπτης (and creating a further catchword connection through the use of διορύσσω in 12:39).

---

30. See above, Chapter 3, pp. 69–70.

31. The presence of Semitisms in Thomas has been suggested on numerous occasions in the literature, but not the redactional creation of sayings even more Semitic or Septuagintal than their synoptic counterparts.

32. GTh 21:5 has a parallel to Q 12:39, including "cut into the house of his domain and steal his possessions." If GTh 21:5 represents an independent tradition, then matters are even more complicated.

There is no obvious motive for the replacement of either substantive; so, redactional tendencies are not much help in this matter. Q's second adversity clause is both more developed, arguably a sign of scribal or redactional accretion, and more descriptive, arguably a sign of prior oral transmission. In the end, Thomas' synonymous parallelism of moths approaching to eat and worms destroying at least appears to be more original because it is more strictly Semitic in style and simpler in overall structure. In a manner of speaking, then, Q, while creating the thief clause, kept the worm, but subsumed it under the more general and abstract (and redactionally-created) "devourer."

Archetype¹²: Q's διορύσσουσιν οὐδὲ κλέπτουσιν or Thomas' ἐγγίζει

To be consistent with my decision for Archetype¹¹, οὐδὲ κλέπτουσιν should not be considered as part of the archetype.

Worms are noted for digging and rooting around—the first Q verb, διορύσσω, could have suggested the use of σκώληξ in Thomas. At the same time, Thomas does not use διορύσσω with σκώληξ, so a reminiscence of διορύσσω in ἐγγίζω is entirely speculative. Furthermore, we would have a case of the replacement of a descriptive action verb with a more general action verb, but no obvious motive for the replacement. Luke's replacement of Q's διορύσσω οὐδὲ κλέπτω with Thomas' ἐγγίζω in Luke 12:33c served the purpose of abbreviating the adversity clauses in order to focus attention on Luke 12:33ab and create a simpler, more terse parallelism. Such motives are not in evidence in GTh 76:3 since the archetype probably contained only one verb. Looking to a Judean time-of-Jesus mud-brick house as the source for Q's verbs does not work—one can dig under rock houses if they're not built on bedrock, and there's no strong evidence that Jesus traveled outside of Galilee before the last year of his life.

Thomas' ἐγγίζω is not as descriptive an action of κλέπται as "digging through and stealing," suggesting that Q had good reason for replacing Thomas' verb with verbs that are much more specific about the actions of a thief. At the same time, since διορύσσω could have been used for a worm's activity, redaction in the Thomasine direction is less likely. With these observations, and in view of previous decisions for Archetypes⁸ and

[11], I would argue that Thomas' verb has better claim to being the more original.

Results

At this point, I suggest a text that underlay both Q and Thomas in the early to mid-first century:

> Ζητεῖτε ὑμῖν θησαυροὺς μὴ ἀπολλύμενους,
>   μένοντας,
> ὅπου οὐ σὴς εἰς βρῶσιν ἐγγίζει
>   οὐδὲ σκώληξ ἀφανίζει.

> Seek for yourselves treasures which do not perish,
>   which abide,
> where no moth approaches to eat
>   nor worm destroys.

CHAPTER 6 | Conclusion

SUMMARY OF THE PREVIOUS CHAPTERS

Chapter 1 was concerned with placing this study in the context of current discussions on the relationship between canonical sayings traditions and the Gospel of Thomas. With regard to synoptic traditions and Thomas, I have focused on a number of studies of individual sayings of Jesus. The conflicting results of these studies demonstrate that the relationship between Thomasine and synoptic traditions cannot be boiled down to a simple argument of dependence or independence. Most scholars addressing the similarities between the Gospels of John and Thomas agree that these similarities suggest an historical relationship of some sort, though there is great disagreement as to the nature of this relationship. Parallel sayings or concepts are found, but not with the degree of verbal similarity one finds with Thomas and the synoptics. Similarities mostly exist on the level of images and underlying concepts. The degree to which Paul used sayings of Jesus traditions is uncertain. Verbal similarities to known collections—especially when "the Lord" is cited—reveal only a few connections. However, Paul's use of community paraenesis—paraenesis itself often embodied or absorbed sayings traditions—shows likely familiarity with sayings traditions, and opens the door to considering possible connections between Pauline and Thomasine traditions.

Chapter 2 reconstructed the Q version of the Treasure in Heaven saying. The position of the pericope in Q is represented by Luke, with the exception of the Lukan insertion of 12:32 between the Free from Anxiety like Ravens and Lilies pericope (Q 12:22–31) and the pericope on Storing up Treasures in Heaven (Q 12:33–34). The text of the Q pericope can be reconstructed with a good degree of accuracy. The Matthean version (Matt 6:20) mostly represents the Q version, the exception being Matthew's singular "heaven" (it was left undecided whether or not Q had a prohibition as represented by Matt 6:19). Luke prefaced the Q saying with an adaptation of Mark 10:21. The rationale for many of the stylistic changes Luke made to the body of the saying can be understood on internal grounds, but where Luke got the idea for the content of many of these changes was left to be discussed in Chapter 3. The original form of Mark 10:21 is unknown. What all four of these versions have in common is a concern for the disposition of wealth. That this is the case for Q is made clear by the position of the saying in Q following 12:22–31.

Chapter 3 found traditional interpretations of John 6:27 lacking with regard to its provenance. The saying was found to be a traditional saying of Jesus—the Treasure saying—modified to introduce the Bread of Life Discourse of John 6. Likewise, traditional interpretations of GTh 76:3's relationship to the canonical sayings traditions were found to be lacking. These problems, combined with the question of where Luke got the idea for many of the changes made to Q 12:33 and the coincidence of Luke 12:33; John 6:27; and GTh 76:3 all having two qualifiers of the object of the imperative, are resolved by the hypothesis that the authors of John and Luke knew of the Thomasine version of the Treasure saying. Luke borrowed a number of elements of the saying in redacting Q 12:33, and John modified the saying when creating the Bread of Life Discourse.

It was further proposed that, while Luke showed no obvious *animus* toward a Thomas tradition in the conflation of GTh 76:3 with Q 12:33, John may have had an anti-Thomasine reason for the severe modification of the Treasure saying.

Chapter 4 found that the author of James was aware of the Q sayings tradition and adapted the Treasure saying for the purpose of an eschatological condemnation of the wealthy who gain their riches by rapacious means (Jas 5:1–6, esp. 2–3). James is consistent with the synoptic tradition in understanding the saying as referring to the disposition of earthly wealth. With regard to Colossians, traditional interpretations of Col 3:1–11 were found to be lacking with regard to the provenance of specific elements; namely, the heavenly-earthly and hidden-revealed dualities (Col 3:1–4), the prohibition against lying (Col 3:9), and the All-predication that concludes the passage (Col 3:11). It was observed that these elements of Col 3:1–11 are found side-by-side in two sections of the Gospel of Thomas, GTh 6:2–6 and 76:3–77:1. If the author of Colossians had used a sayings collection shared by or akin to the Gospel of Thomas, then this would explain the presence of verbal and thematic elements of the Treasure saying in Col 3:1–2. It would also explain why the author treats the Treasure saying as metaphorical (as do Thomas and John).

Chapter 5 drew inferences from the results of Chapters 2–4. Both primary forms of the Treasure saying—represented by Q 12:33 and GTh 76:3—can be dated to the first century CE: GTh 76:3 to 60–85 CE at the latest; Q 12:33 to 30–70 CE. Evidence for a written source or version of the Gospel of Thomas prior to 100 CE was found to be inconclusive. The bifurcation of the tradition history of the Treasure saying observed throughout this study can be understood as the development of two different topoi in Jewish wisdom literature: the proper disposition of wealth and the search for Divine Wisdom.

Finally, an attempt was made to reconstruct an archetype of the Treasure saying from Q 12:33 and GTh 76:3. It was assumed that Q's wisdom topos was original to the saying—whether it came from early tradents or Jesus himself—yet, most of the changes were best understood as having been made by the composer of Q. Only small (but significant) changes in the Thomas tradition reoriented the saying toward the search for Wisdom topos.

Charting the Development
of the Treasure in Heaven Saying

The diagram (Figure 18) charts the transmission history of the known versions of the Treasure saying based on the results of this study (see the following page).

Q 12:33 and GTh 76:3 developed from the archetype and are the basis for the canonical versions of the Treasure saying. Q 12:33 existed in written form prior to its adoption in Matthew and Luke. Whether GTh 76:3 existed in written form prior to adoption in Luke, John, and/or Colossians is uncertain.

Figure 18: Transmission History of the Treasure Saying

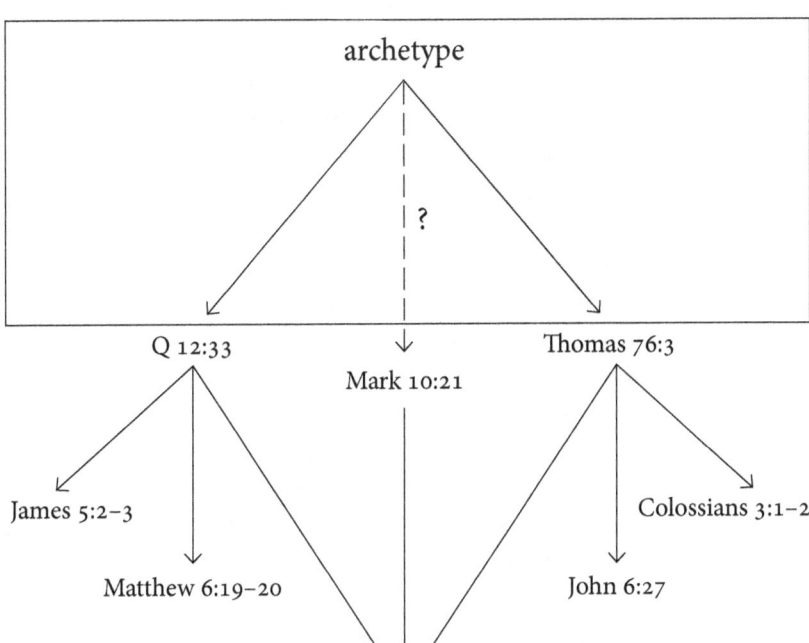

Archetype: exhortation (with appositive attributes and synonymous parallelism that further modifies the object); **Q 12:33**: (prohibition and) exhortation (with synonymous parallelism that further modifies the object); **Thomas 76:3**: exhortation (with appositive attributes and synonymous parallelism that further modifies the object); **Mark 10:21**: motive clause (for two exhortations); **James 5:2-3**: oracular condemnation (including synonymous and three-step parallelism in the service of epistolary paraenesis); **Colossians 3:1-2**: exhortation (with conditional protasis and two appositive object qualifiers); **Matthew 6:19-20**: prohibition and exhortation (with synonymous parallelism that further modifies the object): **John 6:27**: prohibition and exhortation (with two object qualifiers); **Luke 12:33**: three exhortations (the third with appositive, parallel objects, followed by synonymous parallelism that further modifies the second object).

Prior to or in the process of the writing of Mark, a pronouncement story concerning the need to give up what one values most in order to follow Jesus was developed around the Treasure saying. Mark's source and original form are otherwise unknown. The phrase "treasure in heaven" and the concern for the disposition of wealth locates it in the sphere of developing synoptic traditions—Mark therefore did not use Thomas as a source for this saying.

It is uncertain whether James used a written text of Q, a developing oral Q tradition, or some other sayings source as a source for the Treasure saying. What is certain is that the form of the source saying was closest to, if it was not in fact, Q 12:33/Matt 6:19–20. Like synoptic versions, it was interpreted as referring to the disposition of wealth. GTh 76:3 appears to have been part of a collection when it was incorporated in Colossians, but the nature and extent of the collection used by the author of Colossians is uncertain. The Treasure saying was used in Colossians as the keynote saying of the hortatory half of the letter.

Matthew kept the Q version of the Treasure saying largely intact, but relocated it to a cluster of sayings dealing with one's attitude toward wealth. In John, the Thomasine version of the saying was modified and used as the keynote saying for the Bread of Life Discourse. Luke used Q 12:33 as the textual base for the saying and kept it in its Q position, but substantially altered the saying with the help of Mark 10:21 and GTh 76:3. Unlike conventional theories of Thomasine use of gospel versions, redactional rationales can be discerned for each aspect of the Lukan conflation of sources. This is not to say that Thomas 76:3 did not undergo any changes. At some point, the Parable of the Pearl was attached to the Treasure saying as a motive for the search, and it may have replaced a prohibition.

Conclusion

Charting the development of the Treasure in Heaven saying has allowed us at least a small and limited glimpse at the process by which sayings traditions were altered and adapted as they moved through different communities and were taken up in different texts. Broad claims about the Gospel of Thomas as a whole and its relationship to canonical traditions cannot be made on the basis of this study alone. Nevertheless, it is hoped that this study has persuasively demonstrated that at least one saying in the Thomas corpus of sayings and logia was understood to be an authoritative, traditional saying of Jesus—one that was used by two, possibly three, different canonical authors. For this reason, close and careful studies of individual sayings in Thomas—sayings that find their parallels in the canonical literature and elsewhere—must continue to be done in order to gain a more precise and detailed picture of the history and development of the Gospel of Thomas and its historical relationship to sayings traditions represented by other texts, especially those of the canon. If this study is indicative, such studies can only help to provide biblical scholarship with a clearer picture of the development of canonical traditions as well.

Appendix: Reconstructed Text of Q 12:33

Q 12:33 (S. Johnson)	Q 12:33 (CEQ)
°/	°/
¹∫	¹∫
	(«μὴ θησαυρίζετε ὑμῖν θησαυροὺς ἐπὶ τῆς γῆς, ὅπου σὴς καὶ βρῶσις ἀφανίζει καὶ ὅπου κλέπται διορύσσουσιν καὶ κλέπτουσιν·»)²
[( )]²	
(θησαυρίζε)³τε	(θησαυρίζε)³τε
( )⁴	(δὲ)⁴
⟦(ὑμῖν)⟧⁵	(ὑμῖν),⁵
[]⁶	[]⁶
θησαυρο(ὒς)⁷	{θησαυρο}( )⁷
[]⁸	[]⁸
ἐν []⁹	{ἐν ⟦[]⁹⟧
οὐραν[οῖς]¹⁰,	οὐραν⟦(ᾧ)}¹⁰⟧,
ὅπου	ὅπου
¹¹∫ (οὔτε)¹² σῆς	¹¹∫ (οὔτε)¹² σῆς
(οὔτε βρῶσις)¹²	(οὔτε βρῶσις)¹²
(ἀφανίζει)¹³	(ἀφανίζει)¹³
⌉¹¹	⌉¹¹
(καὶ ὅπου)¹⁴	(καὶ ὅπου)¹⁴
¹¹∫ κλέπτ(αι)¹⁵	¹¹∫ κλέπτ(αι)¹⁵
οὐ (διορύσσο)¹⁶(ουσιν)¹⁵·¹⁷	οὐ (διορύσσο)¹⁶(ουσιν)¹⁵·¹⁷
(οὐδὲ κλέπτ)¹⁷(ουσιν)¹⁵·¹⁷ ⌉¹¹.	(οὐδὲ κλέπτ¹⁷(ουσιν)¹⁵·¹⁷ ⌉¹¹.
⌉¹-->Q 12:34	⌉¹-->Q 12:34
\⁰	\⁰

IQP Formatting		Definitions of Variation Units
		0 Is Luke 12:33/Matt 6:(19–)20 in Q?
Sigla	**Grades of Certainty**	1 Position of the pericope in Q.
text	Minimal Q	2 Luke's πωλή-... ἐλεημοσύνην or
(text)	Matthew at an A or B grade	Matt 6:19.
[text]	Luke at an A or B grade	3 Luke's ποιέω or Matthew's
⟦(text)⟧	Matthew at a C grade	θησαυρίζω.
⟦[text]⟧	Luke at a C grade	4 Matthew's δέ.
( )	In Matthew at a D, U, or Luke D	5 Luke's ἑαυτοῖς or Matthew's ὑμῖν.
		6 Luke's βαλλάντια μὴ παλαιούμενα.
[ ]	In Luke at a D, U, or Matthew D	7 Luke's θησαυρόν or Matthew's θησαυρούς.
[( )]	Undecided. Both the IQP and I argue Luke ≠ Q at 12:33² at an A or B grade	8 Luke's ἀνέκλειπτον.
		9 Luke's τοῖς.
		10 Luke's οὐρανοῖς or Matthew's
( )	Not in Matt at a B or higher	οὐρανῷ.
[ ]	Not in Luke at a B or higher	11 Position of adversaries.
⟦( )⟧	Not in Matthew at a C	12 Matthew's ... (τε) ... (οὔτε
⟦[ ]⟧	Not in Luke at a C	βρῶσις).
⌠⌡	Position variant	13 Luke's διαφθείρω or Matthew's
o/\o	In/not in Q variant	ἀφανίζω.
		14 Luke's οὐ[δὲ] or Matthew's καὶ ὅπου.
		15 Luke's κλέπτης or Matthew's κλέπται.
		16 Luke's ἐγγίζω or Matthew's διορύσσω.
		17 Matthew's οὐδὲ κλέπτω.

Works Cited

Adamson, James B. "James and Jesus." In idem, *James: The Man and His Message*. Grand Rapids: Eerdmans, 1989.
Aland, Kurt. *Synopsis Quattuor Evangeliorum: Locis parallelis evangeliorum apocryphorum et patrum adhibitis*. 15th rev. ed. Stuttgart: Deutsche Bibelgesellschaft, 1996.
———, Matthew Black, Carlo M. Martini, Bruce Metzger, and Allen Wikgren, editors. *The Greek New Testament*. 3rd ed. Stuttgart: United Bible Societies, 1975.
Aland, Kurt, and Barbara Aland, editors. *Novum Testamentum Graece*. 27th rev. ed. Stuttgart: Deutsche Bibelgesellschaft, 1993.
Aletti, Jean-Noël. *Saint Paul: Épitre aux Colossiens: Introduction, traduction et commentaire*. Ebib 20. Paris: Gabalda, 1993.
Anderson, Stanley D. Pages 128, 140, 155, and 185 in the database of *Q 12:33–34: Storing up Treasures in Heaven*, edited by Steven R. Johnson. Documenta Q. Leuven: Peeters, 2007.
Arnal, William E. *Jesus and the Village Scribes: Galilean Conflicts and the Setting of Q*. Minneapolis: Fortress, 2001.
———. "The Rhetoric of Marginality: Apocalypticism, Gnosticism, and Sayings Gospels." *HTR* 88 (1995) 471–94.
Asgeirsson, Jon Ma. "Doublets and Strata: Towards a Rhetorical Approach to the Gospel of Thomas." Ph.D. dissertation, Claremont Graduate University, 1998.
Attridge, Harold W. "'Seeking' and 'Asking'" in Q, Thomas, and John." In *From Quest to Q: Feschrift James M. Robinson*, edited by J. Ma. Asgeirsson et al., 295–302. BETL 146. Leuven: Peeters, 2002.
Baarda, Tjitze. "Logion 76 in the Gospel of Thomas." Paper presented at the annual meeting of the AAR/SBL, Chicago, IL, November 20, 1994.
Barrett, C. K. *The Gospel according to St. John*. 2nd ed. Philadelphia: Westminster, 1978.
Bauer, Walter. *A Greek-English Lexicon of the New Testament and Other Early Christian Literature*. Revised and edited by Frederick W. Danker. 3rd edition. Chicago: University of Chicago Press, 2000.
Bauernfeind, Otto. "Ἁπλοῦς, ἁπλότης." In *TDNT* 1 (1964) 386–87.

Becker, Jürgen. *Das Evangelium des Johannes: Kapitel 1–10.* KZNT 4/1. Gütersloh: Gütersloher, 1979.

Bethge, Hans-Gebhard, Christina-Maria Franke, Judith Hartenstein, Uwe-Karsten Plisch, Hans-Martin Schenke, and Jens Schröter. "Evangelium Thomae copticum: Das Thomas-Evangelium/The Gospel According to Thomas (EvThom NHC II,2 p.32,10–51,28)." In *Synopsis Quattuor Evangeliorum: Locis parallelis evangeliorum apocryphorum et patrum adhibitis,* edited by Kurt Aland, 519–46. 15th rev. ed. Stuttgart: Deutsche Bibelgesellschaft, 1996.

Betz, Hans Dieter. *Galatians: A Commentary on Paul's Letter to the Churches in Galatia.* Hermeneia. Philadelphia: Fortress, 1979.

Bieberstein, Sabine. *Verschwiegene Jüngerinnen, vergessene Zeuginnen: Gebrochene Konzepte im Lukasevangelium.* Novum Testamentum et Orbis Antiquus 38. Göttingen: Vandenhoeck & Ruprecht, 1998.

Black, Matthew. *An Aramaic Approach to the Gospels and Acts.* 2nd ed. Oxford: Clarendon, 1954.

Blass, Friedrich, Albert Debrunner, and Robert W. Funk. *A Greek Grammar of the New Testament and Other Early Christian Literature.* Chicago: University of Chicago Press, 1961.

Bonnard, Pierre. *L'Évangile selon Saint Matthieu.* CNT 1. Neuchâtel: Delachaux & Niestlé, 1963.

Bornkamm, Günther. "Der Aufbau der Bergpredigt." NTS 24 (1978) 419–32.

———. "Die Hoffnung im Kolosserbrief: Zugleich ein Beitrag zur Frage der Echtheit des Briefes." In *Studien zum Neuen Testament und zur Patristik,* edited by the Kommission für spätantike Religionsgeschichte, 56–64. TU 77. Berlin: Akademie, 1961.

Brandenberger, Stefan, and Alan Kirk. *Q 11:9–13: The Certainty of the Answer to Prayer.* Edited by Christoph Heil. Documenta Q. Leuven: Peeters, forthcoming.

Bratcher, Robert G., and Eugene A. Nida. *A Handbook on Paul's Letters to the Colossians and to Philemon.* UBSHS. New York: United Bible Societies, 1977.

Braun, Herbert. *Spätjüdisch-häretischer und frühchristlicher Radikalismus: Jesus von Nazareth und die essenische Qumransekte.* Vol. 2. BHT 24. Tübingen: Mohr/Siebeck, 1957.

Brooks, Stephenson H. *Matthew's Community: The Evidence of His Special Sayings Material.* JSNTSup 16. Sheffield: Academic, 1987.

Brown, John Pairman. "Synoptic Parallels in the Epistles and Form-History." NTS 10 (1963) 27–48.

Brown, Raymond E. "The Gospel of Thomas and St. John's Gospel." NTS 9 (1962) 155–77.

———. *The Gospel according to John (I–XII).* 2nd ed. AB 29. Garden City, NY: Doubleday, 1982.

Bultmann, Rudolf. *Die Geschichte der synoptischen Tradition.* 2nd rev. ed. FRLANT 29. Göttingen: Vandenhoeck & Ruprecht, 1931.

———. *The Gospel of John: A Commentary.* Translated by G. R. Beasley-Murray, R. W. N. Hoare, and J. K. Riches. Philadelphia: Westminster, 1971.

———. *History of the Synoptic Tradition*. Rev. ed. Translated by John Marsh. Oxford: Blackwell, 1968.
Burney, C. F. *The Poetry of Our Lord*. Oxford: Clarendon, 1935.
Cadbury, Henry J. "The Single Eye." *HTR* 47 (1954) 69–74.
———. *The Style and Literary Method of Luke*. HTS 6. Cambridge: Harvard University Press, 1920.
Cameron, Ron. "Ancient Myths and Modern Theories of the Gospel of Thomas and Christian Origins." In *Method and Theory in the Study of Religion* 11 (1999) 236–57.
———. "Parable and Interpretation in the Gospel of Thomas." *Forum* 2/2 (1986) 3–39.
Cannon, George E. *The Use of Traditional Materials in Colossians*. Macon, GA: Mercer University Press, 1983.
Carson, Herbert M. *The Epistles of Paul to the Colossians and Philemon: An Introduction and Commentary*. Grand Rapids: Eerdmans, 1960.
Castor, George D. *Matthew's Sayings of Jesus: The Non-Marcan Common Source of Matthew and Luke*. Chicago: University of Chicago Press, 1918.
Cerfaux, Lucien, and Gérard Garitte. "Les paraboles du royaume dans l'Évangile de Thomas." *Mus* 70 (1957) 307–27.
Charles, R. H., editor. *The Apocrypha and Pseudepigrapha of the Old Testament in English*. Vol.1. Oxford: Clarendon, 1913.
Chilton, Bruce D. "The Gospel according to Thomas as a Source of Jesus' Teaching." In *The Jesus Tradition Outside the Gospels*, edited by David Wenham, 155–75. Gospel Perspectives 5. Sheffield: JSOT Press, 1985.
———. "'Not to Taste Death': A Jewish, Christian and Gnostic Usage." *Studia Biblica* 2 (1978) 29–36.
Creed, John M. *The Gospel according to St. Luke: The Greek Text with Introduction, Notes and Indices*. London: Macmillan, 1930.
Crossan, John Dominic. *In Fragments: The Aphorisms of Jesus*. 1983. Reprinted, Eugene, OR: Wipf & Stock, 2008.
———. *The Historical Jesus: The Life of a Mediterranean Jewish Peasant*. San Francisco: HarperCollins, 1991.
Crum, Walter. E. *A Coptic Dictionary*. 1939. Reprinted with a new introduction by James M. Robinson. Ancient Language Resources. Eugene, OR: Wipf & Stock, 2005.
Cullmann, Oscar. "The Gospel of Thomas and the Problem of the Age of the Tradition Contained Therein." *Int* 16 (1962) 418–38.
Davies, Stevan L. "The Christology and Protology of the *Gospel of Thomas*." *JBL* 111 (1992) 663–82.
———. *The Gospel of Thomas and Christian Wisdom*. New York: Seabury, 1983.
Davies, W. D. *The Setting of the Sermon on the Mount*. Cambridge: Cambridge University Press, 1964.
Davies, W. D., and Dale C. Allison. *A Critical and Exegetical Commentary on the Gospel according to Saint Matthew*. Vol. 1: *Introduction and Commentary on Matthew I–VII*. ICC. Edinburgh: T. & T. Clark, 1988.

De Conick, April D. "'Blessed are those who have not seen' (Jn 20:29): Johannine Dramatization of an Early Christian Discourse." In *The Nag Hammadi Library after Fifty Years: Proceedings of the 1995 Society of Biblical Literature Commemoration*, edited by John D. Turner and Anne McGuire, 381–98. NHMS 44. Leiden: Brill, 1997.

———. "John Rivals Thomas: From Community Conflict to Gospel Narrative." In *Jesus in Johannine Tradition*, edited by Robert T. Fortna and Thomas Thatcher, 303–11. Louisville: Westminster John Knox, 2001.

———. *Recovering the Original Gospel of Thomas: A History of the Gospel and Its Growth*. New York: T. & T. Clark, 2005.

———. *Seek to See Him: Ascent and Vision Mysticism in the Gospel of Thomas*. VCSup 33. Leiden: Brill, 1996.

———. *Voices of the Mystics: Early Christian Discourse in the Gospels of John and Thomas and Other Ancient Christian Literature*. JSNTSup 157. Sheffield: Sheffield Academic, 2001.

Deppe, Dean B. *The Sayings of Jesus in the Epistle of James*. Chelsea, MI: Bookcrafters, 1989.

Dibelius, Martin. *From Tradition to Gospel*. Translated by Bertram L. Woolf. New York: Scribners, 1935.

———. *James: A Commentary on the Epistle of James*. Revised by Heinrich Greeven. Translated by Michael Williams. Hermeneia. Philadelphia: Fortress, 1976.

Dillon, Richard J. "Ravens, Lilies, and the Kingdom of God (Matthew 6:25–33/Luke 12:22–31)." *CBQ* 53 (1991) 605–27.

Dodd, C. H. *Historical Tradition in the Fourth Gospel*. Cambridge: Cambridge University Press, 1963.

———. *The Interpretation of the Fourth Gospel*. Cambridge: Cambridge University Press, 1953.

Doresse, Jean. *L'Évangile selon Thomas, ou Les paroles secrètes de Jésus*. Les livres secrets des Gnostiques d'Égypte. Paris: Librairie Plon, 1959.

———. *The Secret Books of the Egyptian Gnostics*. 1960. Reprinted, Rochester, VT: Inner Traditions International, 1986.

Dunderberg, Ismo. *The Beloved Disciple in Conflict? Revisiting the Gospels of John and Thomas*. New York: Oxford University Press, 2006.

———. "From Thomas to Valentinus: Genesis Exegesis in Fragment 4 of Valentinus and Its Relationship to the *Gospel of Thomas*." In *Thomas Traditions in Antiquity: The Social and Cultural World of the Gospel of Thomas*, edited by Jon Ma. Asgeirsson, April D. DeConick, and Risto Uro, 221–37. NHMS 59. Leiden: Brill, 2006.

———. "John and Thomas in Conflict?" In *The Nag Hammadi Library after Fifty Years: Proceedings of the 1995 Society of Biblical Literature Commemoration*, edited by John D. Turner and Anne McGuire, 361–80. NHMS 44. Leiden: Brill, 1997.

———. "Thomas and the Beloved Disciple." In *Thomas at the Crossroads: Essays on the Gospel of Thomas*, edited by Risto Uro, 65–88. SNTIW. Edinburgh: T. & T. Clark, 1998.

———. "*Thomas*' I-Sayings and the Gospel of John." In *Thomas at the Crossroads*, edited by Risto Uro, 33–64. SNTIW. Edinburgh: T. & T. Clark, 1998.
Dunn, James D. G. *The Epistles to the Colossians and to Philemon*. NIGTC. Grand Rapids: Eerdmans, 1996.
Dupont, Jacques. *Les Béatitudes. Vol. 1: Le problème littéraire*. Ebib. 1958. Reprinted, Paris: Gabalda, 1969.
Elliott, John H. "The Evil Eye and the Sermon on the Mount: Contours of a Pervasive Belief in Social Scientific Perspective." *Biblical Interpretation* 2 (1994) 51–84.
———. "The Fear of the Leer: The Evil Eye from the Bible to Li'l Abner." *Forum* 4,4 (1988) 42–71.
Ensor, Peter W. *Jesus and His 'Works.'* WUNT 2/85. Tübingen: Mohr/Siebeck, 1996.
Evans, Craig A., Robert L. Webb, and Richard A. Wiebe, editors. *Nag Hammadi Texts and the Bible: A Synopsis and Index*. NTTS 18. Leiden: Brill, 1993.
Evelyn-White, Hugh G. *The Sayings of Jesus from Oxyrhynchus*. Cambridge: Cambridge University Press, 1920.
Fallon, Francis T., and Ron Cameron. "The Gospel of Thomas: A Forschungsbericht and Analysis." *ANRW* 2.25.6 (1988) 4195–251.
Fitzmyer, Joseph A. "The Oxyrhynchus *Logoi* of Jesus and the Coptic Gospel according to Thomas." *TS* 20 (1959) 505–60.
Fleddermann, Harry T. *Q: A Reconstruction and Commentary*. Biblical Tools and Studies. Leuven: Peeters, 2005.
Fortna, Robert T. *The Fourth Gospel and Its Predecessor: From Narrative Source to Present Gospel*. Philadelphia: Fortress, 1988.
Funk, Robert W., Roy W. Hoover, and the Jesus Seminar. *The Five Gospels: The Search for the Authentic Words of Jesus*. San Francisco: HarperCollins, 1993.
Furnish, Victor Paul. "The Jesus-Paul Debate: From Baur to Bultmann." *BJRL* 47 (1964–65) 342–81.
Gärtner, Bertil. *The Theology of the Gospel according to Thomas*. New York: Harper, 1961.
Gerhardsson, Birger. *Memory and Manuscript: Oral Tradition and Written Transmission in Rabbinic Judaism and Early Christianity*. ASNU 22. Lund: Gleerup, 1961.
Giversen, Søren. "Questions and Answers in the Gospel according to Thomas: The Composition of pl. 81,14–18 and pl. 83,14–27." *AcOr* 25 (1960) 332–38.
Gnilka, Joachim. *Der Kolosserbrief*. HTKNT 10/1. Freiburg: Herder, 1980.
———. *Das Matthäusevangelium 1.Teil: Kommentar zu Kap. 1,1—13,58*. HTKNT 1.1. Freiburg: Herder, 1986.
Grant, Frederick C. "Method in Studying Jesus' Social Teaching." In *Studies in Early Christianity*, edited by Shirley Jackson Case, 239–81. New York: Century, 1928.
Grant, Robert M., and David Noel Freedman. *The Secret Sayings of Jesus*. Garden City, NY: Doubleday, 1960.
Grässer, Erich. "Kol 3,1–4 als Beispiel einer Interpretation secundum homines recipientes." *ZTK* 64 (1967) 139–68.

———. "Der Mensch Jesus als Thema der Theologie." In *Jesus und Paulus: Festschrift für Werner Georg Kümmel zum 70. Geburtstag*, edited by E. Earle Ellis and Erich Grässer, 129-50. Göttingen: Vandenhoeck & Ruprecht, 1975.

Grundmann, Walter. *Das Evangelium nach Lukas*. THKNT 3,2. Berlin: Evangelische Verlagsanstalt, 1961.

Guillaumont, Antoine, Henri-Charles Puech, Gilles Quispel, Walter C. Till, and Yassah 'Abd Al Masih. *The Gospel according to Thomas: Coptic Text Established and Translated*. New York: Harper, 1959.

Gundry, Robert. *Matthew: A Commentary on His Literary and Theological Art*. Grand Rapids: Eerdmans, 1982.

Haenchen, Ernst. *Die Botschaft des Thomas-Evangeliums*. Berlin: Töpelmann, 1961.

———. *Johannesevangelium: Ein Kommentar*. Tübingen: Mohr/Siebeck, 1980.

———. "Literatur zum Thomasevangelium." *TRu* 27 (1961/62) 147-78, 306-38.

Hahn, Ferdinand. "Die christologische Begründung urchristlicher Parärese." *ZNW* 72 (1981) 85-99.

Hanson, K. C. "Jesus and the Social Bandits." In *The Social Setting of Jesus and the Gospels*, edited by Wolfgang Stegemann et al., 283-300. Minneapolis: Fortress, 2002.

Harnack, Adolf von. *Sprüche und Reden Jesu: Die zweite Quelle des Matthäus und Lukas*. BZENT 2. Leipzig: Hinrichs, 1907.

Harris, Murray J. *Colossians and Philemon*. EGGNT. Grand Rapids: Eerdmans, 1991.

Hartin, Patrick J. *James and the Q Sayings of Jesus*. JSNTSup 47. Sheffield: JSOT Press, 1991.

Haupt, Walther. *Worte Jesu und Gemeindeüberlieferung: Eine Untersuchung zur Quellengeschichte der Synopse*. UNT 3. Leipzig: Hinrichs, 1913.

Hawkins, John C. *Horae Synopticae*. 2nd ed. Oxford: Clarendon, 1909.

Hedrick, Charles W. "Thomas and the Synoptics: Aiming at a Consensus." *SecCent* 7 (1989-90) 39-56.

Heil, Christoph. *Lukas und Q: Studien zur lukanischen Redaktion des Spruchevangeliums Q*. BZNW 111. Berlin: de Gruyter, 2003.

Hoffmann, Paul. "Evaluation of Q 12:33-34: Storing Up Treasures in Heaven." In *Q 12:33-34: Storing Up Treasures in Heaven*, Steven R. Johnson, 16, 53-57, 104-5, 114, 117, 120, 127, 133, 138, 142-45, 150-52, 156-57, 162, 168, 171-72, 176, 182, 187, 194-95, 197. Documenta Q. Leuven: Peeters, 2007.

———. "Jesu 'Verbot des Sorgens' und seine Nachgeschichte in der synoptischen Überlieferung." In *Jesu Rede von Gott und ihre Nachgeschichte im frühen Christentum: Beiträge zur Verkündigung Jesu und zum Kerygma der Kirche: Festschrift für Willi Marxsen zum 70. Geburtstag*, edited by D.-A. Koch et al., 116-41. Gütersloh: Gütersloher, 1989.

———. "Mutmassungen über Q: Zum Problem der literarischen Genese von Q." In *The Sayings Source Q and the Historical Jesus*, edited by A. Lindemann, 255-88. BETL 158. Leuven: Peeters, 2001.

———. *Tradition und Situation: Studien zur Jesusüberlieferung in der Logienquelle und den synoptischen Evangelien*. NTAbh 28. Münster: Aschendorff, 1995.

Horn, Friedrich W. *Glaube und Handeln in der Theologie des Lukas.* Göttingen: Vandenhoeck & Ruprecht, 1983.
Houlden, J. L. *Paul's Letters From Prison: Philippians, Colossians, Philemon, and Ephesians.* Philadelphia: Westminster, 1977.
Huck, Albert. *Synopse der drei ersten Evangelien.* 13th ed. revised by Heinrich Greeven. Tübingen: Mohr/Siebeck, 1981.
Jacobson, Arland D. *The First Gospel: An Introduction to Q.* 1992. Reprinted, Eugene, OR: Wipf & Stock, 2005.
Jeremias, Joachim. *The Parables of Jesus.* 2nd ed. Translated by S. H. Hooke. New York: Scribners, 1972.
Jeremias, Joachim. *Die Sprache des Lukasevangeliums: Redaktion und Tradition im Nicht-Markusstoff des dritten Evangeliums.* MeyerK Sonderband. Göttingen: Vandenhoeck & Ruprecht, 1980.
―――. *Unknown Sayings of Jesus.* Translated by Reginald H. Fuller. 2nd ed. London: SPCK, 1964.
Johnson, Steven R. "The *Gospel of Thomas* 76:3 and Canonical Parallels: Three Segments in the Tradition History of the Saying." In *The Nag Hammadi Library after Fifty Years: Proceedings of the 1995 Society of Biblical Literature Commemoration*, edited by John D. Turner and Anne McGuire, 308-26. NHMS 44. Leiden: Brill, 1997.
―――. "The Hidden/Revealed Saying in the Greek and Coptic Versions of *Gos. Thom.* 5 & 6." *NovT* 44 (2002) 176-85.
―――. "The Identity and Significance of the *Neaniskos* in Mark." *Forum* 8/1-2 (1992) 123-39.
―――. *Q 12:33-34: Storing up Treasures in Heaven.* Documenta Q. Leuven: Peeters, 2007.
Jones, Geraint V. "The Parables of the Gospel of Thomas." In *The Art and Truth of the Parables: A Study in their Literary Form and Modern Interpretation*, 230-40. London: SPCK, 1964.
Jongkind, Dirk. "'The Lilies of the Field' Reconsidered: *Codex Sinaiticus* and the Gospel of Thomas." *NovT* 48 (2006) 209-16.
Joüon, Paul. "Note sur Colossiens, III, 5-11," *RSR* 26 (1936) 185-89.
Kasser, Rodolphe. *L'Évangile selon Thomas: Présentation et commentaire théologique.* Bibliotèque théologique. Neuchâtel: Delachaux et Niestlé, 1961.
Kelber, Werner H. *The Oral and the Written Gospel: The Hermeneutics of Speaking and Writing in the Synoptic Tradition, Mark, Paul, and Q.* Philadelphia: Fortress, 1983.
Kilpatrick, George D. *The Origins of the Gospel according to St. Matthew.* Oxford: Clarendon, 1946.
Kirk, Alan. *The Composition of the Sayings Source: Genre, Synbchrony, and Wisdom Redaction in Q.* NovTSup 91. Leiden: Brill, 1998.
Kittel, Gerhard. "Der geschichtliche Ort des Jakobusbriefes." *ZNW* 41 (1942) 71-105.
Klein, Martin. *"Ein vollkommenes Werk": Vollkommenheit, Gesetz und Gericht als theologische Themen des Jakobusbriefes.* BWANT 7. Stuttgart: Kohlhammer, 1995.
Kloppenborg, John S. "Evaluation of Q 12:33-34: Storing Up Treasures in Heaven." In *Q 12:33-34: Storing Up Treasures in Heaven*, Steven R. Johnson, 16, 53, 104, 113–

14, 117, 120, 127, 133, 138, 142, 150, 156, 162, 168, 171, 175, 182, 186, 194, 197. Documenta Q. Leuven: Peeters, 2007.

———. *Excavating Q: The History and Setting of the Sayings Gospel*. Minneapolis: Fortress, 2000.

———. *The Formation of Q: Trajectories in Ancient Wisdom Collections*. SAC. 1987. Reprinted, Valley Forge, PA: Trinity, 2000.

Klostermann, Erich. *Apokrypha II: Evangelien*. Edited by Hans Lietzmann. 2nd ed. KlT. Bonn: Marcus und Weber, 1910.

———. *Das Lukasevangelium*. HNT 5. Tübingen: Mohr/Siebeck, 1929.

Knox, Wilfred L. *The Sources of the Synoptic Gospels*. Vol. 2: *St. Luke and St. Matthew*. Cambridge: Cambridge University Press, 1957.

Koester, Helmut. *Ancient Christian Gospels: Their History and Development*. Philadelphia: Trinity, 1990.

———. "Dialog und Spruchüberlieferung in den gnostischen Texten von Nag Hammadi." *EvT* 39 (1979) 532–56.

———. "Les discours d'adieu de l'évangile de Jean: Leur trajectoire au premier et deuxième siècle." In *La communauté johannique et son histoire: La trajectoire de l'évangile de Jean aux deux premiers siècles*, edited by Jean-Daniel Kaestli et al., 269–80. Geneva: Labor et Fides, 1990.

———. "Gnostic Sayings and Controversy Traditions in John 8:12–59." In *Nag Hammadi, Gnosticism, and Early Christianity*, edited by Charles W. Hedrick and Robert Hodgson, Jr., 97–110. Peabody, MA: Hendrickson, 1986.

———. "Gnostic Writings as Witnesses for the Development of the Sayings Tradition." In *The Rediscovery of Gnosticism: Proceedings of the International Conference on Gnosticism at Yale, New Haven, Conn., March 28–31, 1978*, edited by Bentley Layton, 1:238–61. Leiden: Brill, 1980.

———. "The Story of the Johannine Tradition." *Sewanee Theological Review* 36 (1992) 17–31.

———. *Synoptische Überlieferung bei den apostolischen Vätern*. TU. Berlin: Akademie, 1957.

Koester, Helmut, and Elaine Pagels. "The Dialogue of the Savior [III,5]." In *The Nag Hammadi Library in English*, edited by James M. Robinson, 244–45. 3rd ed. San Francisco: HarperCollins, 1990.

Kuhn, Heinz-Wolfgang. "Der irdische Jesus bei Paulus als traditionsgeschichtliches und theologisches Problem." *ZTK* 67 (1970) 295–320.

Kuhn, Karl H. "Some Observations on the Coptic Gospel according to Thomas." *Mus* 73 (1960) 317–23.

Kysar, Robert. *The Fourth Evangelist and His Gospel: An Examination of Contemporary Scholarship*. Minneapolis: Augsburg, 1975.

Lähnemann, Johannes. *Der Kolosserbrief: Komposition, Situation und Argumentation*. SNT 3. Gütersloh: Gütersloher, 1971.

Layton, Bentley, editor. *Nag Hammadi Codex II,2–7; Together with XIII,2*, Brit. Lib. Or.4926(1), and P.Oxy. 1, 654, 655: Vol I*. NHS 20. Leiden: Brill, 1989.

Levison, John R. "2 *Apoc. Bar* 48:42–52:7 and the Apocalyptic Dimension of Colossians 3:1–6." *JBL* 108 (1989) 93–108.
Liddell, Henry G., and Robert Scott. *A Greek-English Lexicon.* Revised and Augmented by Henry S. Jones. Oxford: Clarendon, 1968.
Lightfoot, J. B. *Saint Paul's Epistles to the Colossians and to Philemon.* 9th ed. London: MacMillan, 1890.
Lindemann, Andreas. *Der Kolosserbrief.* Züricher Bibel Kommentare. Zürich: Theologischer, 1983.
———. "Zur Gleichnisinterpretation im Thomas-Evangelium." *ZNW* 71 (1980) 214–43.
Lohmeyer, Ernst. *Die Briefe an die Kolosser und an Philemon.* KEKNT 2.12. Göttingen: Vandenhoeck & Ruprecht, 1961.
Lohse, Eduard. *Colossians and Philemon: A Commentary on the Epistles to the Colossians and to Philemon.* Translated by William R. Poehlmann and Robert J. Karris. Hermeneia. Philadelphia: Fortress, 1971.
Lührmann, Dieter. *Die Redaktion der Logienquelle.* WMANT 33. Neukirchen-Vluyn: Neukirchener, 1969.
Luz, Ulrich. *Das Evangelium nach Matthäus. Vol. 1: Mt 1–7.* EKKNT 1.1. Neukirchen-Vluyn: Neukirchener, 1985.
———. *Matthew 1–7.* Translated by James Crouch. Hermeneia. Minneapolis: Fortress, 2007.
Mack, Burton L. *Rhetoric and the New Testament.* GBS. Minneapolis: Fortress, 1990.
Mack, Burton L., and Vernon K. Robbins. *Patterns of Persuasion in the Gospels.* Sonoma, CA: Polebridge, 1989.
Manson, Thomas W. *The Sayings of Jesus: As recorded in the Gospels according to St. Matthew and St. Luke arranged with Introduction and Commentary.* London: SCM, 1949.
Marriot, Horace. *The Sermon on the Mount.* London: SPCK, 1952.
Martin, G. Currie. "The Epistle of St. James as a Storehouse of the Sayings of Jesus." *Exp* 4 (1907) 174–84.
Martin, Ralph P. *Colossians and Philemon.* Greenwood, S.C.: Attic, 1974.
Massebieau, L. "L'Épitre de Jacques est-elle l'oeuvre d'un Chrétien?" *RHR* 32 (1895) 249–83.
Mayor, Joseph B. *The Epistle of St. James.* London: MacMillan, 1892.
McLean, Bradley H. "On the Gospel of Thomas and Q." In *The Gospel behind the Gospels: Current Studies on Q*, edited by Ronald A. Piper, 321–45. NovTSup 75. Leiden: Brill, 1995.
Merklein, Helmut. *Die Gottesherrschaft als Handlungsprinzip: Untersuchung zur Ethik Jesu.* 3rd ed. FB 34. Würzburg: Echter, 1984.
Minear, Paul S. *Commands of Christ.* Nashville: Abingdon, 1972.
Mineshige, Kiyoshi. *Besitzverzicht und Almosen bei Lukas: Wesen und Forderung des lukanischen Vermögensethos.* WUNT 2/163. Tübingen: Mohr/Siebeck, 2003.
Montefiore, Hugh W. "A Comparison of the Parables of the Gospel according to Thomas and of the Synoptic Gospels." *NTS* 7 (1961) 220–48.

Moreland, Milton C., and James M. Robinson. "The International Q Project: Work Sessions 31 July—2 August, 20 November 1992." *JBL* 112 (1993) 500–506.

———. "The International Q Project: Work Sessions 23–27 May, 22–26 August, 17–18 November 1994." *JBL* 114 (1995) 475–85.

Moulton, Harold K. *Colossians, Philemon and Ephesians*. Epworth Preacher's Commentaries 10. London: Epworth, 1963.

Moulton, James H., and George Milligan. *Vocabulary of the Greek Testament*. 1930. Reprinted, Peabody, MA: Hendrickson, 2004.

Moxnes, Halvor. *The Economy of the Kingdom: Social Conflict and Economic Relations in Luke's Gospel*. OBT. Philadelphia: Fortress, 1988.

Neirynck, Frans. "Paul and the Sayings of Jesus." In *L'apôtre Paul: personnalité, style et conception du ministère*, edited by Albert Vanhoye, 265–321. BETL 73. Leuven: Leuven University Press; Peeters, 1986.

Neller, Kenneth V. "Diversity in the Gospel of Thomas: Clues for a New Direction." *SecCent* 7 (1989–90) 1–18.

Norden, Eduard. *Agnostos Theos: Untersuchungen zur Formengeschichte religiöser Rede*. Leipzig: Teubner, 1913.

Onuki, Takashi. "Traditionsgeschichte von Thomasevangelium 17 und ihre christologische Relevanz." In *Anfänge der Christologie*, edited by Cilliers Breytenbach and Henning Paulsen, 399–415. Göttingen: Vandenhoeck & Ruprecht, 1991.

Pagels, Elaine. *Beyond Belief: The Secret Gospel of Thomas*. New York: Random House, 2003.

———. "Exegesis of Genesis 1 in the Gospel of Thomas and John." *JBL* 118 (1999) 477–96.

Patterson, Stephen J. "The Gospel of Thomas and Christian Beginnings." In *Thomas Traditions in Antiquity: The Social and Cultural World of the Gospel of Thomas*, edited by Jon Ma. Asgeirsson, April D. DeConick, and Risto Uro, 1–18. NHMS 59. Leiden: Brill, 2006.

———. *The Gospel of Thomas and Jesus*. FFNT. Sonoma, CA: Polebridge, 1993.

———. "The Gospel of Thomas and the Synoptic Tradition: A Forschungsbericht and Critique." *Forum* 8.1-2 (1992) 45–97.

———. "The Gospel of Thomas: Introduction." In *Q-Thomas Reader*, edited by John S. Kloppenborg et al., 77–123. Sonoma, CA: Polebridge, 1990.

———. "Paul and the Jesus Tradition: It is Time for Another Look." *HTR* 84 (1991) 23–41.

———. "Wisdom in Q and *Thomas*." In *In Search of Wisdom: Essays in Memory of John G. Gammie*, edited by Leo G. Perdue, B. Brandon Scott, and William J. Wiseman, 187–221. Louisville: Westminster John Knox, 1993.

Percy, E. *Die Botschaft Jesu: Eine traditionskritische und exegetische Untersuchung*. Lund universitets årsskrift 49/5. Lund: Gleerup, 1953.

Perrin, Nicholas. "Recent Trends in *Gospel of Thomas* Research (1991–2006): Part I, The Historical Jesus and the Synoptic Gospels." *CBR* 5.2 (2007) 183–206.

Pesch, W. "Zur Exegese von Mt 6,19–21 und Lk 12,33–34." *Bib* 40 (1960) 356–78.

Piper, Ronald A. *Wisdom in the Q-tradition: The Aphoristic Teaching of Jesus*. SNTSMS 61. Cambridge: Cambridge University Press, 1989.

Pöhlmann, Wolfgang. "Die hymnischen All-Prädikationen in Kol 1:15–20." *ZNW* 64 (1973) 53–74.

Pokorny, Petr. *Colossians: A Commentary*. Translated by S. S. Schatzmann. Peabody, MA: Hendrickson, 1991.

Polag, Athanasius. *Fragmenta Q: Textheft zur Logienquelle*. Neukirchen-Vluyn: Neukirchener, 1979.

Popkes, Enno Edzard. "'Ich bin das Licht'—Erwägungen zur Verhältnisbestimmung des Thomasevangeliums und der johanneischen Schriften anhand der Lichtmetaphorik." In *Kontexte des Johannesevangeliums: Das vierte Evangelium in religions- und traditionsgeschichtlicher Perspektive*, edited by J. Frey et al., 641–74. WUNT 175. Tübingen: Mohr/Siebeck, 2004.

Porter, Stanley D. "POxy. 655 and James Robinson's Proposals for Q: Brief Points of Clarificatiton." *Journal of Theological Studies* 52 (2000) 84–92.

Radford, Lewis B. *The Epistle to the Colossians and the Epistle to Philemon*. London: Methuen, 1931.

Rahlfs, Alfred, ed. *Septuaginta: id est: Vetus Testamentum graece iuxta LXX interpretes*. 2 vols. Stuttgart: Deutsche Bibelgesellschaft, 1935. Reprinted, 1979.

Richter, Georg. *Studien zum Johannesevangelium*. Edited by Josef Hainz. BU 13. Regensburg: Friedrich Pustet, 1977.

Riley, Gregory J. "The *Gospel of Thomas* in Recent Scholarship." *Currents in Research: Biblical Studies* 2 (1994) 227–52.

———. "Influence of Thomas Christianity on Luke 12:14 and 5:39." *HTR* 88 (1995) 229–35.

———. *Resurrection Reconsidered: Thomas and John in Controversy*. Minneapolis: Fortress, 1995.

Robbins, Vernon K. "Rhetorical Composition and Sources in the Gospel of Thomas." In *Society of Biblical Literature 1997 Seminar Papers*, 86–114. SBLSP 36. Atlanta: Scholars, 1997.

Robinson, James M. "Q 12:49–53: Evaluation of Children against Parents." In Albrecht Garsky, Christoph Heil, Thomas Hieke, and Josef E. Amon, *Q 12:49–59: Children against Parents; Judging the Time; Settling out of Court*, edited by Shawn Carruth, 119–21. Documenta Q. Leuven: Peeters, 1997.

———. "Evaluation of Q 12:33–34: Storing Up Treasures in Heaven." In *Q 12:33–34: Storing Up Treasures in Heaven*, Steven R. Johnson, 16, 53, 102–4, 113, 116, 120, 127, 132, 138, 142, 149, 156, 161–62, 167–68, 171, 175, 182, 186, 194, 197. Documenta Q. Leuven: Peeters, 2007.

———. "The International Q Project: Work Session 16 November 1990." *JBL* 110 (1991) 494–98.

———. "The International Q Project: Work Sessions 12–14 July, 22 November 1991." *JBL* 111 (1992) 500–508.

———. "Kerygma and History in the New Testament." In James M. Robinson and Helmut Koester, *Trajectories through Early Christianity*, 20–70. 1971. Reprinted, Eugene, OR: Wipf & Stock, 2006.

———. "LOGOI SOPHON: On the Gattung of Q." In James M. Robinson and Helmut Koester, *Trajectories through Early Christianity*, 71–113. 1971. Reprinted, Eugene, OR: Wipf & Stock, 2006.

———. "A Pre-Canonical Greek Reading in Saying 36 of the *Gospel of Thomas*." In idem, *The Sayings Gospel Q: Collected Essays*, 845–84. BETL 189. Leuven: Peeters, 2005.

———. "The Pre-Q Text of the (Ravens and) Lilies: Q 12:22–31 and P. Oxy. 655 (*Gos. Thom.* 36)." In *Text und Geschichte: Facetten theologischen Arbeitens aus dem Freundes- undSchülerkreis. Dieter Lührmann zum 60. Geburtstag*, edited by Stefan Maser and Egbert Schlarb, 143–80. Marburger theologischer Studien 50. Marburg: Elwert, 1999. Reprinted in *The Sayings Gospel Q: Collected Essays*, 729–76. Reprinted in *The Sayings Gospel Q*, 729–76.

———. *The Sayings Gospel Q: Collected Essays*. Edited by Christoph Heil and Joseph Verheyden. BETL 189. Leuven: Peeters, 2005.

———. "The Study of the Historical Jesus after Nag Hammadi." *Semeia* 44 (1988) 45–55.

———. "A Written Greek Sayings Cluster Older than Q: A Vestige." *HTR* 92 (1996) 61–77. Reprinted in *The Sayings Gospel Q: Collected Essays*, 777–94.

Robinson, James M., and Christoph Heil. "The Lilies of the Field: Saying 36 of the *Gospel of Thomas* and Secondary Accretions in Q 12.22b–31." *NTS* 47 (2001) 1–25. Reprinted in *The Sayings Gospel Q: Collected Essays*, 809–34.

———. "Noch einmal: Der Schreibfehler in Q 12,27." *ZNW* 92 (2001) 113–22. Reprinted in *The Sayings Gospel Q: Collected Essays*, 795–808.

———. "P.Oxy. 655 und Q: Zum Diskussionsbeitrag von Stanley E. Porter." In *For the Children, Perfect Instruuction: Essays in Honor of Hans-Martin Schenke on the Occasion of the Berliner Arbeitskreis für koptisch-gnotische Schriften's Thirtieth Year*, edited by H.-G. Bethbe, S. Emmel, K. L. King, and I. Schletterer, 411–23. Nag Hammadi and Manichaean Studies 54. Leiden: Brill, 2002. Reprinted in *The Sayings Gospel Q: Collected Essays*, 835–44.

———. "Zeugnisse eines schriftlichen, griechischen vorkanonischen Textes: Mt 6,28b ℵ*, P.Oxy. 655 I,1–17 (EvTh 36) und Q 12,27." *ZNW* 89 (1998) 30–44. Reprinted in *The Sayings Gospel Q: Collected Essays*, 713–28.

Robinson, James M., Paul Hoffmann, and John S. Kloppenborg, editors. *The Critical Edition of Q: Synopsis including the Gospels of Matthew and Luke, Mark and Thomas with English, German, and French Translations of Q and Thomas*. Managing editor, Milton C. Moreland. Hermeneia Supplements. Minneapolis: Fortress, 2000.

———, editors. *The Sayings Gospel Q in Greek and English: With Parallels from the Gospels of Mark and Thomas*. Minneapolis: Fortress, 2002.

Roulet, Philippe, and Ulrich Ruegg. "Étude de Jean 6: La narration et l'histoire de la rédaction." In *La communauté johannique et son histoire: La trajectoire de l'évangile de Jean aux deux premiers siècles*, edited by Jean-Daniel Kaestli, Jean-Michel Poffet, and Jean Zumstein, 231–47. Geneva: Labor et Fides, 1990.

Sanders, E. P. "Literary Dependence in Colossians." *JBL* 85 (1966) 28–45.
Sato, Migaku. *Q und Prophetie: Studien zur Gattungs- und Traditionsgeschichte der Quelle Q*. WUNT 2/29. Tübingen: Mohr/Siebeck, 1988.
Schmid, Josef. *Matthäus und Lukas: Eine Untersuchung des Verhältnisses ihrer Evangelien*. BibS(F) 23. Freiburg: Herder, 1930.
Schnelle, Udo. *Antidoketische Christologie im Johannesevangelium: Eine Untersuchung zur Stellung des vierten Evangeliums in der johanneischen Schule*. FRLANT 144. Göttingen: Vandenhoeck & Ruprecht, 1987.
Schrage, Wolfgang. *Das Verhältnis des Thomas-Evangeliums zur synoptischen Tradition und zu den koptischen Evangelienübersetzungen*. BZNW 29. Berlin: Alfred Töpelmann, 1964.
Schröter, Jens. "Vorsynoptische Überlieferung auf P.Oxy. 655? Kritische Bemerkungen zu einer erneuerten These." *ZNW* 90 (1999) 265–72.
Schulz, Siegfried. *Q: Die Spruchquelle der Evangelisten*. Zürich: Theologischer Verlag, 1972.
Schürmann, Heinz. "'Das Gesetz des Christus' (Gal 6,2): Jesu Verhalten und Wort als letztgültige sittliche Norm nach Paulus." In *Neues Testament und Kirche*, edited by Joachim Gnilka, 282–300. Freiburg: Herder, 1974.
———. "Das Thomasevangelium und das lukanische Sondergut." *BZ* 7 (1963) 236–60.
———. *Traditionsgeschichtliche Untersuchungen zu den synoptischen Evangelien*. KBANT. Düsseldorf: Patmos, 1968.
Schweizer, Eduard. *Der Brief an die Kolosser*. EKKNT. Neukirchen-Vluyn: Neukirchener, 1976.
———. *Das Evangelium nach Matthäus*. NTD 2.13. Göttingen: Vandenhoeck & Ruprecht, 1973.
Sell, Jesse. "Johannine Traditions in Logion 61 of the Gospel of Thomas." *Perspectives in Religious Studies* 7 (1980) 24–37.
Sellew, Philip H. "Reconstruction of Q 12:33–59." In *Society of Biblical Literature 1987 Seminar Papers*, edited by David J. Lull, 617–68. Atlanta: Scholars, 1987.
Shepherd, Massey H. "The Epistle of James and the Gospel of Matthew." *JBL* 75 (1956) 40–51.
Sieber, John H. "A Redactional Analysis of the Synoptic Gospels with Regard to the Question of the Sources of the Gospel according to Thomas." Ph.D. dissertation, Claremont Graduate School, 1965.
Snodgrass, Klyne R. "The Gospel of Thomas: A Secondary Gospel." *SecCent* 7 (1989–90) 19–38.
Spitta, Friedrich. *Der Brief des Jakobus*. Zur Geschichte und Literatur des Urchristentums 2. Göttingen: Vandenhoeck & Ruprecht, 1896.
Stanley, D. M. "Pauline Allusions to the Sayings of Jesus." *CBQ* 23 (1961) 26–39.
Steinhauser, Michael. *Doppelbildworte in den synoptischen Evangelien*. FB 44. Würzburg: Echter, 1981.
Temple, Sydney. *The Core of the Fourth Gospel*. London: Mowbrays, 1975.
Tuckett, Christopher M. "1 Corinthians and Q." *JBL* 102 (1983) 607–19.

Turner, H. E. W., and Hugh W. Montefiore. *Thomas and the Evangelists*. SBT 1/35. Naperville, IL: Allenson, 1962.

Uro, Risto. "Neither Here Nor There: Luke 17:20-21 and Related Sayings in Thomas, Mark, and Q." Occasional Papers of the Institute for Antiquity and Christianity 20. Claremont, CA: Institute for Antiquity and Christianity, 1990.

―――. "'Secondary Orality' in the Gospel of Thomas? Logion 14 as a Test Case." *Forum* 9.3-4 (1993) 305-29. Revised version published as "*Thomas* and Oral Gospel Tradition." In *Thomas at the Crossroads: Essays on the Gospel of Thomas*, edited by R. Uro. SNTIW. Edinburgh: T. & T. Clark, 1998.

―――. *Thomas: Seeking the Historical Context of the Gospel of Thomas*. London: T. & T. Clark, 2003.

Valantasis, Richard. *The Gospel of Thomas*. NTR. London: Routledge, 1997.

Verheyden, Joseph. "Evaluation of Q 12:33-34: Storing Up Treasures in Heaven." In *Q 12:33-34: Storing Up Treasures in Heaven*, Steven R. Johnson, 16-17, 57-59, 105-7, 114, 117, 120-21, 127, 133, 138, 145, 152-53, 157, 162-63, 168, 172, 176, 182-83, 187, 195, 197-99. Documenta Q. Leuven: Peeters, 2007.

Walter, Nikolaus. "Paul and the Early Christian Jesus-Tradition." In *Paul and Jesus: Collected Essays*, edited by A. J. M. Wedderburn, 51-80. JSNTSup 37. Sheffield: JSOT Press, 1989. Translated from "Paulus und die urchristliche Jesustradition." *NTS* 31 (1985) 498-522.

Wendling, Emil. *Die Entstehung des Marcus-Evangeliums: Philologische Untersuchungen*. Tübingen: Mohr/Siebeck, 1908.

Wilkens, Wilhelm. *Die Entstehungsgeschichte des vierten Evangeliums*. Zollikon: Evangelischer, 1958.

Wilson, Robert McL. *Studies in the Gospel of Thomas*. London: Mowbray, 1960.

―――. "'Thomas' and the Growth of the Gospels." *HTR* 53/54 (1960) 231-50.

Wischmeyer, Oda. "Matthäus 6,25-34 par: Die Spruchreihe vom Sorgen." *ZNW* 85 (1994) 1-20.

Wise, Michael O., Martin G. Abegg, Jr., and Edward M. Cook. *The Dead Sea Scrolls: A New Translation*. San Francisco: HarperCollins, 1996.

Wrege, Hans-Theo. *Die Überlieferungsgeschichte der Bergpredigt*. WUNT 9. Tübingen: Mohr/Siebeck, 1968.

Zeller, Dieter. *Die weisheitlichen Mahnsprüche bei den Synoptikern*. FB 17. Würzburg: Echter, 1977.

Index of Ancient Documents

OLD TESTAMENT

Genesis

1:29	74n, 143n
1:30	74n, 143n
2:9	74n, 143n
3:6	74n, 143n
9:3	74n, 143n
47:24	74n, 143n

Exodus

16:19–24	76
20:1–17	103n
20:4	103n
20:5	103n
20:17	103n

Leviticus

19:18b	84
25:7	73n, 143n

Deuteronomy

5:6–21	103n

2 Samuel

16:2	73n, 143n

Job

25:6	74n

Psalms

110:1	102, 118

Proverbs

2:4–6	108
2:4	129
8:17–19	129
8:17	108
11:25	52n
24:28	108
25:20	74n
30:8	108

Isaiah

14:11	74n
51:8	74n
55:10	143n
64:3	25

Jeremiah

7:33	143n
15:3	143n

Index of Ancient Documents

Jeremiah (*continued*)

19:7	143n
41:20	143n

Ezekiel

29:5	143n
47:12	143n

Malachi

3:1	144n
3:11	74n, 99n

DEUTEROCANON AND PSEUDEPIGRAPHA

2 Apocalypse of Baruch — 108n

Baruch

3:15	130

2 Baruch

14:12–14	51n
24:1	51n

1 Enoch

97:8–10	90n, 99n

2 Enoch

50:5—51:3	54n

Epistle of Jeremiah

13	99n

2 Esdras

7:76–77	129n
7:77	51n, 141n
8:33	51n, 141n

Psalms of Solomon

9:5	51n

Pseudo-Phocylides

7	108
110	100n

Sirach

3:30–31	128
4:11–12	108
4:11	129
4:18	108, 111n
6:27	108, 130
7:12–13	108
11:17–19	96n
11:18–19	100n
17:22	128
18:1	108
20:24–26	108
20:30	128
24:34	108
29:10–13	54n
29:11–12	128
41:14	128
43:26–27	108
43:27	107n, 108
50:13–22	108

Testament of Levi

13:5	54n

Tobit

4:6b–11	54n
4:7–11	54
4:8–10	54, 128
12:8–9	54n, 128

Index of Ancient Documents

Wisdom of Solomon

1:14	106n, 108
6:12	108, 111n, 130
7:13–14	113n
7:13b–14b	130
7:14	42n, 141n
7:21–22	108, 111n, 113n
7:24–27	106n, 108, 113n
8:1	106n, 108, 113n
8:5	106n, 108, 113n, 130
8:18	108, 113n, 141n
9:1–2	106n, 108
14:28	108
15:1	106n, 108

DEAD SEA SCROLLS

4Q185

2.10–12	108n, 130

4Q525

2.2.2–4	108n, 130

NEW TESTAMENT

Q

3:9	38n
4:1	38n
6:20	xv, 81n, 88n, 90, 90n
6:21	90n
6:23	44n, 141–42, 141n
6:36–37	82n
6:38	37n
6:41	38n
6:44b	82n, 95
6:46–49	xv, 91, 92
7:24	38n
7:31–32	37n
9:58	141n
9:59	38n
10:2–12, 13–16	40n
10:4	40
10:5	38n
10:7	38n
10:9	49
10:15	43n, 43n, 44n, 141n
10:21–22	24n
10:21	141n
10:23–24	24, 24n
11:13	43n, 44n, 141n
11:33–35	93
11:34–36	30
11:34–35	52
11:39	37n
11:41	37n
12:2–40	30
12:2–12	31, 31n
12:4–7	31, 31n
12:7	31n
12:8–9	31n
12:11–12	31, 32n
12:11	31n, 38n
12:12	32n
12:22–34	42n
12:22–31	10, 29, 30, 31, 31n, 32–33, 32n, 34, 46n, 51–52, 93, 124, 125n, 132, 137–39, 148, 149
12:22–24	10, 31, 32n
12:22–23	37n
12:22	30, 31, 31n, 32, 32n
12:23	138n
12:24ff.	32n
12:24	31, 31n, 51, 137
12:25	38n, 138n
12:27	10, 51
12:29–31	34, 137–38
12:29–30	137–38
12:30–31	137–38
12:30	139

Q (*continued*)		
12:31	30, 32, 38–39, 39n, 54, 137–38, 139	
12:33–34	5, 29, 30, 31, 32, 32n, 33, 34, 35n, 41, 48n, 51–52, 138, 148–49	
12:33	xv, 4, 27–50, 51, 52, 53, 54, 57, 63, 64, 72–73, 76, 97–100, 117, 121, 124–25, 125n, 129, 131–47, 149, 150, 151, 152, 155	
$12:33^0$	27–29	
$12:33^1$	29–33, 39	
$12:33^2$	33–37, 38	
$12:33^3$	37–38, 38n, 99n	
$12:33^4$	38	
$12:33^5$	38–40	
$12:33^6$	40–41	
$12:33^7$	41–42	
$12:33^8$	42, 68n	
$12:33^9$	43–44	
$12:33^{10}$	44–45	
$12:33^{11}$	45–46	
$12:33^{12}$	46, 48	
$12:33^{13}$	47	
$12:33^{14}$	47–48	
$12:33^{15}$	48–49	
$12:33^{16}$	49–50	
$12:33^{17}$	50	
12:34	29, 32n, 41	
12:39–40	31, 124	
12:39	29n, 31, 38n, 46, 48–49, 145, 145n	
12:45	38n	
12:51–53	10	
12:52	9–10	
12:56	141n	
13:19	141n	
14:11	xv, 94	
15:7	141n	
16:13	30, 52	
16:17	141n	
17:1–2	37n	
17:3	88n	
17:23–37	13	

Matthew

5:3	86n, 89
5:7	82n, 89
5:9	23n
5:11–12	89
5:11	9
5:18–19	89
5:21–30	103n
5:22–26	103n
5:27–30	103n
5:39ff.	23n
5:39–40	23n
5:44	23n
6	29
6:1–18	30, 34, 35, 36, 51
6:2–4	34
6:5–6	34
6:10	45n
6:16–18	34
6:16	47, 47n
6:17	35n
6:18	30
6:19–24	30, 52n
6:19–21	29, 30, 35, 51–52, 55, 55n
6:19–20	xv, 27–29, 29n, 29n, 31n, 33n, 34, 35, 36, 37n, 38, 39, 46, 47, 52, 53, 54, 63, 67n, 68n, 71n, 75n, 89, 90n, 99n, 129, 132, 135, 151, 152
6:19	4, 34, 35, 35n, 35n, 36, 36n, 38, 39n, 42, 45, 47, 51, 52, 54, 64n, 69, 100n, 116, 121, 134, 137, 149
6:20–34	35

6:20	34, 36, 36n, 37, 38, 42, 45, 47n, 48n, 52–53, 55, 71, 86n, 134, 149
6:20b	50
6:21	42
6:22–34	36
6:22–23	52, 93
6:22–24	29, 30, 34, 36
6:24	52, 89
6:25–34	10, 29, 30, 34, 52
6:25–33	30, 93
6:25	35n
6:31–33	34
6:34	35n
7:1	23n, 35n, 82n, 89
7:6	35n
7:7	89
7:8	89
7:11	89
7:16	3, 89
7:16b	2, 93, 95
7:24	89
7:26	89
10:16b	23n
10:26	35n
10:39	60, 61n
11:23	43n
13	5
13:16–17	24, 24n
13:44	136n
13:45–46	66n, 136n
13:45	136n
15:11	70
16:19	44n, 45
18:15	89
18:18	44n, 45
19:21	43n
21:25	43n
22:39–40	84
23:12	xv, 89, 94
24:31	43n
24:43	29, 29n, 49
28:2	43

Mark

1:10	44
1:11	44
1:17	56n
1:18	56n
2:14	56n
2:15	56n
2:21–22	12, 77n
3:7	56n
4	5, 114
5:24	56n
6:1	56n
6:4–5	77n
7:15	9, 23n
8:34	56n
8:35	60
9:1	78n
9:38	56n
9:42	23n
9:48	66
9:50	23n
10:17–31	56n
10:17–22	23n, 55, 55n, 55n
10:17–21	56n, 121
10:17–21c	56
10:17	57n
10:17a	55n
10:18	56n
10:21–25	100
10:21	5, 29n, 33, 41, 44, 53–54, 55–57, 56n, 69, 76, 129, 149, 151, 152
10:21bc	56n
10:21d	56n
10:21e	56
10:23	55, 55n
10:23b	56
10:25	55, 55n, 56
10:28–31	56
10:28	56n
10:29–30	57n

Mark (continued)

10:30	57n
10:32	56n
10:52	56n
11:20–26	44
11:25	44
12	23, 114
12:17	23n
12:25	44
12:28–30	23n
15:41	56n

Luke

1:1	125
1:2	126
2:11	41n
2:14	43n
2:22	44
3:21	44
3:22	44
4:23–24	77n
4:25	81n, 81n
5:36–39	12
5:39	11
6:20	81n, 86n, 89
6:21	41n, 81n
6:22–23	89
6:23	89
6:24	98
6:25	81n, 86n
6:25b	81n
6:27ff.	23n
6:27–28	23n
6:29	23n
6:36–37	82n, 89
6:37	23n, 89
6:43–45	95
6:44	3, 89
6:44b	2, 82n, 93, 95
6:45	41n
6:46–49	89
9:25	39n
9:47	39n
10:4	40n
10:8–9	9, 70
10:20	45
11:9	89
11:10	89
11:13	89
11:16	44
11:21	39n
11:33–36	52n
11:33–34	52n
11:35	93
11:36	52n
12:1	39n
12:13–21	30, 31, 33, 37n
12:13–20	31
12:13–14	11, 77n
12:14	11
12:15–21	33n
12:15–20	37, 96n
12:16–21	38
12:16–20	82n, 100n
12:21	31, 32, 33, 33n, 34, 36, 37, 37n, 38–39, 100n, 135
12:22–34	29n
12:22–31	10, 32, 33, 93
12:32	30, 32, 33, 148
12:33–34	29n, 30–31, 33, 33n, 38
12:33	xv, 4, 27–29, 29n, 29n, 33n, 41n, 49, 49n, 53–54, 55, 58, 63, 68n, 69, 71, 71n, 72–73, 77, 86n, 89, 129, 132, 149, 151
12:33ab	146
12:33a	33, 33n, 34, 36n, 38, 39, 48, 53–54, 69, 135
12:33b	41, 48, 143n
12:33c	41, 46, 47, 48, 146
12:34	41n, 42

12:35–38	29n, 49	**John**	
12:35	41n	3:16	59, 60
12:38	29n	4	59, 65
12:39–40	29n	4:14	61n
12:39	29, 49	6	59, 61, 135, 149
12:52	9–10	6:1–14	65
13:19	39n	6:1–5	61
13:34	39n	6:12	59, 59n, 60
13:44	41n	6:25–59	76n
13:52	41n	6:26–58	61
14:8–10	82n, 96n	6:26–34	59n, 121
14:11	82n, 89	6:26–27	61n, 78n
14:26	39n	6:26	61, 77, 136
14:27	39n	6:27	4, 5, 34, 46, 58–66,
16:1–8	37		68, 71, 71n, 72, 75n,
16:9	37, 38–39, 42		77, 78, 122, 129, 135,
16:13	89		136, 143, 149, 151
16:17	89	6:27a	59, 59n, 60–61,
17:3	89		69, 75
17:20–21	8, 8n, 12–13, 13n	6:27b	58–59, 59n
		6:28	59n
17:20–21a	13n	6:28–58	65
17:20	13n	6:28–34	121
17:20a	13n	6:28–33	61
17:21	13n	6:28–29	61
17:21b	13n	6:29	77
17:22	13n	6:30–34	59
17:23	12–13, 13n	6:30–33	61
17:33	60	6:31–34	78n
18:22	33, 41n	6:32	78
19:21	41n, 42, 44–45	6:35–47	61
19:38	43n	6:39	59, 60
20:20	39n	6:48–58	61
20:36	44	6:48–50	78n
21:30	39n	6:51–55	61
21:34	39n	6:51b–58	58–59, 59n
22:17	39n	6:52–58	75n
22:32	42	6:53–58	78
22:35	40n	6:56	75n
22:36	40n	7:24	61n
23:2	39n	7:37	61n
23:28	39n	8	65n
23:45	42	8:12–59	65n, 79n

178 Index of Ancient Documents

John (continued)

8:12	65n, 131n
8:51–52	78–79n
8:52	78–79n
9:5	131n
10:10	59, 60
10:28	59, 60
11:50	59, 60
12:24–25	60n
12:24	60n
12:25	60, 60n, 65
12:26	61n
12:34	59n
12:35	61n
14:1	61n
14:27	61n
15:4–9	61n
15:5	60
16:24	61n
17:12	59
18:9	59
20:24–29	19
20:29	19

Acts

13:41	47

Romans

2:25	114n
2:29	109n
6:4	118
8	107, 119
8:5	102
8:18–25	107
8:18–23	118
12–14	21, 23, 25, 26, 83
12–13	84
12:3–8	23
12:9—13:14	23n
12:9–21	23
12:14	23n
12:17	23n, 24
12:18	23n, 24
12:21	23n
13–14	23n
13:1–7	23n
13:7	23n, 23n
13:8–10	23n
13:9	23n
14:1—15:6	23
14:10	23n
14:10a	23n
14:10b–12	23n
14:13	23n
14:14	23n
14:20	23n
16:19	23n

1 Corinthians

1–4	21, 24–25, 26
2:9	24, 24n, 25
3:1	24n, 25
4:8	25
5–7	22
6:12—11:1	23, 23n
7	22n
7:10–11	22, 22n
8–10	22
8:5–6	111n
9:14	22, 22n
11	22n
11:17–34	22
11:23–25	22, 22n
12	23
12:13	105, 111n, 112
15:28	102, 102n, 105, 106, 106n, 106n, 111n
15:28ab	106, 106n
15:28b	106
15:28c	106, 106n

2 Corinthians

9:10	64n

Galatians

3	104
3:28	102, 104, 105, 111n, 112
5:14—6:10	23n

Ephesians

1:23	111n
3:9	111n
4:10	111n
4:17—6:17	23n
4:22–32	101n

Philippians

3:17–21	102
3:19–20	102, 118, 119
3:21	102, 111n
4:4–9	23n

Colossians

1–2	122
1:5	141n
1:14	109
1:15–20	102, 102n, 106, 108, 111n, 114n, 120
1:15ff.	111n
1:15	141n
1:16–17	105, 109n, 111n, 114n
1:16	109n, 111n, 114n, 141n
1:17–18	109n
1:17	105, 109n, 111n, 114n
1:20	141n
1:23	141n
1:24—4:6	107n
2:8	104n
2:11	109n, 114n
2:12–15	100
2:12–13	100
2:12	101, 118
2:16—3:4	107n
2:20–23	100
2:20	100, 118
3:1—4:6	26n, 103
3	108, 113, 135
3:1–17	101–2, 107, 121
3:1–11	26, 100, 102, 105, 107, 109, 112, 114, 117, 120, 124, 126, 131, 149–50
3:1–5	108n
3:1–4	xv, 100, 107, 108, 114n, 117, 118, 141, 150
3:1–2	xv, 4, 6, 64n, 103, 109, 110, 112, 116, 117, 119, 120–22, 122–23, 129, 131, 131n, 135, 141, 142, 143, 150, 151
3:1	101, 101n, 120
3:1a	100–101, 103, 118
3:1b	101, 103, 107, 108
3:2	101, 102, 103, 107, 119, 121
3:3–4	101, 102, 103, 107, 109, 110, 112, 119, 120, 126
3:3	118
3:5—4:6	23n
3:5–17	120
3:5–8	101, 102, 103, 107, 119
3:5–6	103n
3:5	101, 103n, 104, 104n, 120, 122
3:6–7	119, 120
3:7–8	103n
3:8	101, 103, 103n, 104, 104n, 111n, 113n, 119, 120
3:9–11	104, 107
3:9	109n, 110, 112, 119, 150
3:9a	101, 103–5, 104n, 104n, 107, 108, 109, 119, 120
3:9b–10	120

Colossians (continued)

3:9b–11	101–2
3:9b–11a	102n, 105, 120
3:11	102, 106n, 106n, 109n, 110–11n, 150
3:11a	120
3:11b	102, 105–6, 107, 108, 109, 110, 112, 114n
3:12–17	101, 120, 122, 135
3:12–14	101n
3:12	120, 131
3:13–17	120
3:14	131
3:15–16	131
4:1	141n
4:6	100

1 Thessalonians

1–3	22
4–5	21
4:1–9	23n
4:15	22
5	25, 26, 84
5:1–11	23n
5:12–22	24
5:12–14	23n
5:12	24
5:15–22	23n
5:15	24

Hebrews

2:9	78n
13:1–9	23n
13:17	23n

James

1:1	80n
1:2	88n, 89
1:3—5:11	23n
1:5	89
1:17	89
1:22–33	89
1:22–25	xv, 91–93
1:23	96
1:25	91n
2:1–12	91
2:1	80n
2:2–3	82n, 96n
2:5	xv, 81n, 86, 89, 90–91, 90n
2:8	84
2:10	89
2:13	82n, 89
2:14—3:11	88
3:9–11	94n
3:11–12	94n, 95, 96
3:12	3, 82n, 82–83n, 89, 94, 94n
3:12a	2
4:3	89
4:4	89
4:9	81n, 81n, 86n, 90n
4:10	xv, 82n, 89, 94
4:11–12	89
4:13–14	82n, 96n, 100n
4:14	47, 47n
5	134
5:1–6	149
5:2–3	xv, 4, 6, 34, 38n, 46, 47, 89, 90n, 97–100, 121, 122–23, 129, 134, 137, 149, 151
5:2	98–99, 99n
5:3	99
5:4–6	129
5:4	99
5:7	100
5:8	100
5:10	89
5:12	82n
5:17	81n, 81n
5:19–20	88n, 89

1 Peter

2:11—4:11	23n
5:1–11	23n

1 John

3:6	60

2 John

8	60
9	60

EARLY CHRISTIAN LITERATURE

Apocryphon of James   16–17

Book of Thomas   16

Clement, Stromateis

4.33	71n

1 Clement

23:1	52n

Dialogue of the Savior   16–17, 16n

Didache

1–2	83
1:3—2:1	84

Gospel of Thomas

1	69, 78–79n
2	16n, 25n, 136
3	9, 13, 13n, 141n
3:3a	8n, 13n
4	25n
5	109n, 113n
6	109n, 113n, 141n
6:2–6	112, 114n, 115, 150
6:2–3	110
6:2	112, 120, 133
6:3	114n
6:4–6	112, 117, 126, 133
6:4–5	110
6:5–6	113, 113n, 114n
6:5	112, 113n
6:6	113n
9	67n
9:4	70n
11	141n
12	141n
14	8, 9
14:4	9, 70
14:5	8–9, 12, 70
16	10
16:1–2	10
16:3	10, 12
17	24, 24n
18	69
19	69, 109n
20	141n
21	25n, 70
21:5	70n, 145n
21:7	70n
22	25n
24:2	66n
31	77n
35	70
36	10–11, 10n
37	25n
38	136
39	70
44	141n
46	25n
47	12, 77n
47:3–5	12
47:3–4	11

Gospel of Thomas (continued)

53	109n, 114n
54	141n
59	136
61	109n
63	100n
72	11–12, 77n
76	67n, 114n, 129n, 136n
76:1–2	29n, 35, 64, 66, 70, 121, 134, 135, 136n, 140
76:3—77:1	112, 115, 150
76:3	xv, 4, 28–29n, 29, 34–35, 36n, 46, 49–50, 49n, 50n, 58, 66–76, 77, 78, 78n, 110, 112, 113, 114n, 116, 117, 119, 120–22, 124–25, 126, 127, 129, 130, 131–47, 149, 150, 151, 152
77	109n, 111n
77:1	78n, 109n, 110, 112, 114n, 114n, 131, 131n, 133
81	25n
85	69
91	141n
92	136
94	136
103	70, 70n
107	136
109	25n, 67n
110	25n
111	69, 141n
113	8, 8n, 9, 13
113:1–2	13n
113:3	13n
114	141n

Hermas, *Similitudes*

9.42.2	52n

Letter of Barnabus

19:2	52n

Letter of Polycarp

	24n

Oxyrhynchus Papyri

1	14
654	14
654.15–16	13n
654.36–40	141n
654.38	109n
655	10, 10n
655.1–17	137–38

Tertullian, *De resurrectione carnis*

23.4.13	131n

OTHER ANCIENT WRITINGS

Aristotle
Nichomachean Ethics

IV	52n, 129

Josephus
Against Apion

2.82.6	64n

Antiquities

3.230.4	64n

P. London

1223.9	64n

Plutarch
Moralia

	52n

Philo
De specialibus legibus
1.256.3   64n

Sophocles
Fragments
181.2   64n

Strabo
Geography
16.1.7.4   64n

www.ingramcontent.com/pod-product-compliance
Lightning Source LLC
Chambersburg PA
CBHW031432150426
43191CB00006B/476